W9-DCZ-926

PAUL K.T. SIH

Decision for China

Asia in the Modern World, No. 10

Decision for China

By

PAUL K. T. SIH
Director
Center of Asian Studies
St. John's University, New York

Published by the St. John's University Press
under the auspices of the Center of Asian Studies

NIHIL OBSTAT: Msgr. Joseph H. Brady, S.T.D.
Censor Librorum

IMPRIMATUR: ✠ Thomas A. Boland, S.T.D.
Archbishop of Newark

Library of Congress Catalog Information

Hsüeh, Kuang-ch'ien, 1909–Decision for China: communism or Christianity [by] Paul K. T. Sih. Chicago, H. Regnery Co., 1959. 262p. 21 cm. Includes bibliography. 1. China— Church history. 2. China—Civilization. 3. Communism—China. 4. Chinese rites. I. Title, BR1285.H74
275.1 59—9061 ‡

First Printing – Henry Regnery Company, 1959

Dedicated to the persecuted Catholics of China and their heroic martyrs and confessors.

CONTENTS

Preface to the Second Edition

This book was written in 1958. When it was first published by Henry Regnery Company, Chicago, in 1959, Communist China was wholeheartedly carrying out its commune system. China-watchers in the United States appraised the situation with expectancy and awe. Some of them anticipated that, with the eventual development of the communes, Communist China would achieve great power status which no nation in the world, not even the United States, could afford to ignore. It was not until 1966, when the Cultural Revolution broke out in mainland China,[1] that these same China-watchers suddenly realized that not only did the commune system not work, but instead, there was brought upon its heels another tremendous upheaval which was without even an ostensible constructive purpose, and which, as we now see, has been and is still creating nothing but nation-wide chaos, over-all stagnation, multi-level strife, and self-imposed isolation—in a word, a "great Power" hollower than ever.

The fate of my book seems to have followed this turn of events. When it came off the press in 1959, it drew little attention from the reading public. Increasing demand for it began in 1966 as the Chinese mainland was engulfed in total turmoil by the Red Guards of the Cultural Revolution. Within a short time, the first printing was sold out. The reason for this is very simple.

In 1959, few people believed or cared to believe what I wrote about the communes:

"How far the Chinese Communists can go with this new system, we do not know. What we already know is that with more than ninety-five per cent of the peasants organized into co-operatives, the Reds still could not achieve their objectives because the co-operatives killed the family spirit. How, then, can they expect to succeed with this new organization which aims at a more radical destruction of the family? Stalin's forced collectivization of Russian agriculture in the 1930's—a program less radical than the establishment of the Chinese communes—was achieved only at the cost of more than ten million Russian lives. Whether Mao can succeed without resistance on a similar scale in China remains to be seen. . . .Most probably, this new system, like the birth-control campaign, must be slowed down because it has already invited serious opposition from the peasants. . . .We do not know all the reasons for the present unrest or for Mao's resignation announced by the Peiping radio on December 17, 1958, but we do know that resistance to the new communes is one of the main factors involved." (pp. 132-133)

Again, on the intra-party conflicts among the Chinese Communists themselves, I noted:

"There have been no executions, no spectacular public trials in the crackdown on the critics of the regime. It has been done 'new style,' as in Russia, with demotion and degradation. A province-to-province Communist party purge is under way, and Chekiang, Hunan, Anhwei, Sinkiang, and even Chinghai, have been affected. The Communist governor of Chinghai province, Sun Tso-pin, a member of the Chinese Communist party for approximately thirty years, was accused of sabotaging party unity and aiding anti-Communists. High ranking generals and officials have lost their positions. Party leaders have been purged. Spies are set on agents, and agents are planted on spies. 'Who will guard the guard?' This is the question that tears at the whole fabric of totalitarian control. There is no end to Red China's internal troubles."(p. 116)

In view of the current situation on the Chinese mainland in 1970, these pertinent observations seem to be prophetic. This most probably has brought more and more readers to my book since 1966 so that a second edition is warranted.

There is, however, one point in the book which may call for an explanation. When I discussed the problem of Titoism (p. 115), I attached little importance to the deviation of the Chinese Communist leadership from Moscow. This seems to be not in keeping with the current development of the Sino-Soviet conflict. As a matter of fact, after Mao Tse-tung resigned in December 1958, Liu Shao-chi was in power. Mao decided to eliminate Liu in the name of anti-revisionism. Had Liu survived the struggle and established firm leadership, there would have developed no crises of revisionism and anti-revisionism whatsoever, and a united Moscow-Peking front would have been sustained. Now Mao has gained the upper hand, but the struggle, however, is not over yet. The next phase of the development of Moscow-Peking relationship is yet to be revealed in the making.

Furthermore, the present Moscow-Peking conflict has not been a disadvantage to both Communist camps. "The different tactics applied by Moscow and Peking towards the West," as Franz Michael of George Washington

University put it, "have not necessarily weakened the Communist course but may have broadened the scope of the Communist political offensive. The purpose of Moscow's and Peking's Communist policy, after all, has been the same—the advance of Communism on the global scene. Only the methods or the emphasis on methods used has varied. The Soviet emphasis has been on strategic 'peaceful coexistence,' meaning largely a political and propaganda warfare, which, in my view, has been highly successful. The Chinese Communist emphasis has been on violence. Those revolutionary-inclined Communists to whom violence appeals have found leadership in the Communist center in Peking. In contrast, Soviet policy has looked peaceful indeed, especially to those who believe that 'peaceful coexistence' means peace. And so the two policies have reinforced each other."[2]

So far as Communist China is concerned, the Cultural Revolution since 1966 produced a bizarre situation no one had anticipated. In the words of Louis Barcata who visited Communist China for the third time in the spring of 1967: "It became more and more obvious that its [the Cultural Revolution's] tendency was to alienate and disrupt, and that total success was out of the realm of possibility."[3] L. La Dany, Editor of *China News Analysis* in Hong Kong, noted that "the situation inside China is utterly different from that of a few years ago. There is a curious political vacuum in Peking. Most of the orders that appear are concerned with a single subject, in pursuit of those opposed to the new order, *i.e.* the political purge, which since 1967 has been called *tou-p'i-kai* (fight, criticize, change)." In cautioning the free world not to seek a hasty and easy way in dealing with the China problem, La Dany had this to say: "There is no easy solution at hand. The problem of the Republic of China in Taiwan cannot be bypassed. Normal dealings with Peking are extremely difficult, and, as the examples of Britain's and West Germany's trade with China show, not even profitable. To this must now be added the fragile political situation inside China, where the 'red flag' is still opposed to the 'red flag,' where the ruling military are meeting wide and stubborn opposition among the ever-growing younger generation and where the regional leadership is hesitant in executing Peking's orders."[4]

In the same tone, Wm. Theodore de Bary of Columbia University observed that "as witnesses of these tragic struggles on the mainland of China, we must develop the capacity to see them, not just in terms of the danger or advantage they present to us, but of how from these agonies China may be able to gain her sense of self-respect."[5]

However, this process has a long way to go. Within the Communist Party there is persistant factional struggle, and the army continues to provide the backbone of day-to-day administration. Economic dislocations are widespread. It will take years for Peking's economic and political machinery to recover from the damage done by Mao's Cultural Revolution. In his recent book, *Party Leadership and Revolutionary Power in China.*, John Wilson Lewis of Stanford University thus wrote: "As a result [of the Cultural Revolution], it is no longer possible to hold a simple view of power and leadership in which the actions at the top ramify neatly to the base, nor can the actions of the 'base' in any one part of the country be considered typical of those in any other. While it is necessary to consider this power situation as transitional. . . the transition to a fundamentally different political system will thus take years if not decades. Even the death of Mao Tse-tung will probably not change, basically, the fact that power resides in many hands and that doctrine has innumerable interpreters."[6]

With all these in mind, it is indispensably important that we look at Taiwan under the Republic of China, where people are enjoying increasing economic success, social well-being and political stability. In contrast with Taiwan under Japanese rule, they have never had so much prosperity, share of government, and civil rights and liberties. Oftentimes, it is suggested that the China problem may be solved through an arrangement for the "self-determination of Taiwan." This is entirely illogical and unprincipled. For centuries, Taiwan has been an integral part of China. To hold a plebiscite in Taiwan for self-determination would be tantamount to a plebiscite among the Hawaiians or Californians for their separation from the Union. Furthermore, both the Communist regime on the mainland and the Republic of China in Taiwan will not accept such a "China–Taiwan" solution. If proposed, it would only mean a declaration of no confidence in the Republican government and would thus introduce a new element of instability into the area. We are already confronted with the chaos in Laos and Cambodia, the insecurity in Thailand, and the delicate situation in South Vietnam. Should we now introduce further disarray into this region by upsetting the forward stance and stabilizing influence of a government and people who have achieved so much progress and contributed so much to the cause of the Free World?

It is assumed by some that somehow something must be done to Taiwan to exchange for a Chinese Communist agreement on a general peace in East and Southeast Asia. To this we would like to raise a fundamental question. Is an international agreement with a Communist nation, notably Communist China, adequate for only a reasonable assurance of peace? We need not cite the numerous instances wherein Communist China has never lived up to international principles and practices. Then another question may be validly raised: Will the admission of Peking to the United Nations' membership improve its international behavior and make it a responsible member in the world parliament system? On this, Professor de Bary made a very pertinent point: "It is not he [Mao] who agitates for China's admission to the UN. He leaves that to Western liberals who cannot live without Mao as he can easily live without them. . . Admission of Red China to the UN would be regarded by Mao as a purely formal and symbolic matter. Participation would be judged by him in terms of its possible contribution to world revolution, not world parliamentarianism."[7] If such is the case, what is the logic, or shall we say profit, then, in trying to upset the currently viable situation of Taiwan which is contributing so much to the security of Asia[8] for the sake of some new formula which will be untried and unreliable? As we are witnessing the utterly confused situation on the Chinese mainland, it is most important for us to develop the wisdom to wait and see. Developments in the future have to be taken care of by evolution.

Time is in our favor. We need more patience and more perseverance. We must remain firm. We must always stand on our principles for human freedom and unity. We have nothing to change. What we must do now with great vigor is to unite all the non-Communist nations diplomatically, politically, and economically so as to place greater pressures on the Communist world, particularly on Communist China. This will finally force the Communists to change their basic position. On the other hand, every gain made by the Communists would lead to greater, not lesser, national arrogance.

In this balance of nuclear terror, we must accept co-existence in this limited sense. The kind of co-existence that we uphold is not negative, but positive. It does not retreat before the despotic power, but advances. It gives up nothing, but demands a real change that will expand, not reduce, the area of freedom throughout the entire world!

This second edition is a reproduction of the original work with only a few corrections of typographical errors and a revised note relating to Yen Fu on page 239. The original note should apply to Lin Shu. This was an oversight on the part of the author due to a last-minute re-arrangement of notes in that chapter.

The Epilogue, "American Policy Towards China: A Reappraisal," is newly added. It is a reprint of my article published by *The Catholic World* in its August 1964 issue. Although written more than six years ago, it appears increasingly valid and relevant. I am most thankful to Reverend John B. Sheerin, C.S.P., editor of *The Catholic World,* for allowing me to reproduce it in this new edition.

The author is also indebted to Mr. Harvey Plotnick, President of Henry Regnery Company, for his courtesy in allowing the transfer of the copyright of the book to the St. John's University Press for reprinting. He wishes to thank Dr. Blaise J. Opulente, Administrative Vice President, and Dr. Paul T. Medici, Dean of the Graduate School of Arts and Sciences, St. John's University, for their sincere encouragements, and the editorial and production staff of the St. John's University Press for their kind assistance.

Paul K. T. Sih
Director, Center of Asian Studies
St. John's University

October 1970

NOTES:

[1] There has never been any formal announcement of the day on which the Cultural Revolution was inaugurated, but reference is often made to the middle of 1966, the time of the first appearance of the Red Guards.

[2] Michael, Franz, "What the United States Should Do with Regard to the Peking-Moscow Controversy," a lecture delivered at the Symposium on Asia and Contemporary World Problems, St. John's University, July 23, 1970.

[3] Barcata, Louis, *China in the Throes of the Cultural Revolution,* New York: Hart Publishing Company, 1967, p. 283.

[4] La Dany, L., "China: Period of Suspense," *Foreign Affairs,* July 1970, p. 711.

[5] de Bary, Wm. Theodore, "China in Perspective," *Columbia Forum,* Spring 1970.

[6] Lewis, John Wilson, *Party Leadership and Revolutionary Power in China,* Cambridge: Cambridge University Press, 1970, pp. 27-28.

[7] For a scholarly study of the importance of Taiwan in relation to the situation in Asia, please read "The Republic of China and Asian Security," by Richard Walker, a lecture delivered at the Symposium on Asia and Contemporary World Problems, St. John's University, July 24, 1970.

[8] "China in Perspective," *op. cit.*

Author's Note

In the present world struggle there are two major contenders, the Soviet Union and the United States; but neither the Soviet Union nor the United States forms an isolated unit of power. Each constitutes a center of power, which seeks to draw additional areas, additional nations, and peoples within its sphere.

Thus the position of the so-called "uncommitted third" of the world, Asia, Africa, and Latin America, is vital. Of the three, the situation in Asia is most critical. The Communist base in Red China has become a center from which aggressive activity radiates in all directions, threatening to engulf the world.

Both the Soviet Union and the United States are trying to win this "uncommitted third" to their side. Two primary elements are involved: the material and the cultural; of the two, the cultural is basically more important than the material. This is so because physical or material elements are organized, reinforced and sustained by the historical, psychological, moral, and religious elements of the cultural system—not vice versa. It is for possession of this cultural area that the Soviet Union and Red China on the one hand, and the United States on the other are waging a serious battle for the minds and hearts of the Asian peoples.

The culture which the United States represents is Western civilization, a civilization with Christianity as its core. The culture which the Soviet bloc propagates derives its major strength from the defects of the Western cultural system. It makes the Asian peoples believe that Western culture is nothing but Western domination which is to be identified with imperialism. However, in this ideological struggle, it is evident that Western culture is gaining acceptance in the Eastern world.

Many nations in Free Asia are now under Christian leadership.

President Chiang Kai-shek of China is a devout Christian; so are President Syngman Rhee and Vice President John Chang of Korea, President Ngo Dinh Diem of Viet Nam, the late President Ramon Magsaysay and his successor Carlos Garcia of the Philippines, Chief Justice Kotaro Tanaka and former Premier Yoshida of Japan. Among them, Ngo Dinh Diem, Garcia, John Chang, and Tanaka are active Catholics. In religious belief, all are faithful adherents to Western Christianity.

I met and talked to most of these leaders in person during my three visits to the Far East in 1955 and 1956. The general consensus of their opinions can be summed up in two points: the future of Asia is with Christianity; Asia can achieve its economic recovery and growth with the help of Western technology. This is particularly true of Free China.

Free China, with her present base in Taiwan (Formosa) is the testing ground. Here it has been definitely shown that with the revitalizing force of the Christian faith the Chinese can live a fuller and more religious life, and that with American aid the basic economic problems can be solved.

More than 96 per cent of school-age children in Taiwan are in school. Land reform for the double purpose of giving land to the tiller and equalizing land rights has been carried out without resorting to class struggle. Seventy-eight per cent of the farmers own all or part of their land. Rural economy with American cooperation, involving 1,852 reconstruction projects, has had a helpful effect recognized by over 90 per cent of the rural population. Power supply has been increased five times in the last ten years. Production of all kinds has made gains ranging from 165 to 1090 on the index of production (1952 equals to 100). Popular elections for local self-government are held regularly and according to democratic principles. Above all, Church activities, Catholic and Protestant alike, have entered a more vigorous phase than ever before. A similar situation is found among the Chinese residing abroad. More Christians are made secretly on the mainland than is generally realized. Christianity, not Communism, is China's hope for salvation. As China is the key to Asia, the decision between those two is a vital factor in determining the destiny of Asia.

Asia needs help from the West. However, no help is valid and conducive to unity unless it is made on the basis of genuine partnership. This sense of fraternal fellowship must be expressed not merely in words, but also in deeds. Both must recognize that only through helping others can each be benefited.

There are several reasons for Asia's predominantly neutral attitude. One of these is the short-sightedness of some of the comparatively young nations which have yet to learn the true nature of Communism. Of equal importance, however, is the wavering attitude of the West in its anti-Communist policy. If these nations are not too sure where the West stands, why should they commit themselves? Speculation feeds on inconsistency and confusion.

It is now not a question of whether the East will permit the West, with its spiritual as well as material resources, to share the common task of counteracting Communism in strategic and cultural spheres. It is a question principally of how the West responds to this challenge, of how soon and how adequately she is able to hasten this moral and spiritual development as a needed complement to military protection.

The true enemy of Christianity in Asia is not Communism. It is secularism. Secularism in culture is neutralism in international politics. Whenever culture loses its spiritual and religious basis, it becomes unstable, unconvincing—neutral. It is difficult for the Asian peoples to understand that, while Christianity is from the West, the West is not always Christian. This contradiction is precisely what Communist propaganda utilizes most effectively throughout Asia.

In the matter of religion, the West seems to be a river with two streams running in opposite directions. The surface stream carries the spiritual as a value in life, while the stream underneath, which is secularism, denies the spiritual as the basic element in life. Oftentimes, the stream underneath appears to run more strongly than the surface stream. On the other hand, no matter to what religious creed they are attached, the Asian peoples believe in God and in the spiritual destiny of man. All have faith, all practice a morality. This being so, they consider secularism no less a threat than Communism to their basic philosophies of life.

If there be friction or misunderstanding between East and West, it cannot spring from the higher traditions of either culture. Conflict can only arise when the East has forgotten to practice its morality and the West has been unfaithful to its Christian traditions.

Thus, the immediate answer to the problem in Asia lies not in telling the Asian peoples how to fight Communism physically, but in working toward a union of both spiritual traditions, with Christianity taking the leadership. This will give an inner spiritual vigor to our efforts which Communism cannot match. It is in this light that the present work is offered.

Upon the completion of this manuscript, I wish to express my deep gratitude to Right Reverend Monsignor John L. McNulty, President of Seton Hall University, for his kindness in taking in a particularly busy period to write the foreword. To Reverend

Edward J. Fleming, Dean of University College, Seton Hall University, I owe special thanks for his constant encouragement and practical advice all along the way. Thanks are owed to Reverend Raymond J. de Jaegher, Regent, Institute of Far Eastern Studies of the same University, and my colleague, Dr. John B. Tsu, for their constructive counsels.

Further thanks are due to Right Reverend Monsignor Joseph H. Brady, Sister M. Zita of the Sisters of Charity, Mother Mary Columba and Sister Coleman of Maryknoll, for their generosity in reading the manuscript and for their suggestions in matters of expression. I also wish to record here my appreciation for the assistance of Monsignor Stanislau Lokuang of the Chinese Legation to the Holy See, of Reverend C. H. Vath of the Catholic Truth Society, Hong Kong, of Reverend Francis A. Rouleau, S.J. of Institutum Historicum, Rome, of Reverend John T. S. Mao, of Reverend Joseph S. McGrath, C.S.C., University of Notre Dame, of Professor Paul Chiang Fu-tsung, Director of the National Central Library, Taipei, and of the *Chinese News Service*, New York, in verifying certain historical and current materials embodied in this work.

Finally, I wish to express my sincere appreciation to the editorial staff of Henry Regnery, especially to Mr. Charles E. Lee, General Editor, and Mr. Daniel R. Hayes, Catholic Editor, for many excellent suggestions that have resulted in substantial improvement in this book. Above all, however, I am anxious to acknowledge my great indebtedness to Reverend Thomas Berry. He has given many hours of his time to discussion of the manuscript and has made many helpful suggestions.

Needless to say, none of these friends is responsible in any way for the judgments or interpretations in this volume.

PAUL K. T. SIH

Institute of Far Eastern Studies
Seton Hall University, Newark, N. J.
December 1958

Foreword

In 1951, Seton Hall University established an Institute of Far Eastern Studies for the primary purpose of fostering better understanding between the American people and the peoples of the Far East.

In our Institute—and in most Asian Institutes in America—China merits special interest for several reasons:

Physically, we are closer to China than to any other mainland country of Asia.

Historically, we have been intimately associated since that February morning in 1784 when the *Empress of China* sailed out of New York and around Cape Horn to Canton, the great port of South China.

Politically, we have defended the interests of China against the aggressive policies of other World Powers.

Academically, we have educated more Chinese students than has any other Western nation.

It is appropriate, therefore, that Dr. Paul K. T. Sih, Director of the Institute, should publish his study of the present crisis in China. This, his first full-length study of China, is the natural outgrowth of his years of lecturing in Canada, Europe, Asia, Central America, and in thirty of the forty-eight states in America.

Particular attention is given in this work to the spiritual conflict that is in progress for the very soul of China. For what we witness now is not the ordinary conflict of political parties to determine who shall administer the laws of the country—not a revolution such as those which are prevalent in Latin America—but rather a titanic struggle to decide whether the Chinese people shall preserve and reestablish their noble traditions which are in danger of extirpation on the mainland.

Dr. Sih, who reached maturity when China was entering her thirty-year struggle for survival, has witnessed the violent strife. Through his own experience, he knows the turbulence, the fears and the hopes within the Chinese people. Thus his words flow, not from an ink-dipped pen, but from a heart that has known the tears and the bloodshed of a war-torn land.

The author recognizes the tragic turmoil China has experienced in reshaping her ancient way of life to prepare her survival in modern times. He is cognizant also of the external influence that have frequently served to confuse rather than to assist China in maintaining her strength and peace and freedom. But, like many others who have participated in the agonies and tensions of these last decades, he is more concerned with designating a way to the future than with reminiscing over the past.

On two points he is adamant. The future of China is with America and with Christianity. Only through the principles of the Christian faith can China find spiritual rebirth. Only through American assistance can she attain economic recovery.

With his intellectual training and political experience, Dr. Sih combines a profound understanding of Christianity and of the universal need of the Asian world with belief in the teachings of Christ.

Decision for China is an analysis of the past, an evaluation of the present, and the projection for the future.

RIGHT REVEREND JOHN L. MCNULTY, PH.D.
Seton Hall University, South Orange, N. J.
Office of the President

Prologue

A STUDY of Asia is an immediate and universal need for all educated people of the Western world. Some Western scholars characterize the "shift of world politics from Western Europe to Asia" as "the major political fact of our time."[1] However to be aware of this change as an accomplished fact does not suffice to give a full understanding concerning the present developments in world affairs. For this, it is necessary to study the underlying causes which motivated this shift, and made it possible. While the motivating causes are several, the most important is the grand strategy of Soviet Russia. Its dominant role in world politics is (or should be) a well recognized fact.

Nearly thirty years ago Stalin in his *Marxism and the National and Colonial Question* and *China in Revolt* revealed the Communist world strategy. Only recently did the West bother to study this plan: (1) Subjugate the little nations on Russia's western border, securing the homeland of Communism against counterattack from the west. (2) With the front door locked, conquer China by fraud, deception, and civil war. (3) Hand China the sword to conquer the rest of Asia for Communism. (4) Foment revolution in the colonial and semi-colonial lands of the Middle East. (5) Deny Asia's strategic materials to the

West and obtain for Communism an inexhaustible supply of man power. (6) When the West becomes exhausted through lack of supplies and commerce, strike at the tottering bastion of free society and wipe it out.

It is of no importance whether "Stalinism" or "anti-Stalinism" now controls the Kremlin. What is important is that the Communist plan for world conquest has been in progress in nearly every country of Asia and the Middle East and has been succeeding—exactly as Stalin planned a quarter of a century ago. When Stalin's mantle fell upon the shoulders of the Kremlin's present rulers, they inherited an empire which sprawls across one fourth of the earth's surface and dictates to a third of its people.[2]

The Communist grand plan is based on Lenin's mottoes: that "the way to Europe is through Asia—China and India" and "Peking is the gateway to Paris." While Communist methods change as convenience dictates, their objective of world domination through the subjugation of Asia always remains the same.

In the light of this principle, we can understand why in the Red lexicon there was no Korean war, no Malayan war, no Indo-Chinese war. There is only an all-Asia war, on the all-Asia front, involving Japan, China, Korea, Hong Kong, Indo-China, Malaya, the Philippines, Indonesia, Burma, Thailand, India, Pakistan, and Ceylon—each a sector on this front. Supporting these aggressive movements in Asia is the militant force dominating the China mainland, and from here, all the Communist Asian activities originate.

The problems of Asia cannot be fully understood without prior knowledge of the situation in China. Henry R. Luce once wrote in a magazine article that "China is truly the middle kingdom of all Asia, and in this first epoch of global history China is the ultimate test of East-West relationship." Truly, China long ago constituted the stabilizing element in the Far East. Had the China mainland not succumbed to the Red contagion, there need never have been a war in Korea, to say nothing of the surface and sub-surface aggression in Viet Nam, Laos, and Malaya.

The story of China's conquest by the Communists is a long one. As it is to be treated, in its entirety, in this book, I do not here intend to go into detail. However, I do wish to point out that, with China under Communist rule, Stalin's blueprint Number Two—to conquer China by fraud, deception and civil war—was well implemented.

The Asian continent is now completely under the threat of Communism. For reasons which I explain in this work, Communism will not, and cannot take root in China. It will remain a yoke, not an inner principle of life. However, we can never minimize the vast potential of Communist China for evil, and its bearing on neighboring countries in the Asian world.

Its area of 3,750,000 square miles compares with 2,975,000 for the United States. It occupies one-fifth of the Asian continent, has common borders with almost every other Asian country, faces the Soviet Union and Outer Mongolia on the north, Korea on the east, and Afghanistan, Pakistan, India, Burma, and Indo-China on the west and south. A relatively short stretch of the Pacific separates it from Japan. Thailand is not far away from its southernmost point. This strategic position in Asia's heartland creates both opportunity and difficulty for its present rulers, particularly today when the airplane has diminished the importance of those mountain barriers that cut off China from many of its neighbors.

China's vast population is another fact that we must never forget. It numbers, by recent Communist count, about 585,000,000—almost three times the population of the Soviet Union. The mere size of the Chinese Communist armed forces constitutes a great threat not only to Free China in Taiwan, but also to all neighboring nations.[3] Though China's Chiang Kai-shek, Korea's Syngman Rhee, and Viet Nam's Ngo Dinh Diem stand staunch as ever, Communism gains ground elsewhere in Asia. In fact, the real danger of Communism lies in its ceaseless expansion and conquest. Red China is pushing and will push its campaign slowly, even cautiously, but always relentlessly.

Recent developments in Southeast Asia have shown that Communist China is involved in an international conspiracy rather than in a domestic revolution and reform. Threats from Red China have been felt in all neighboring countries.

In the Philippines, Chinese Communists have openly supplied help to the Hukbalahap terrorists. In Malaya the British authorities reported that in security operations against the terrorists more than 90 per cent of those captured are Chinese Communists. Indo-China was used as a staging area and as a supply base for the Vietminh dissidents led by the Communist Ho Chi Minh with a view, not only of undermining the free Republic of Viet Nam, but also of threatening Laos and Cambodia. The totalitarian controls over Tibet are another active phase of the Communist conspiracy against liberty, as is the pressure on Nepal, the infiltration into Thailand and Burma, and the agitation in Indonesia. In India, where Nehru is trying to placate neighboring Communists while suppressing his own, Communism has developed considerable strength in Kerala, just above Ceylon.

In the light of these facts, we note that Communist China, in accord with Stalin's blueprint Number Three, has been handed the sword to conquer the rest of Asia. More than this, Red China is now fulfilling Stalin's blueprint Number Four—the stirring of revolution in the colonial and semi-colonial lands of the Middle East.[4]

All this is possible because China is the core of Asia. Although the troubled Southeast is not so well known as the troubled Middle East, the fundamental problem in both areas is similar—how to stop the advancing Communists. We know how the Communists work through subtle infiltration and subversion in the midst of tangled domestic politics. This was noted in SEATO's (Southeast Asia Treaty Organization) annual report published in March 1957, which characterized the Communist effort as "an integrated subversive attack in all fields of national life to undermine the stability of free nations and thus prepare them for Communist domination."[5]

The Communist subversion campaign is comprehensive. It is directed ultimately from Moscow, but immediately from Peiping. It applies different techniques to different areas as political convenience dictates. Where the Communist party is underground, as in Burma, Malaya, and the Philippines, it is pressing for the right to emerge and attain legality. Where it is already legal, it is pressing for a role within the government as in Indonesia. However, legal or illegal, Communism uses the following tactics: (1) it forms inter-party alliances of united-front elements; (2) it engages in a constant propaganda campaign conducted through Communist agents infiltrating the area as refugees; (3) it uses trade and aid programs to tie participating nations into the Communist orbit; (4) it infiltrates labor unions and schools with Communist teachers and textbooks.

At the same time, Communists are increasing pressure on the Chinese overseas with a view to compelling their allegiance, without which no Communist action, overt or covert, could be effective. To understand this, we need only examine the excellent article "Red China 'Attack the Heart' of Southeast Asia" by John C. Caldwell.[6] By "attack the heart," the Communists mean to work on the minds of the Chinese people overseas throughout that region.

We should never neglect the important role played by the overseas Chinese in dealing with China and, indeed, with Southeast Asia as a whole. Scattered over all the countries of the region are more than twelve and one half million Chinese.[7] They are both numerous and economically powerful. They represent a great force in the national life of China as well as in the communities in which they live. Dr. Sun Yat-sen, founder of the Republic of China, succeeded in guiding the revolutionary movement and overthrowing the Manchu dynasty in 1911 chiefly because of the moral and financial help he received from Chinese living overseas.[8]

What, at present, is the general attitude of the Chinese throughout Southeast Asia? They are anti-Communist to the core. They remain loyal to Free China. Everywhere they retain their native culture and have a strong sense of solidarity. This they will continue to do so long as they are assured that Free China will continue to exist. Since many of them are intellectuals, esteemed by their countrymen, they are a major source of moral strength in the conflict with Communism, which attacks and rejects everything sacred in the Chinese heritage.

The Chinese overseas offer another great advantage. With the mainland behind the Bamboo Curtain it is difficult for the free world to have contact with the Chinese people there. However, this is not true of the Chinese overseas. The great majority have maintained very close relationships with their families and relatives on the mainland. Many things have been destroyed by the Communists, but not this family solidarity.

This being so, if we want to penetrate the Curtain and to win the hearts of the enslaved people on the mainland, there is no better way than to win, first of all, the hearts of the Chinese overseas wherever we find them. To consolidate our effort in the struggle against Communism in Southeast Asia, we must of necessity make full use of the Chinese throughout the area. They constitute a dominant force for good. If we fail to unite ourselves with this force, we may find that we are unable to do anything about the future of China except through military operations. We deprive ourselves of a most intelligent and effective means of meeting the challenge in this region.

SEATO, which was established to unite the governments of the area with the West and to insure a common action against further threat, is both useful and necessary. However, it is unable to do everything. To oppose Communist military aggression, yes; to exercise vigilance over Communist subversive activities, yes; but to counteract Communist warfare in psychological or ideological fields, especially among the Chinese overseas, no!

It is true that Communism feeds on the extreme poverty prevailing among the great masses of mankind. However, in the case of China, Communism went there primarily to fill a spiritual vacuum. It has, of course, only deepened the vacuum. Now it is our opportunity to win the hearts and minds of the Chinese. We must grasp the opportunity by offering them a truly spiritual program of life. This is especially true of the Chinese overseas who are even more religious than the people on the mainland.

The success of Communism as well as its point of great weakness lies in its ability to disguise its aggressive policy which, when exposed, clashes with every spiritual tradition of the world. The religious thought of the East can never tolerate a materialistic ideology, and this incompatibility of atheistic Communism with the traditional Oriental belief in supernatural goodness is of great significance in the struggle. It is a struggle between those who believe in the spiritual and those who do not. China has never claimed to have a true religion of its own, but even so the Chinese are among the most spiritual-minded people of the world. There are many approaches to the problem in China, but it is this issue that is most fundamental—the need for religion.

What a splendid field for Christianity to work in! Christianity does not conflict with any morally good culture. Its purpose is to develop and to supernaturalize culture. It offers mankind belief in something higher and deeper than ourselves or national boundaries, with which we can commune and in which we can find genuine peace and universal harmony. The overseas Chinese now have a great opportunity for spiritual renewal which they can later communicate to the mainland. Success or failure here may well determine the destiny of China and of Asia.

It is clear that this task is not limited to Catholics. Men of goodwill and high principles should answer the call in concerted action. As a Catholic, I place much hope in the religious field on those of my own faith.

In the past, the Catholic Church has done a great work among the Chinese residing in various foreign countries.[9] Missionaries, after many bitter experiences in Red China, have returned to the free world to intensify the spiritual work of the Church with the Chinese overseas so that now in these dark and unhappy days they may be a source of strength and a beacon of hope to the fatherland.

Communism entered China not as a political or social system, but as a new religion. We can expect only limited results from military power or economic programs. But where international or diplomatic deliberations stop, Christianity can take up with its spiritual action.

Communism has caused intense suffering in China. In this suffering we see a glimmer of the Christian story of sorrow as a preparation for joy, of crucifixion as a prelude to resurrection. We hope that with prayer and work, peace and happiness will come to China in God's good time.

Part One

ESSENTIALS OF CHINESE CULTURE

"Whatsoever things are true, whatsoever modest, whatsoever just, whatsoever holy, whatsoever lovely, whatsoever of good fame, if there be any virtue, if there be any praise of discipline, think on these things."

—*Phil.* 4, 8

Breadth and Depth

THE TASK OF Christianity in China implies an understanding of Chinese culture, since Christianity, as a universal religion, cannot be, and is not, indifferent to the culture of any people.

Chinese culture has two dimensions, depth and breadth. Depth is expressed in its continuity: from ancient times until the present, there has existed in China an unbroken code of cultural values—a code which has formed the principle of unity in Chinese life. Even under foreign rule, which has occurred several times in Chinese history,[1] Chinese culture has shown a rare power for absorbing alien elements and resisting foreign influences. As Dr. Chang Chi-yun puts it, "The vital strength of the Chinese nation lies in its power to assimilate elements both internal and external. The term Chinese must be considered as a purely cultural rather than a racial term."[2] Professor Alfred North Whitehead says: "The more we know of Chinese art, of Chinese literature, and of the Chinese philosophy of life, the more we admire the heights to which that civilization attained. Having regard to the span of time, and to the population concerned, China forms the largest volume of civilization which the world has seen."[3]

The breadth of Chinese culture is found in the extensive influence which China during her long history has exercised on almost every country in Asia. Speaking of another civilization of the East, Laurence Binyon observes, "There is one country in the world which has formed and fostered a tradition of art and life even more powerful and persistent, and in the end more exclusive; and that is China. Everywhere in Asia it is the art of China which, like Greek art in Europe, has enjoyed the greatest prestige."[4] This is why Dom Pierre-Célestin Lou Tseng-tsiang, O.S.B., remarks that Chinese culture represents the "precious pearl of human life in the Far East."[5]

These two characteristics of Chinese culture—continuity in depth and extensiveness in influence—have significant bearing on the present ideological war against Communism; since Chinese traditional values, stimulated by the Communist attack, are powerfully reasserting themselves, not only among the Chinese people of the mainland, but also and especially among those who reside in Taiwan and throughout Southeast Asia, where a cultural renaissance can take place in freedom.

On the Chinese mainland, where military and political activity is now secondary to the war which the Communists are waging against the people on cultural and ideological levels, Christianity and the Chinese cultural tradition have been joined in a natural alliance. In the present struggle Chinese Christians, Catholics and Protestants alike, find in their Faith complete assurance of ultimate victory; but their great sacrifices have been made easier by their cultural heritage which is rooted in the ethical teachings of Confucius.

The Communist military menace to the regions of Southeast Asia is already evident. But more serious than this, the Communists, as we indicated in the Prologue, are conducting in the area an intensive propaganda campaign through cultural and social movements. SEATO is not able to counteract this kind of

Communist intrigue. In these circumstances we must make use of the cultural force of the Chinese residing in this part of the world to meet the Red challenge. This struggle in the cultural and social order is really the key struggle.

First of all, this war of ideas cannot be won without revitalizing the Chinese culture among the Chinese people throughout Southeast Asia. Chinese culture cannot be preserved, developed, and propagated by China alone. Like all cultures, Chinese culture needs external help for its growth and enrichment. The fact that Communism prevails today on the mainland is a clear indication of the inadequacy of an isolated Chinese people to meet its urgent need for self-preservation and rejuvenation.

China had an excellent opportunity to revitalize her cultural heritage in the beginning of the seventeenth century when Father Matteo Ricci brought to China the Christian faith together with the new scientific discoveries of the West. How this Western contact influenced the cultural and religious life of China will be treated in later chapters. It will suffice here to note that no outside influence can assist a people unless they themselves are disposed to receive it and integrate it with their past traditions. This was the case of China in the seventeenth century.

China derived her cultural heritage mainly from Confucius. Confucianism, at the time of Christ's birth, was a thing of grandeur, needing only Christianity to fulfill and complete it.[6] During the sixteen centuries before the arrival of Matteo Ricci, Chinese culture underwent many changes and developments. These changes so altered the original spirit of Confucianism that it was unable to receive influences from without which earlier it would have welcomed.

It is in this light that we discuss, in the following chapter, the origins and developments of Confucianism, and, to a lesser extent, Taoism and Buddhism.

Origins and Developments

CHINESE CULTURE emphasizes the supremacy of the practical over the abstract. Supremacy of the practical not only means the application of human philosophy to a way of life in the everyday relations with one another, but also implies a contempt for mere speculative thought as such. The aim of Chinese wisdom is not to satisfy intellectual curiosity, but to enlighten human life by farsight, foresight, and insight.

In Confucianism there is an aim toward human perfection that teaches people how to live morally. Taoism is more subtle than Confucianism, yet its chief object is also to heighten moral sensibility and strengthen the impulses toward good.[1] Even in a detached state the bond with the world must not be completely cut or severed. Compared with Confucianism and Taoism, Buddhism is more spiritual. But its basic idea of reenforcing the ethical note of righteousness and its teaching that suffering is a certain consequence of unrighteousness pertains, after all, to this world. In short, Chinese natural wisdom opens its eyes to all the realities of life, and thus becomes fruitful and attractive in all human activities. This results in a splendid humanism combined with practical living, constant emphasis on morality and character as the supreme good, and moderation in all things.

These ideals are symbolized by the ancient coin which is a round piece with a square hole in the center. The circumference of the coin represents the external harmony between man and man, the self-mastery philosophy of Confucianism. By practicing self-mastery one is to conform oneself to the way of the world. The central square hole signifies the pure, detached mind of man and the self-abnegation of Taoism or Buddhism. By practicing self-abnegation one becomes free from the toils of life. Thus, the combination of inner virtue (self-abnegation) and outer accomplishments (self-mastery) is necessary for the development of that independent and mature personality which enables man to joyfully accept life and yet be constantly prepared for death.

This synthesis of the ideal and the practical, of the finite and the transcendent, may be illustrated by the national pastime of kite-flying. In the Orient, it engrosses the whole population, young and old. One reason why this pastime has enjoyed enduring popularity is the feeling that through the bit of bamboo and paper soaring high in the sky, a contact with an infinite and sublime power is experienced in the tug of the string between the fingers. It is a detached sport enjoyed in a practical way.

Chinese unity is thus to be found in this basic dichotomy of attitude, rather than in any one philosophy or one school of thought. No Chinese can be strictly called a Confucianist, a Taoist or a Buddhist. He follows all three at one and the same time. They constitute one tradition, one way of life, one wisdom. As Professor Kenneth S. Latourette notes:

> Just why this is so must be in part conjectural. It may have been because the practically minded Chinese have been eager to take advantage of every possible benefit from each of the systems which have come to their attention. It may have been because of a fundamental religious uncertainty—a lurking suspicion that all religions are at least in part false and a lack of confidence in the finality of any one of them—and yet fear that each may possess elements of truth.[2]

On the same subject, Rev. Thomas F. Ryan, S.J. writes:

> It has sometimes been said of the Chinese that they are not a religiously-minded race, and in fact it has been often declared that they are too matter-of-fact to be much given to any form of abstract speculation. Matter-of-fact they certainly are, but not in a crude materialistic sense, and it would be difficult to find any literature which is inspired by such a consistently idealistic spirit as theirs.

Oftentimes the Chinese say: "There are three religions (they refer to Confucianism, Taoism, Buddhism), but there is only one faculty: 'reason.' " The word "reason," however, is not to be interpreted as something intellectual, but to indicate that there is only *one* reason (truth), which stands *above* the religions. They have, therefore, confidence in a higher Wisdom.

Both Confucianism and Taoism, in their pure and original forms assume a fitting attitude toward the Supreme Being—an attitude of ingenuousness and simplicity. Even Buddhism, originally atheistic, assumed an attitude of reverence in the Amidist tradition.

The notion of "Heaven" in Confucianism indicates a Personal God, which man must not ignore, but can never adequately know. As to the "Tao" in Taoism, it assumes a very flexible attitude toward the supernatural. Certain Buddhists do not envisage the existence of a Supreme Being, yet their fervent devotion to Kuan-yin and compassion for human suffering prepares them to understand the essence of Revelation and Redemption. In fact, the devotion of the Chinese to Amida Buddha comes very close to the reverence for God as the enlightener and rescuer.

The most distinctive attribute of the Chinese moral character and strength is an inherent honesty about those spiritual things which cannot be known with certitude. The silence of the Chinese thinkers about God, as far as I can determine, is the silence of the surface-water of a pool reflecting stars in the sky. It is the silence pointing to a higher affirmation leading implicitly to the true religion, a silence which is, in sentiment at least, the best attitude toward reality.

This negative concept of God in the Chinese mentality is a source of both strength and weakness. It is a source of strength because it acts as a barrier against increasing superstition or further speculation about supernatural problems. We realize today that this attitude is not adequate for a full religious life. Nevertheless, it allowed the Chinese freedom for the acceptance of the revealed religion. But this same attitude can become a source of weakness. In the absence of a definite and transcendental outlook, life on the spiritual level can be developed only within the limits of human imperfections. In fact, the central difficulty of humanist teaching, as that of any moral code, is the danger of self-righteousness. If the only standards are human ones, in man himself, self-righteousness is almost inevitable.

Self-righteousness or self-centeredness is an intellectual error; no living creature is in truth the center of the Universe. It is precisely due to this defect that the essentials of Chinese culture, Confucianism, Taoism, and Buddhism, reveal a variety of changes, so apart from their original forms that these traditions have often been misinterpreted. The fact that Communism prevails in China at the present time is enough to show the inadequacy of the old system. At the same time, and for the same reason, the Chinese have not been capable of combating the new evil of Communism. But under the Communist outrages the original values of Chinese culture, once prominent and then obscured, have been forced to the surface. Once more they are operating stronger than ever.

But what, in reality, are these changes? The heart of Confucian ethics is a striving for perfection based on the growth of a full and ordered personality. As Lily Abegg puts it, "Perfection in any achievement depends on the degree of perfection in the personality behind it, whether it be a work of art, a philosophic doctrine, a piece of craftsmanship, or skill in music or archery."[4] Thus, the true concept of human perfection does not lie merely in individual development, but in adapting oneself to the community, and in such a capacity to carry a good share of social responsibility, especially in one's family. In the Confucian tradition, a Chinese is primarily son and father and only secondary an individual. This is why filial piety stands out above all other ethical virtues.

This family devotion and filial piety is certainly a good thing.

The difficulty is not that the Chinese has too much family love, but that he does not use it as a starting point for the great love of society, community, country, and world, as envisaged by Confucius himself.[5] Why? The most important reason is the fact that the Confucian conception of eternity is obscure, and the Chinese simply cannot put the sense of love in its proper place. This explains a paradoxical fact: in spite of the family system, a Chinese can remain at heart an individualist, and he frequently is.

Confucius, for instance, taught that in order to keep family continuity, every married couple should be encouraged to have children. The average Chinese well knows the popular saying: "There are three unfilial things in one's life: not to have posterity is the greatest of the three." This axiom has formed the development of family ties. However, not a few Chinese tended to over-emphasize, in a most distorted way, the bearing of children. Under the pretense of filial piety, they took concubines when their wives happened not to give birth to a male descendant. This practice gave rise to polygamy, thereby defeating the very purpose of Confucian ethics.

In short, family love in accordance with the orginal intention of Confucius was nothing more than a sentiment of, and a basis for altruism. But lacking a spirit of objectivity, the family system became self-centered.

Regarding woman's social position we note the popular proverb of the Chinese: "It is virtuous for women not to possess any talent." Here the word "talent" is subject to interpretation. To possess no talent means, in a very general way, to be a fool. No one, of course, wants to be considered a fool. The meaning of this proverb, in other words, is that the wife should not interfere in her husband's business. Woman is made to be the helpmate of man and his mother. A man is likely to be wrapped up in his affairs, but a woman's gifts and satisfactions are in shaping another person's life. Therefore, woman must be woman, and man must be man.

What was here expressed in the Confucian tradition corresponds rightly to the biblical demand for woman's obedience to man as her head. However, this sense of family solidarity rooted in a genuine partnership between man and woman often degenerated, consciously or unconsciously, into an unreasonable demand for woman's subordination to man—a distorted conception erased from the Chinese mind recently.

One of the finest men who developed Confucian thought was Mencius (371-289 B.C.), whose position in Confucianism may be compared to that of St. Paul in Christianity. Like St. Paul, who centers all his thought around Christ, Mencius referred everything to Confucius. So far as the basic concept of natural theology is concerned, Mencius' ideas are in essential harmony with those of Confucius. In fact, he elaborated to a considerable degree the theological notion of Confucius with regard to the law of nature.[6]

According to Mencius, "He, who has completely developed his mind, knows his nature. He, who knows his nature, knows Heaven."[7] To him, Heaven is the Supreme Ruler over all the universe, while nature is what Heaven "confers" on men. In other words, the law of nature is implanted in man by Heaven. Mencius' interpretation of human nature would be unthinkable without this notion of the law of nature.[8] To him, natural law is the expression of the perfectibility of man and of the internal power and natural reason leading to man's perfection.

Mencius was opposed by Hsun Tzu (298-238 B.C.) who was largely responsible for a trend in Confucian thought different from the Confucianism elaborated by Mencius. He began the deviation of Confucianism. In direct opposition to Mencius, Hsun Tsu declares that human nature is essentially evil. He holds that every man has a capacity for knowing; he denies that man has an innate ethical constitution. According to him, men establish social and political order and make progress in civilization because of their acquired knowledge, and not because they are inclined by nature to be moral. On this philosophical basis, he upholds his positivist theory of the supremacy of law and of the regulation of human thought and conduct through the setting up and enforcement of rational measures. This positivist and rationalist philosophy constitutes a direct contrast to the original Confucianism represented by the natural-law philosophy of Mencius. This also provides a basis for the birth of Neo-Confucianism which began with the cosmological ideas of Tung Chung-shu (*circa* 179-104 B.C.). Tung preached a doctrine "in which morality was inextricably mingled with an elaborate technique for the reading of omens and the practice of magic on a cosmic scale. In each of these cases, the later philosophy flourished centuries nearer to our own day, yet intellectually they seem incomparably more remote from us than the earlier."[9]

It was on this cosmological element that in later days Chang Tsai (1020-1077) formed a complex system of pantheist and rationalist ideas.[10] This system was to become the basis of Neo-Confucianism—a philosophy so distant from its origin that "Confucius would not have understood it,"[11] and that Father Matteo Ricci was led to remark: "This is not Confucius!"[12]

So much for Confucianism. Let us now make a few remarks on the historical evolution of Taoism.

In its pure and original form Taoism preached the virtue of the simple life and communion with nature, the denial of selfishness, and mystical union with the Tao. However, Taoists in old China drifted away from this original thought. As centuries passed, the Taoist philosophy slowly descended to gloomy levels of idolatry and superstition.

Loaded down with an incubus of sorcery, fortune-telling, charm-selling, geomancy, and alchemy, it became more akin to voodooism than to the noble philosophy of Lao Tzu. Worship became magic and its object was solely the attainment of earthly blessings. Its priests were hired employees who performed rituals. They were without any conception of spiritual leadership. Secret societies were formed for various worldly purposes, rather than for moral elevation. Long before the end of the nineteenth century, as a consequence of the spread of scientific awareness, Taoism as a religion was dying. The later Taoism was thus not the Taoism of Lao Tzu, but something which had become very much distorted. But his noble concept and spirit of Tao, whence comes enlightenment, is still vital in the hearts of the Chinese.

So far as Buddhism is concerned, it could hardly escape the same deterioration experienced by Confucianism and Taoism. Buddhism which owed its origin to India had become extinct in the land of its birth and lived on mostly in the countries farther east, such as Tibet, China, Japan, Thailand and Indo-China.

Very much like Taoism, Buddhism in China became mixed, in popular estimation, with superstitious practices such as fortune-telling and image worship. Belief in an after-life, desire of some means of communicating with those who were dear in life, readily led untutored minds to superstitious ghost-stories.

From this, the Buddhist devotees among the masses turned their attention to fantastic idols, garbled the testimony of conscience to the soul's dignity, substituted for the aspirations toward salvation vain attempt for material success. It is fair to say that except among the educated classes, not one fundamental element of original Buddhist teaching has remained. For the general multitude, Buddhism has become another form of utilitarianism.

The causes leading to this situation are many and various. The fundamental factor, however, lies in the very nature of man. Chinese culture, like all cultures, is something human, something limited. It can never rise above its human limitations.

All schools and system of philosophy have their periods of development and the periods of decline. Only Christian spirituality will grow in depth and breadth until the end of the world. "Every man at first setteth forth good wine, and when men have well drunk, then that which is worse. But thou hast kept the good wine until now."[13] Therein lies the difference between the work of God and the work of man. As Dr. John C. H. Wu says, "All human teachers can only bequeath to posterity their words; only Christ promised the Paraclete, whose mission is to teach us 'all the truth' and to bring to our mind what He had said."[14] This insight is borne out, negatively, by the saying prevalent among certain Buddhists that when Buddha was living his disciples followed Buddha, but after his demise we have to follow his law.

It is clear that the kernal of Chinese culture is a devout and trustful submission to the Supreme Being, without any adequate understanding of his nature and attributes. The strength of Chinese culture is its child-like simplicity—a simplicity which gives ample room for the influx of Divine power to compensate for man's weak reason, his all-too-human conception of God.

We all know that Confucius did not discuss religion, in content or in ideas. This shows his deep reverence before the greatest of mysteries. It is in itself a sublime religious attitude though inadequate for human need. But if there is this deficiency on the doctrinal side of religion, we do find an abundance of spiritual wisdom which contains the most integral study of human relations known to the ancient cultures of mankind. Our present need is to complete what was left out by Confucius. The Chinese culture must be, and can be completed. Christianity offers this completion. The Chinese tradition needs the supernatural perfection of Christianity. Christianity needs the natural perfection of the Chinese tradition. Each needs the other; each has a place for the other; each attains its perfection in the other.

In this connection, there is no one who has expressed a better view than Dr. Paul Chiang Fu-tsung, Director of the National Central Library in Free China. In his autobiography telling of his conversion to Catholicism, he writes: "The teaching of Confucius has nothing incompatible with that of Christ. The basic idea of Confucius originated in the way of Heaven. However, Confucius undertook the primary responsibility of teaching the six techniques to his pupils. He seldom discussed or elaborated the way of Heaven. The reason why I embrace the Catholic faith is because I wish to comply with the basic teaching of Confucius and to seek what Confucius had left out in his explanation of the way of Heaven."

What is most needed is the development of a true Confucian-Christian humanism transcending all narrow secularist limits. It is particularly important that the Gospel should be preached in such a way as to allow its incarnation in non-Western cultures. This is precisely what Christianity is able to offer the Chinese people, an infallible, spiritual teaching that will preserve all that is best in the wisdom and virtue of the Chinese tradition. It was against this background that the missionaries from the West began to make contact with the land of Confucius. Under Divine guidance, they worked to correct and elevate the imperfect yet noble tradition of China.

Part Two

THE WESTERN IMPACT

"But if, while we seek to be justified in Christ, we ourselves also are found sinners, is Christ then the minister of sin? God forbid!"

—*Galatians,* 2, 17

The Early Contacts: The Question of Adaptation

WHILE SOME eminent Chinese scholars, including the Catholic writer, Professor Soo Hsueh-lin, maintain that early Chinese thought was influenced by the Hebrew teachings of the Old Testament,[1] and while tradition tells us that China was visited by St. Thomas the Apostle,[2] the earliest contemporary reference to Christianity in China appears in the works of Arnobius, a Christian writer of about 300 A.D. In a rhetorical passage, supporting the truth of Christianity by the evidence of the successes already achieved, Arnobius writes: "For the things done in India may be counted and come in for the purpose of reckoning, among the Seres (Chinese), Persians, and Medes, in Arabia and Egypt, in Asia and Syria, among the Galatians, Parthians, Phrygians, in Achaia, Macedonia, Epirus, in every island and province upon which the sun at its rising or its setting shines. And lastly what has been done in the Mistress Rome herself, where although men are taken up with the arts of king Numa and with ancient superstitions, they have not hesitated to leave their native ways and join the Christian truth."[3] Apparently Arnobius thought that the Gospel had been preached to the Chinese before the end of the third century.

Whatever be the truth in regard to these early centuries we

can with certainty state that Christianity did reach China before the seventh century, brought there in an imperfect form by the Nestorians.[4] From the seventh to the ninth centuries, Christians in China were numerous; and later on envoys came from the Pope to the court of Genghis Khan and his successors, and missionaries followed in their wake. It was not until late in the thirteenth century, however, that the Catholic mission to China was definitely established.[5] The first friar to reach China proper was John of Monte Corvino, a Franciscan appointed on July 15, 1289, by Pope Nicholas IV (1288-1292). He arrived in Peking in 1294, having come by way of India, where his companion, a Dominican, had died. Gaining the favor of the Emperor, he built two churches, and by 1305 had baptized about six thousand converts, including Prince George of Tendue. In 1307 seven more Franciscans were sent by Pope Clement V to act as Monte Corvino's assistants, and Monte Corvino was made Archbishop of Cambaluc (later called Peking) and Primate of the Far East.[6] He seems to have had no unified program and to have attained only limited success, but his work, considering his resources, was truly monumental.

The last Roman Catholic missionary to penetrate China during the Middle Ages was a papal legate, John of Marignolli. Following the overland route, he reached Peking in 1342, remaining there for a few years before returning to Avignon in 1353. Shortly thereafter, a national revolution drove the Mongols out, and the Chinese Ming dynasty (1368-1644) took their place. The Mings reacted against all the foreign doctrines the Mongols had favoured, especially Christianity, and although Rome continued to send missionaries out none of them seem to have gotten as far as China. When the Italian Jesuits went into the country in the sixteenth century, they found no trace of the first Christian communities.[7]

These early missionaries were comparatively ineffective, not because they lacked a noble purpose or true teachings, but rather because of human frailty and the difficult situation that they had to face.

Christian missionaries generally have been divided by their preference for one of two practices in their approach to pagan peoples. The first approach takes little note of the cultural, social, or religious backgrounds of the people to be converted, and offers them, as from a foreign land, a religion developed chiefly according to alien standards. The other makes every effort, in accordance with the catechetical need, to speak in terms of the native culture so that its people may be brought to a more rapid understanding of the Christian message. This was the practice of St. Paul, the Apostle of the Gentiles, during the first years of the Church in the Greco-Latin world,[8] and it was also the program of the catechetical school of Alexandria in the second century which integrated Christian traditions with the ancient traditions of Greece.

From early times missionaries in China continued using the European traditions, and made little serious effort to adapt themselves to the new peoples among whom they worked. They were so busy with pastoral activities that they had no time or energy to develop such knowledge, even if they had wished to do so. It was only natural, therefore, that they continued their European attitudes, desiring as they did to sow the seeds of Christianity without any risk of compromise. For the same reason, however, Church doctrine could not be easily absorbed by the Chinese. These missionaries made little progress.

This European approach remained unchanged until the arrival of the Italian Jesuit Father Matteo Ricci in 1582. Father Ricci first lived at Macao. After several attempts, he was finally allowed to establish his residence on the Chinese mainland. After entering China, he mastered its language and literature. He developed an extensive and deep knowledge of the Chinese classics making it possible for him to change from the traditional approach to another approach, that of "adaptation." In so doing, Ricci attained a success never known by his predecessors. His new expression of Christian faith also made it possible for the Chinese Ming Empire to review her policy. The Empire, as we noted before, showed an unfavorable attitude toward Christian doctrine, partly because it was of alien origin, and partly because it was favored by her former enemy, the Mongols. Now they realized that Christianity tempered by Ricci's conciliatory attitude toward the Chinese traditions was, after all, not a totally "foreign" product. In describing the success of the Jesuits' mission in Asia, Arnold Toynbee writes: "The Jesuits stripped Christianity of its accidental and irrelevant Western accessories, and offered the essence of it to China in a Chinese, and to India in a Hindu, intellectual and literary dress in which there was no incongruous Western embroidery to jar on Asia sensibilities."[9]

So far as Father Ricci was concerned, he made no new discovery. He simply took a positive approach to Chinese learning and believed that it could be united with Christian revelation to form one complete pattern of Christian Wisdom, one integral Christian Humanism, in which reason and revelation sustained, defended, and, each in its own way, perfected the other.

Ricci's method of "adaptation" was immediately successful. He became convinced that China could be gained for Christ if only the missionaries would, imitating his method, accommodate themselves to the traditional ways of the Chinese people. Many of these customs, he found, were not contrary to faith or morals, and could not be condemned. For instance, it seemed to Ricci that the institution of ancestor worship, which was a genuine product of the Chinese family system, could be considered "a ceremonial which had been thoroughly and scrupulously purified from all taints of superstitions."[10] He thus allowed the Chinese Christians to perform these ceremonies.

Ricci's plan for winning China was to win first the lettered or educated classes. After he was accepted by the upper class of scholars who virtually ruled the country, "his house became a rendezvous for civil and military authorities, afterwards known in Europe as mandarins";[11] and he so impressed them by his combined intellectual, moral, and humanist method that he was called another Confucius. In later years, Ricci was even empowered by the imperial authorities to establish a novitiate at Peking. He was well on in years by that time, but continued valiantly in his work, making saints as well as scholars out of his Jesuit associates.

Through Ricci's influence the Chinese faithful increased from a few in 1584, to more than 500 in 1603.[12] The most significant event in his apostolate was, however, the conversion of the greatest official scholar of the court, Paul Siu Kwang-k'i (Paul Siu),[13] an event which was a triumph in itself and marked the beginning of many other conversions in intellectual circles.

Under the enthusiastic direction of Paul Siu and with the help of his friends, a Chinese encyclopedia of all European sciences, sacred and profane, was planned and partially realized. A Chinese literature of the West was thus inaugurated, and under its aegis Christianity was able to spread quietly and peacefully throughout most of the provinces by the efforts of a relatively small number of missionaries. Christianity gradually acquired an established position—a position which was greatly strengthened by Ricci's writings in Chinese on general moral principles as well as on Christian doctrine. To show how his works pleased the people, let the Jesuit missionary speak for himself:

> Copies of the Commandments were printed in Chinese and given out to all who asked for them. Many who received them said they would live in the future according to these Commandments, because as they claimed, they were in such accord with the voice of conscience and with the natural law. Their reverence for the Christian law increased with their admiration for it.[14]

This shows how the moral precepts of Christianity can be readily accepted by the Chinese because they are in harmony with the traditional moral teachings of the Chinese people.

Ricci's first work in Chinese was *De Amicitia (Treatise on Making Friends)*, written, according to Reverend Maurus Fang Hao, Professor of History at National Taiwan University, during the period from November 4 to December 15, 1595.[15] A discussion on friendship based on translations of one hundred maxims of noted Western writers, it was reprinted in many collections and "must have been very popular to go through many editions."[16]

Ricci's famous book of apologetics, *T'ien Chu Shih-I,* appeared in 1604. An important work, it was addressed primarily to non-Christians, and used arguments from reason concerning the existence of a Lord of Heaven, Creator of all beings. It dealt with the immortality of the human soul, the reward and punishment hereafter, and the falsity of the theory of metempsychosis. The arguments were supported by quotations from the Chinese classics, which conferred upon the book an aura of singular authority and fascination.

As Clement of Alexandria (150-217) in his writings drew much of his thought from the best writers of Greece, especially Homer and Plato, and added much richness to Christian culture, so Ricci called on Confucius to expound the wisdom of Christianity. He tells us that in compiling his treatise, he

> made every endeavor to draw over to our side the leader of the sect of the learned, that is Confucius, by interpreting in our sense some things that he presented in an ambiguous form; and therefore our fathers won much esteem among the learned who adore no idols.[17]

This work enjoyed a very wide circulation and exercised an extensive influence on the Chinese. Within five years (1604-1609), it was reprinted four times. Two of these printings were made possible by the gifts of two prominent official scholars who were still non-Christians. The book was so loved that even Emperor Ch'ien-lung (1736-1796), who later adopted a rather hostile attitude toward the Church, included it in the Imperial Encyclopedia.

For catechumens and Christians, Ricci published in 1605 a revised verison of the catechism, which he called *Dottrina,* intended for uniform use in all missions of the country. It contained sections on the common prayers, the Decalogue, the Creed, the Sign of the Cross, the works of mercy, the Beatitudes, the seven capital sins and their opposite virtues, the senses of the body and the faculties of the soul, the three theological virtues, and the seven sacraments.[18]

A few days before his death he finished a most valuable and lovely book which he entitled *Entrata della Compagnia di Giesù e Cristianità nella Cina (The Entrance of the Society of Jesus and Christianity in China).*[19] Therein he handed down his exposition of the Chinese way of thinking and some hints about his pastoral approach. He discussed such problems as "Chinese Ethics," "Primitive Religion," "The Three Sects," "The School of the Learned," "Cult of Heaven," "Ancestor Worship," "Rites of Confucius," "Syncretism"—problems which he had faced and tried to solve for others.[20]

When Ricci died in 1610 he was accorded unusual court honors, and he left behind him more than 2,500 converts in China.[21]

The most important successor of Ricci was a German, a native of Cologne, Adam Schall (1591-1666), who arrived in China in 1628.[22] In the course of his work there, the rule of the empire shifted from the Ming dynasty (1368-1644) to the Ch'ing dynasty (1644-1911), also known as the Manchus; but Schall won the favor of the new rulers and was able to continue the missionary method begun by Ricci.

The splendid services Schall rendered to Chinese science made him a favorite at the Court. He brought about the reform of the calendar and in addition made many converts to the Catholic faith. He was made a Mandarin and President of the Board of Mathematics for the Empire. He was given access to Emperor

Shun-chih (1644-1661) at all times and might have made him a Christian, had not the Emperor's favorites induced him to resume the pagan practices from which Schall had weaned him.[23]

Shun-chih died in 1661, leaving his eight-year-old child, K'ang-hsi (1662-1722), as his successor; and in pursuance of Shun-chih's command, Schall was appointed instructor of the young Emperor. This appointment, however, so aroused the jealousy of the Court that in 1664 Schall and thirty-one missionaries (among them, twenty-five Jesuits) were thrown into prison. Schall died in prison in 1666, after thirty-seven years of fruitful labor in the service of the Church and of China.

This anti-Christian feeling was not modified until the young Emperor K'ang-hsi reached the age which allowed him to manage state affairs by himself. In 1669, he issued an imperial order denouncing the trial as iniquitous, and although Schall had then been dead three years unusually solemn funeral services were performed in his honor. His remains were laid beside those of Ricci, and the Emperor himself composed the eulogistic epitaph which was inscribed on the tomb. A policy of toleration toward Christianity followed.

During Schall's trial, another Jesuit, Ferdinand Verbiest (1623-1688), a native of Pilthem near Courtral in Belgium, stood out prominently. Thrown into prison with Schall, he was later freed and, benefiting from the toleration policy of K'ang-hsi, advanced the cause of the Church and taught Western science to the Chinese. His career at the capital equalled that of Schall's in brilliance. K'ang-hsi followed his astronomical classes, appointed him to the highest grade in the mandarinate, and gave him permission to preach Christianity anywhere in the Empire.

While missionaries of different orders, among them the Dominicans and the Franciscans, made further progress in the propagation of the Christian faith,[24] the most significant event in the missionary activity of the time was Verbiest's petition for the use of the native language in the liturgy. This he considered necessary to establish a more effective apostolate. Otherwise, he argued, the conversion of China might prove impossible.

As a matter of fact, the idea of a Chinese liturgy was first brought up by Father Nicolas Trigault long before Verbiest's time. A Jesuit priest and a native of Douai, Trigault began his work in China in 1610, the year when Ricci died. Being a faithful follower of Ricci, he advocated the use of Chinese in the liturgy. For this purpose he went to Rome and presented his petition to Pope Paul V.[25] It was largely due to his efforts that the Decree of the Holy Office was issued on March 26, 1615, which was supplemented by a Pontifical Brief, *Romanae sedis antistes,* dated June 27, 1615.[26] In the Decree and the Brief three essential liturgical concessions—wearing of a Chinese cap during liturgical functions, translation of the Bible into literary Chinese, and the use of Chinese by Chinese priests in celebrating Mass and administering the Sacraments—were made to China. Trigault returned to China in 1619 with a sense of triumph. However, of the three privileges granted, only the first (wearing of a Chinese cap) was introduced. Adverse circumstances prevented the application of the other two.

It was for the renewal of these two important concessions that Verbiest submitted his petition to the Holy See. He did the necessary translation and, in 1681, he was able to dedicate his Chinese missal to Pope Innocent XI. In accepting it, the Pope sent him a brief which "contained the greatest praise for 'using the profane science to promote Christianity.'"[27] However, the Pope considered a liturgy in Chinese impolitic and, at the time, premature.

This Pontifical decision delayed the Jesuits' program for the creation of a secular clergy in China. In the meantime a controversy arose which sidetracked altogether this liturgical endeavor; this was the issue of the Chinese Rites.

The Chinese Rites Controversy

FOR OVER a century Christian missionary work in China, as we have seen, was dominated by men who believed in the principle of "adaptation"—of speaking, writing, and acting in terms of Chinese culture, so long as local ways were not in basic conflict with the doctrines of the Church. From the arrival of Ricci in 1582 to the death of Verbiest in 1688, the outstanding missionaries followed this approach. With Verbiest's failure to gain permission to use the native language in the liturgy, the tide flowed in the opposite direction. Succeeding missionaries emphasized the European ways and deplored the earlier attempts at adaptation. This emphasis, however well-meaning, led to the famous "Chinese Rites" controversy, to the eventual expulsion of the Society of Jesus, and to an incalculable setback in the missionary work of the Church itself.

The rites controversy began with the arrival in China of missionaries from religious orders other than the Jesuit. For some fifty years following Ricci's arrival the only Christian missionaries in China were Jesuits; but in the following century the Jesuits were joined by Dominicans (1631), Franciscans (1633), Augustinians (1680), and Paris Foreign Missioners (1683). With the arrival of these different groups, unity of action was lost, and many of the Jesuit policies relating to methods and procedure were challenged. The disputes concerned essentially the cult of Confucius (Master K'ung), the ancestral rites, and veneration of Heaven.

The crux of the controversy lay in the meaning of the words "ancestor worship," a misleading phrase which makes Westerners think of the Chinese custom as a religious institution, when in fact it does not have any religious significance whatever. The non-religious character of "ancestor worship" is seen in its exclusion of anything supernatural, and in the fact that it can exist side by side with belief in a Christian, Buddhist, or Moslem religion. Ancestral spirits, believed to be immortal, are conceived less as gods than as human souls. No prayer is made to them either for favors or for the cure of sickness. The practice is merely a civil and family celebration—no more than an occasion for pious remembrance of one's departed ancestors on a day consecrated to family reunion, and to grateful reflection on what the family owes its forebears. At best, the observance is a poor substitute for the celebration that would take place if the ancestor were still alive. In spirit it differs in no way from the celebration of Mother's Day or Father's Day in the United States. In short, the purpose of the institution is to honor ancestors, to continue human relations which should not be terminated by death, and to express a belief in the unending nature of man.

Perhaps, the matter which actually led Christian missionaries to prohibit Chinese converts from participating in the communal feasting and merrymaking of ancestor worship is that celebrants are required to perform the "kow-tow," a prostration in which the head touches the ground before a fifteen-inch wooden tablet inscribed with the names of ancestors. Objection to the "kow-tow," however, showed a complete lack of understanding on the part of the Christian missionaries. Chinese knees are not quite as unyielding as Western knees; they are instinctively more flexible, for the Chinese have been accustomed to "kow-tow" to emperors, to magistrates, and to their own parents on New Year's Day. The "kow-tow" expresses respect, not religious worship; and kneeling before a wooden tablet inscribed with the names of one's ancestors is not a religious act. The tablet itself is no more religious than the picture of a President on an American postage stamp.

On the other hand, if a Chinese is not allowed to participate in the general feasting that accompanies "ancestor worship" he is compelled to cut himself off from community life and even from the life of his own family—a thing so serious that no Chinese can do it without losing his sense of identity.

Thus, not only is the practice of "ancestor worship" entirely compatible with Church doctrine; it is almost essential to the establishment of any widespread Christian community in China, unless the almost impossible task of eradicating Chinese culture is accepted. How is it that this could be understood in those early missionary times by some missionaries, mainly the Jesuits, but not by all—even though all were equally eminent in apostolic works?

The answer lies in the fact that different missionaries came into contact with different aspects of Chinese culture and naturally saw things in the particular light of these aspects. The breadth of Chinese culture, of which we have written earlier, escaped the eyes of early Western observers, even as it does today; the first missionaries, without realizing their errors, were inclined to identify all Chinese culture with the small parts they saw. Even Ricci, for all his understanding, was received by his intimate contacts with the Confucian scholars. While he correctly divided Chinese religious life into three sects, he held that the Confucianists were an enlightened group, but the Taoists and Buddhists were idol-worshipers.[1]

The truth of the matter is that there were many Taoists and Buddhists who held their religious views in a way as noble and enlightened as the way of the Confucian scholars, and there were many Confucianists, as well as Taoists and Buddhists, whose beliefs and practices approached idolatry. Ricci was right in dividing the followers of Chinese religions into enlightened and unenlightened groups; but he was wrong in his identification of Confucianism with the former group exclusively, and he was equally wrong in thinking that devotion to one of the "three religions" precluded devotion to the other two.

It is more accurate to say that there were, and are, two levels of religious thought among the Chinese—that of the enlightened and that of the masses. By the masses is meant perhaps eighty-five per cent of the Chinese people, who are on the whole religiously devout but ignorant. By the enlightened is meant the intelligentsia, whose approach to the spiritual problem is of a more intellectual than religious character. Both groups embrace the "three religions," but with different motives and intentions.

The enlightened group regards the Chinese "religions" as literary traditions, as objects for intellectual study. So they call Confucianism, *Ju Hsüeh* (The Literature of the Scholars); Taoism, *Tao Hsüeh* (The Literature of Tao), and Buddhism, *Foh Hsüeh* (The Literature of Buddha).

The masses embrace these three systems with a different feeling and with a greater sense of mystery. They gave each a different name: Confucianism, *K'ung Chiao* (the cult of Confucius or Master K'ung); Taoism, *Tao Chiao* (the cult of Tao); and Buddhism, *Foh Chiao* (the cult of Buddha).

While the enlightened pursue the three systems in order to achieve a higher moral perfection, the masses seek immediate favors from the three cults in ways which at times may involve elements of idolatry. Whether the enlightened have always been really sincere in living up to what they morally professed or not, they made people believe they were consistent in profession and conduct.

Generally speaking, the enlightened group, especially in early days, have been city-dwellers, while the masses have resided in the country; and the Jesuit missionaries of the sixteenth and seventeenth centuries were usually assigned stations in the cities. Thus they had more opportunities for meeting the enlightened group through cultural and social gatherings and also had the best chance to learn from these educated persons the true meaning of their customs and religious practices. It was only natural that Ricci and his associates gained a deeper understanding which led them to adopt a more tolerant policy toward the native traditions.

Most of the other missionaries, especially the Dominicans and Franciscans, were stationed in the countryside. The rural classes, with whom they were in touch, in spite of having, on the average, a high moral standard, were less responsive to a spiritual and intellectual outlook on life—a fact which led the missionaries to believe that Chinese customs and traditions were not free from superstitious beliefs and practices incompatible with the teachings of Christ.

Numerous practices attest to the difference of religious thought manifested by the two levels of people. For instance, the Buddhist Goddess of Mercy, Kuan-yin, is presented differently by the different groups. The enlightened group held that Kuan-yin was the central figure of Buddhism, and they studied and took an interest in her as a matter of art or philosophical thinking, but it would never occur to them to think of her as an object of religious devotion. The masses, however, regarded her as a child-sending goddess, as folklore proclaimed her to be, and they would pray to her for many earthly blessings.

A similar difference in attitude and practice was true of ancestor veneration—the center of controversy in the "Chinese Rites" question. It was difficult for the enlightened to understand and see that the basic principle of this institution could be interpreted as anything but the cultivation of moral virtue. As the *Book of Odes* counsels: "With your ancestors ever in mind, cultivate virtue in you." And, "Rising early and going to bed late, do not disgrace those who gave you birth."

Abuses of ancestor veneration did, however, exist among the masses, who were inclined to think of the custom as a prerequisite for assuring temporal gain, and who in their petitions to their forefathers came close to idolatry.

Ricci agreed with the enlightened group that ancestor veneration was a "ceremony instituted more for the living than for the dead; that is, to teach children and ignorant people how to honor and serve their living relatives."[2] Others considered the institution religious idolatry, since they saw the practices of the masses, who "during such sacrifices and through divination constantly asked the dead for advice, assistance, help, protection and blessings of various sorts."[3]

Henri Doré, S.J., who had more than twenty years of close association with the Chinese, has made a very fair comment on this controversial issue:

> Originally ancestral rites were merely expressions of reverence for progenitors together with a native desire to do for them after death what was done during life. To a considerable extent, however, Buddhist ideas on protecting spirits have introduced the superstition of asking the ancestors for help. The learned missionary is not prepared to call the observances religious worship.[4]

There is a great deal of wisdom in these words; but a missionary's judgment on the ancestral rites in the early days did not depend exactly on whether he was "learned" or not. Rather his judgment depended on his opportunities to observe Chinese culture in its various manifestations. During the first centuries the missionaries who knew only the scholarly intelligentsia of the cities, and the missionaries who came into contact only with the ignorant masses of the countryside became sharply divided into two schools of opinion. The two schools were poles apart on the issue, but each would have moved to the other's pole had they exchanged missionary posts!

In short, each school from its limited experience and point of view was right. The advocates of the European traditional method were unquestionably right in opposing the idea that the Church could adapt itself to the semi-idolatrous, degenerated forms of Confucianism, Taoism, and Buddhism with which they were familiar. The advocates of "adaptation" were equally right in seeing no impediment to the Church's acceptance of the three great philosophies in their pure forms. Resolution of the controversy lay, of course, in the Church's adapting itself to the high traditions of Chinese thought as it was found among the scholarly class, but also in its mission among the masses to work at one and the same time for the Gospel of Christ and for a purification of the vulgarized traditions. The method called for was that of St. Paul on Mars Hill.

We can hardly blame the missionaries of the seventeenth and eighteenth centuries, however, for not showing a wisdom that we, with our greater experience and opportunities for knowledge, are only beginning to practice in the twentieth century. Sincerely differing because of their varying experiences, the early missionaries first raised the rites question in the 1630's as an issue among themselves.[5] Holding Ricci's position, the Jesuits generally maintained that the rites were merely civil ceremonies and contained "nothing that is essentially contrary to the Catholic faith."[6] The Dominican and Franciscan missionaries, by and large, condemned the rites as idolatrous and insisted on their discontinuance.[7]

The controversy was intensified when Bishop Charles Maigrot, M.E.P., Apostolic Vicar of Fukien, on March 26, 1693, condemned the rites and threatened to interdict all missionaries who did not conform to this decision.[8] As the situation grew more and more involved, the matter became an issue between the Chinese court and the Papal authorities. In November, 1699, the Jesuit Fathers at court drew up a petition to the throne, asking the Emperor K'ang-hsi to clarify the meaning of worshiping Master K'ung (Confucius) and offering sacrifices. To this petition the Emperor replied in 1700: "What is here written is very good, and is in harmony with the Great Way. To reverence Heaven, to serve ruler and parents, to be respectful towards teachers and elders—this is the code of all people of the empire. So this is correct, and there is no part that requires emendation."[9]

In 1705 Pope Clement XI, with a view to ending the disquieting discussion, appointed Patriarch Maillard de Tournon as legate to China. Full of holy zeal and Christian charity, De Tournon arrived in China with ample faculties for settling all problems of ecclesiastical discipline, but with limited knowledge of the Chinese social conditions. On January 28, 1707, he issued the famous order forbidding the cult of the ancestors.[10]

Generally speaking, throughout Chinese history, the emperors did not pass judgment on religious beliefs, interfere with religious practices, or determine religious creeds. This was especially true in the case of K'ang-hsi. He had been educated by the Jesuits, and was able to interpret Christianity in a Christian way. By nature and culture, he was among those who saw the essential nature and the value of Catholicity. But when the traditional rites, particularly the veneration of ancestors, were directly challenged by De Tournon's order of 1707, the kind soul of K'ang-hsi was so vexed that he felt impelled to decree on April 1, 1707, that unless the missionaries observed the rules of Matteo Ricci, they would be expelled from China. It is significant that even in this order of expulsion, K'ang-hsi showed his love and concern toward the missionaries who might have difficulty in complying with the papal directives expressed in De Tournon's action.[11] De Tournon was escorted by two Imperial officials to Macao, where he was reported to have died in prison on June 8, 1710.[12]

K'ang-hsi still hoped for a solution to the question. In fact, he "seemed pleased to know that Pope Clement XI would permit the use of ancestral tablets provided that they were corrected" in a manner which made clear that ancestors were objects of veneration, not of religious worship.[13] However, the Apostolic Decree *Ex illa die* of 1715, which moved cautiously toward a suitable settlement on the matter of the rites, was badly mishandled; it was made public before it reached the court—a breach of etiquette that made K'ang-hsi indignant.[14]

The awkward situation had to be reviewed by a second papal legate. Patriarch Carlo Ambrogio Mezzabarba, who arrived in 1721. He bore himself with greater circumspection and did his best, but could make no impression on K'ang-hsi. There was no lack of polite exchange of gifts and pleasant amenities, but the mission itself was a complete failure.

K'ang-hsi died on December 20, 1722, and the succession of Yung-chêng (1723-1735) to the throne signalized a sharp change of policy, since he was hostile toward the Church. A third papal legation sent by Pope Benedict XIII and headed by Gotthard Plaskowitz of St. Mary, arrived in 1725 to congratulate Yung-chêng on his succession to the throne, but failed to improve Church-State relations.

As the controversy continued, Pope Benedict XIV closed the debate among the missionaries by his decree of 1742. His Apostolic Constitution *Ex quo singulari* strictly forbade participation in the rites in question and required all missionaries to abjure them by oath before entering the mission field.[15] With the Church thus committed to a policy in opposition to "adaptation," court officials who were enemies of the Church were able to lead the successor of Emperor Yung-chêng, Ch'ien-lung (1736-1796), finally to suppress the Society of Jesus in 1773, bringing to an end 190 years of most fruitful work by no less than 472 Jesuit missionaries.

We can hardly underestimate the harm done to the Church by this expulsion policy, but it is important that the action of the Chinese Emperor should not be misunderstood. The court was by no means fundamentally hostile to Christianity or to the Church. Even in the edict of persecution it was clearly stated that the Christian religion ought not to be considered a bad religion; on the contrary, it exhorted man to practice virtues. The only reproach against it was the prohibition of the ancestral rites imposed by the foreign missionaries without the court's "authorization." As Rev. Thomas F. Ryan, S.J., puts it very rightly, "Historians are agreed that never have the people of China turned against the Church itself and persecuted Christianity for the doctrine it brought."[16]

While in retrospect it seems most unfortunate that the misunderstanding between the Church and the Chinese throne should have been perpetuated by the expulsion of the missionaries from the fields cultivated so laboriously by Ricci, Schall, Verbiest and their successors,[17] it is highly conjectural whether China would have been converted to Christianity had not the issue of the rites arisen. It is true that China did have a good chance of becoming Christian during Ricci's time; but the change of political power made missionary activity more difficult. Cooperation between Church and State was hard even under the Emperor K'ang-hsi, who in his early days assumed a most favorable attitude toward the Church, and of course accommodation with his successor, Yung-chêng, who adopted a strong anti-Christian policy, was impossible.

More important, man cannot be converted entirely and truly by external accommodation—much less so through political influences. Conversion must take its root in the heart; it must come from man himself. If there can be any criticism of Ricci's method of apostolate, it would be that his close relationship to the court bordered on the aristocratic and the political at the possible expense of the spiritual. In this connection, it might be recalled that the high respect in which Buddhism is held in China arose in part from the aloofness towards the emperors practiced by certain Buddhist monks during Chinese history.

Although it was and may still seem difficult to perceive the wisdom hidden in the earlier papal deliberations with regard to the controversy of the rites, it is an obvious historical fact that Christian truth is often made manifest through controversy. China had its own specific difficulties, largely of an intellectual order; but without intense intellectual effort, and even a certain amount of strife, the asssimilation of Chinese culture with Christianity could never have been perfected.

Three centuries of discussion, controversy, and association took place before finally, in 1939, the question of the Chinese rites was solved, thanks to the great wisdom of the late Pope Pius XII. On December 8 of that year, the Sacred Congregation for the Propagation of the Faith issued an instruction regarding *Certain Ceremonies and the Oath on the Chinese Rites.* All priests are thereby dispensed from the obligation of taking the oath. It is permitted: (1) to be present at commemorative functions held before a likeness or tablet of Confucius; (2) to place his image in Catholic schools and to make the ceremonial bow to it; (3) to assist, if ordered to do so, at public ceremonies which bear some resemblance of superstition provided that, in accordance with Canon 1258, they remain passive and participate only in some outward marks of respect as may be regarded as purely civil in character; (4) to bow the head and give other signs of civil respect in the presence of the dead or before their image.[18]

The issue which has weighed heavily upon the minds of missionaries and converts has thus been wonderfully settled by authoritative pronouncements. Henceforth, under the prudent direction of their spiritual guides, Chinese Christians may be loyal both to their traditional culture and to their Catholic faith.

Nevertheless, the early missionaries firmly laid the foundation for Christianity in China. This is borne out by the present resistance to the ruthless persecutions of Christianity by the Communists on the Chinese mainland. This vitality of the Church in China is a tribute to the memory of those early missionaries who, at the price of heroic hardships, made such a splendid contribution to the present and the future Christian work in the Far East.

This point will become significantly clear when we come to a later chapter dealing with the Communist persecution of the Church. For the present, let us consider two questions. What was the result of the expulsion of foreign missionaries in the eighteenth century? What future was at stake? To find the answers it is necessary to discuss, at least in outline, the opening of China to the West by invasion during the following century.

Entry By Force

FOLLOWING THE controversy over rites, China refused to accept not only Christianity but also the Western technology which the missionaries had brought along with them to China. As a state, China remained without significant contact with the outside world, taking pride in her ignorance of science and technology—or to put it succinctly, priding herself on her material backwardness as an index to, and a sign of her spirituality. But while the Chinese resisted the culture of Europe, they could not resist its armies. Following the armed conflict known as the Opium War, which took place between the Chinese Empire and Great Britain in the middle of the nineteenth century (1839-1842), China was opened, against her will, to the West.

The story of the Opium War is too well-known to be retold here. It suffices to say that the conflict, which resulted from opium traffic, was condemned morally, if not politically, even by noble-minded statesmen of Great Britain.[1] China offered virtually no resistance during the course of this war. The peace which was sealed by the Treaty of Nanking (1842) ceded Hong Kong to Great Britain and five ports were opened to foreign trade. The rights granted by China in this treaty were soon extended to France (1844), the United States (1844), Belgium (1845), Sweden and Norway (1847), and Russia (1851).

The terms embodied in the Treaty of Nanking satisfied neither Great Britain nor China; from the Chinese standpoint too much had been granted, and from the foreign standpoint not enough. Local friction led to another clash between the two countries.[2] The murder of Auguste Chapdelaine of the Paris Foreign Missioners in Kwangsi on February 29, 1856, was chosen by the French government as a pretext for joining England in a military action against China. Both Russia and the United States stood aloof from the conflict, which came to be known as the Arrow War. Through their mediation a peaceful settlement of the dispute was concluded by the Treaty of Tientsin (1858) and in supplementary Conventions (1860). At the insistence of France, special privileges were awarded to missionaries in the treaties.[3]

The United States asked nothing as reward for its services; but Russia, posing as a friend of China, secured compensation for her friendship in the cession of the region north of the Amur and east of the Ussouri. This Russian advance has a great bearing on the present world situation. Had this area, as large as the combined area of France and Germany, not been conceded through default to Russia, the Soviet Union would not have been able to establish continental contact with Korea, and thus there might be a completely different picture in the Far East today. In methods of aggression there has been practically no difference between the Tsarist and the Soviet regimes.

The international troubles resulting from the Opium War and the Arrow War so weakened China that she was an easy victim of her jealous neighbor, Japan, in the first Sino-Japanese War (1894-1895), which was fought over the territory of Korea. In the Treaty of Shimonoseki (1896), China had to cede several of her sovereign rights, including the Liaotung Peninsula, where Port Arthur and Dairen are located. Russia, however, considered that the Japanese acquisitions threatened her interests in the Far East, and in cooperation with France and Germany, she was able to force Japan to restore the Liaotung territory to China.[4] For this new benevolent intervention, Russia was able to establish herself in a special position in Manchuria—a position which she lost to Japan in the Russo-Japanese War (1904-1905), but recovered forty years later by acquisition of Port Arthur and Dairen under the Yalta Agreement.[5]

Russia's success in Manchuria in 1895 gave rise to an international scramble for territorial rights in China; and with the exception of the United States, almost every great power took a share. China's difficulties were also intensified by internal strife. In the course of the Arrow War, the Tai Ping Rebellion, a kind of peasants' revolt, put a great strain on China's national life;[6] and after the first Sino-Japanese War the Boxer Uprising almost brought about a partitioning of China by the great powers. The proclamation of the American Open Door Policy by Secretary John Hay saved China from this fate.[7]

Out of the events in China's tangled international relations during the nineteenth century emerged three attitudes which remain of extreme importance today.

In the first place, since throughout the entire course of hostilities the United States maintained a friendly attitude toward China and never took advantage of the situation by asking any privilege or reward for her friendship, the Chinese people became convinced that American policy toward China was governed by altruism.

The United States condemned the Opium War;[8] mediated the Arrow War; helped to conclude the Treaty of Shimonoseki which sealed the first Sino-Japanese War;[9] refrained from any territorial exploitation during the international scramble for "sphere of interest" in China, and—above all—declared the Open Door Policy safeguarding China's political independence and integrity. The United States is the only one among the foreign powers who has never conceived any design on the Chinese territory, and this is something the Chinese people can never forget.

The United States' behavior was in direct contrast to that of the Russian. Russia's traditional policy was exemplified in its attempt to establish a stronghold in Manchuria through a clever practice of double-talk and double-play, through posing as China's friend but collecting substantial benefits for herself.

It is true that under the so-called "most-favored-nation" principle the United States automatically acquired those treaty rights which had been accorded to the other powers. But the Chinese fully understood, even at that time, that the American participation in these treaty rights often made it possible for the United States to defend effectively the interests of China itself. The Open Door Policy speaks for itself.

The American record has led the Chinese to place an unswerving trust in the United States. In the days following her opening to the West, China listened almost unreservedly to what the United States said or advised. On the other hand, the Chinese not only distrusted Russia, but also gained their knowledge of that country—its political, social, and intellectual life—almost exclusively through American literature. The United States could make China believe or disbelieve almost everything.[10]

To the common people, the idea of the United States as a loving, friendly, and trustworthy country is even deeper. The very Chinese name for the United States, "Mei," signifies "beauty" or "perfection." Even in the midst of intensified "anti-America" and "hate-America" campaigns, the Chinese Communists have been unable to change this time-honored nomenclature. When the Communists shouted, "The 'Beautiful Country' is imperialistic and ugly," we can be sure that the people have not believed the slander.

A second attitude generated in the Chinese people by their experience in the nineteenth century is an undying hatred of "extraterritoriality." Despite the valuable friendship of the United States, China suffered greatly from Western imperialism.

Among all the injuries made to China by the European nations since the Opium War, there were three which hurt the most: the violation of Chinese territorial integrity, as exemplified most strikingly in the French, British, and international concessions in Shanghai; the encroachment on China's independence in her loss of tariff autonomy through international control of import and export duties; and the bypassing of China's judicial authority through the exercise of juridical power by the consular authorities of foreign powers.

Although all these violations of Chinese integrity, contained in the so-called "unequal treaties," were finally terminated at the initiative of the United States during World War II, the damage done to the Chinese mind is beyond calculation. To this day we can still find strong feeling among the Chinese against extraterritorial jurisdiction, as, for example, in the Reynolds case in Taiwan.[11]

Thirdly, since as a result of the Arrow War the non-persecution of Christians was made a political condition in the treaties, missionary work in China was considered by many to be part and parcel of the hated foreign concessions.[12] This was most unfortunate from the standpoint of the Christianization of China.

On the surface the provision gave Christians, both aliens and Chinese, the privilege of propagating Christianity and assured them of toleration in the practice of their faith. In reality, it led to many abuses. Frequently Chinese of unreliable character professed conversion with the sole motive of obtaining undeserved assistance from the missionaries or foreign consuls; and the consuls often almost blindly defended unworthy converts at the expense of justice and the dignity of the Chinese civil and judicial authorities.

Even though the Chinese were sometimes wrong in their interpretation of foreign motives, ability, and generosity, their resentment of Westerners often had good basis in fact. For instance, at the entrances of the Shanghai public parks under the jurisdiction of the international concessions there were posted signs, "No Dogs or Chinese Allowed." Christian missionaries, however full of religious enthusiasm in teaching the Chinese about the equality of mankind, with few exceptions seemed to make no effort to do anything about these signs, or to uphold principles against prejudice of the rights of persons against the claims of power.[13] Little wonder that the Chinese, contemplating Western ways, thought, "We seem to worship different gods."

While Chinese and Westerners were thus forming attitudes toward each other that would have future consequences, the Catholic Church intensified its activity among the Chinese. When the international treaties opened the doors to the outside world, missionaries began to re-enter the Chinese Empire from foreign lands, and by the middle of the nineteenth century, there were five Catholic religious Orders functioning in China.[14] Among these were the Jesuits who partially resumed their activities in 1814 and re-established their work in 1842. Five years later they founded their headquarters at Zikawei, a suburb of Shanghai, where the well-known Chinese convert of the seventeenth century, Paul Siu, was buried. Later several other missionary societies came to China;[15] and remarkable contributions were also made in the social field by the religious Orders of Sisters.[16] The Church enjoyed steady progress, and the faithful increased from about 200,000 in 1800, to 369,441 in 1870, and to 741,562 in 1900.

One fact, however, should be remembered. Among the faithful, the great majority belonged to the rural classes and were not well-organized. In retrospect, one realizes that this apparent weakness was a hidden strength, which was to enable the Church in Red China to survive Communist persecution in our own day. Bishop Francis X. Ford of Maryknoll, who died a martyr in 1952 at the hands of the Chinese Communists, seemed to possess the special gift of a prophet when he pointed out this strength in answer to the self-imposed question, "Can the Church continue to function in Communist China?" In 1949 Bishop Ford wrote:

> The answer is yes, provided continuity be not lost and the minimum of tolerance allow the administration of the sacraments. The Catholics of China are not, for the most part, city dwellers. They live in small towns and villages, fairly evenly distributed over the vast land, and history has shown that the Chinese farmer depends on his own resources to survive all hardships. Even if persecution reaches the stage where the Church can no longer function openly, the stamina of the sturdy Catholic farmers will aid them to persevere in the faith. The traditional Catholic life of Chinese villagers has been centered on family prayers rather than on Church services. It is more independent of the liturgy than in Western lands, and thus more capable of survival under persecution.[17]

On the other hand, we should note that since Catholic missionaries went mainly to the rural classes in the nineteenth century, they had little contact with the intellectuals; and the difficulties that the Church faced in dealing with the intellectuals were made even greater by the special privileges granted missionaries in the "unequal treaties." When China's present leader, Chiang Kai-shek, remarked that "even the teachings of Christianity suffered by their connection with the unequal treaties,"[18] he certainly was not expressing a merely personal view.

Thus the "unequal treaties" imposed on China directly affected the progress of Christian mission work. They were also to have great indirect effects. The international pressures on China during the nineteenth century were such that national reform became imperative, and the attempts to bring about this reform had much to do with the development of our situation today—in which the alternative, Communism or Christianity, is posed not only to China but the world.

Part Three

A TOWER OF BABEL

"Now whilst Paul waited for them at Athens, his spirit was stirred within him, seeing the city wholly given to idolatry."

Acts 17, 16

The Struggle For Reform

THE YEARS between 1894 and 1898 may be considered the initial stage of the reform movement in China. After China's defeat in the Sino-Japanese War, 1894-1895, the prestige of the traditional leaders could no longer be maintained, and a political revolutionary force began to emerge. The "unequal treaties," in spite of all their evil effects on the Chinese mind, did make the Chinese aware that they must act to restore Chinese's ancient vitality. But in spite of dark shadows, the twentieth century held the promise of a new dawn. The Chinese came to realize they were living in a spiritual ghetto, and that they must adjust their traditions to modern thought and attempt to meet on equal terms the challenge of the West. Guidance from the intellectuals was sought.

The intellectuals were divided into three groups: conservatives, moderates, and revolutionaries. (1) The conservatives held that China's traditional pattern of life and thought was superior to all others; that the Chinese found themselves in difficulty not because they had been too conservative but because they had not lived up to traditional ideals. If they were to do so, China would become so strong her troubles would vanish. (2) Others maintained a more moderate view. They believed that Chinese culture had provided the soundest basis for China's development in the past. They wished now to modify Chinese culture to meet the conditions of the modern world, and to take over such Western techniques as appeared to be advantageous. (3) A third group insisted that China's entire traditional pattern of political, social, and economic organization was unsuited to the world of today, and that the whole manner of life and thought must be radically revised.[1] However, these three groups were all confronted by a rather awkward age in the West—an age dominated by the philosophy of Positivism.[2]

In 1842, Great Britain completed her opium enterprise in China, and it was in this year that Auguste Comte published his vast *Cours de Philosophie Positive.* This coincidence of dates determined the direction in which the West would influence Chinese thought. Religion was conveniently labelled by Comte's contemporaries as "the opium of the people."

But Comte was not alone responsible. Along with his positivism came the humanist religion of Hegel, Feuerbach, and Nietzsche. Thomas Huxley's *Evolution and Ethics* was translated into Chinese by Yen Fu (1853-1921), and was enthusiastically received in 1898.[3] He also translated the classic works of John Stuart Mill, Spencer, David Hume, Adam Smith, Montesquieu, and E. Jenks. Ma Chiun-wu, in 1891, make known to the Chinese people the works of Darwin and Haeckel. Other doctrines, derivatives of the above, began to be assimilated with the anarchism of Kropotkin, voluntarianism of Nietzsche and, above all, the positivist philosophy of Comte.[4]

As a complete discussion of Comtian positivism is not our purpose here, it suffices to say that Comtian thought was especially influential. It offered the Chinese intellectuals a Tower of Babel which, as Dostoevsky writes in *Brothers Karamazov,* "is being built without God, not to reach heaven from earth but to bring heaven down to earth."

It should be mentioned that Neo-Confucianism, in its extreme rationalistic form, found a certain compatibility with the teachings of atheistic humanism, and thus the "Tower of Babel" greatly attracted the Chinese, making them believe the day of hope and fulfillment was at hand. "Let us be modern" was the current slogan.

This longing for a "modern" scientific mode of life was manifest in the first efforts at industrialization. Railways, telegraphs, arsenals, and factories were initiated by such men as Li Hung-chang, Tso Tsung-tang, Chang Chih-tung, and others. Their primary idea was to strengthen the national defense and make China less dependent on foreign arms and munitions. Important influence on the reform movement was exerted by Weng T'ung-ho. He advocated, however, a program of reform borrowing Western methods in economic and military matters without modifying institutional structure or abandoning the traditional values of the empire.[5]

Unfortunately for the modernization movement in general and the Weng T'ung-ho program of reform in particular, the Imperial Court at this time was dominated by the Empress Dowager, Tsu Hsi, who had no interest in any reform at all. Although immensely clever and courageous, she was also ignorant, superstitious, grossly extravagant, and shortsighted. Throughout her rule, she failed to recognize the nature of Western pressure upon the troubled empire. She ruled by fear and deepened the corruption of an already corrupt court by her constant resort to extreme conservatism. As Regent she overruled the weak Emperor, Kwang-hsü. He was, however, ambitious enough to advocate a reform program submitted by K'ang Yu-wei. Compared to the "moderate" program of Weng T'ung-ho, this program may be characterized as "radical." It called for more extensive changes in the existing system and a high degree of Westernization. K'ang organized the "Strength Through Study Society" to enlist the aid of intellectuals in spreading his ideas. He attracted several disciples, of whom the most influential was Liang Chi-chao.

In the summer of 1898, there began what were later known as the hundred days of reform projected by K'ang Yu-wei. China was to have able diplomatic representation abroad, a new order was anticipated in which all nations would unite in a movement of unending progress, high officials were advised to seek education in Europe. Edict after edict was issued introducing radical changes: the old education was to be replaced by "practical" subjects; the Confucian essay and examination system was to be abolished; modern schools and colleges were to be established in every province. Also a transportation and mining bureau was to be set up in Peking; the army was to be reorganized; useless government posts were to be abolished; foreign works on politics and science were to be translated.[6]

As for religious beliefs, K'ang Yu-wei tended to be conservative. He wanted to make Confucianism a State religion—an idea much ridiculed even at that time by most of the Chinese intellectuals. They considered that Confucianism was not a religion at all—it is not a religion in the true sense of the word.

All these measures for making China a progressive nation had the blessing of the Emperor, Kwang-hsü. They met, however, with stern opposition from the Empress, Tsu Hsi. She made the Emperor a virtual prisoner and terminated all the proposed reforms. The leaders of this reform movement, including K'ang Yu-wei and his able disciple, Liang Chi-Chao, fled for refuge to Japan.

The movement lasted only a hundred days and ended in complete failure. More than that, the Empress, Tsu Hsi, who blamed the Westerners for all these national misfortunes and undesired reforms, developed an anti-foreign policy, thus creating the situation which led to the Boxer Uprising of 1900.

This uprising was primarily an anti-foreign movement. The

slogan of the Boxers was "Cherish the dynasty and exterminate the foreigners." Since foreigners and Christians were, in public estimation, synonymous because of their common association with the unequal treaties, the anti-foreign campaign became also anti-Christian.

During the first half of the year 1900, many Westerners were attacked and some killed, but for the most part the Boxers concentrated their attacks on what they called the "lesser devils," or native Christians. So far as the Roman Catholics were concerned, there were thirty or forty thousand martyrs, fifty-six of whom were beatified recently in April 1955.[7]

The Chinese native clergy was not persecuted, simply because they were so few in number. Though a tragedy in itself, the persecution showed that heroism and sanctity were not wanting among the Chinese faithful. This had an important bearing on the Church's later decisions to settle the questions of the rites in 1939, to establish the native clergy, and in 1946 to institute the Hierarchy together with an internunciature.

The Boxer Uprising brought upon China more "unequal treaties" and foreign encroachments on her sovereign rights.[8] The Empress who had opposed reforms and placed hope in the Boxers to drive the "foreign devils" out of the empire learned the bitter lesson that the foreigners could not be expelled by force. Now aware of her country's weakness and humiliation, she saw the urgent need for responding to the exigencies of the modern world.

Reluctantly, she initiated a comprehensive program of reform, including an educational reform, a new army and navy, a constitutional reform, a campaign against opium.[9] They bore striking resemblances to the reforms of K'ang Yu-wei which she had so ruthlessly suppressed in 1898.

During 1902, edicts removed the ban on intermarriage between Chinese and Manchus, and advised the Chinese to abandon the practice of binding the feet of their women, though men were encouraged to wear their pig-tails as a kind of national make-up. In 1904, five distinguished scholars were sent to Japan, the United States, Great Britain, Germany, and France, to study the constitutional systems and governmental structure of the various countries. Partly as a result of this, a constitution was drafted in 1908 projecting plans for a constitutional monarchy.

Sincere or not, the Empress made her conversion too late. The government faced social, political, economic, and international problems of such magnitude that it appeared to be utterly incapable of adjusting the empire to the nineteenth-century Western impact—the empire failed.

Trial And Error

As THE ENTIRE structure of the State crumbled, change just for sake of change seemed to be inevitable. But the most significant of all these changes was that made in the government—the Empire became a Republic. As the Manchu dynasty failed to adjust itself to the new environment created by the Western impact, the revolutionary movement swept over the land. The Republic of China was founded in 1911.

The man who played the leading role in the revolutionary movement and who founded the Republic of China was Dr. Sun Yat-sen. He was born in 1866 in the district of Hsiangshan, Kwangtung. From 1879 until 1882 he attended Iolani College and Aohu College in Honolulu, and in 1892 he received his M. D. from the College of Medicine for Chinese at Hong Kong. He organized revolutionary societies all over the world and solicited funds for their support from the Chinese living in other countries.

The first revolutionary organization founded by Dr. Sun Yat-sen in Honolulu in 1894 was the Hsing Chung Hui or "Renaissance Party." Its aims were: the expulsion of the Manchus, the restoration of China, and the establishment of a united government. The members were all overseas Chinese nationals. The organization had chapters in Hong Kong, Japan, and the United States. On the eve of the Revolution of 1911, Dr. Sun Yat-sen was residing at Denver, Colorado. Many of his revolutionary ideas were echoed in the "Chinatowns" of great cities throughout the world—in New York, San Francisco, Paris, London, and Singapore.

The Chinese overseas have been known as the "mother of the Revolution." This gives ample evidence of the fact that Dr. Sun's revolutionary effort depended largely on Western help, especially that of the North American continent, and that a close kinship in sentiment was developed.

Even the foreign concessions, generally considered by the Chinese as an international evil, helped the revolutionary cause by granting freedom of press, assembly, and political asylum. This explains why the Republic of China founded by Dr. Sun Yat-sen and now headed by Chiang Kai-shek with its temporary site in Taiwan has always pursued a sympathetic and friendly policy toward the democratic West in general, and the United States in particular.

The most influential and best organized of the revolutionary force was the T'ung Meng Hui, or "Alliance Society." It was organized by Dr. Sun Yat-sen in 1905 while he was living in exile in Tokyo. After several changes it was reorganized into the Kuomintang, or the Nationalist Party of China, which exists today.

By nature and culture, Dr. Sun had a deep concern for the democratic way of life of the people. This is clear in his outline of the four fundamental objectives of the T'ung Meng Hui, which were: (1) to overthrow the Manchus; (2) to implement the sovereignty of the Chinese people which implied the establishment of a "Nationalistic" regime; (3) to create a republican government, based on the principles of equality, in which all citizens would be represented and governed by a popular elected president and legislature, and (4) to equalize the ownership of land so that all the people might enjoy the blessings of modern civilization.

Dr. Sun's later political, social, and economic doctrine better known as *San Min Chu I,* or the *Three Principles of the People* (The Principle of Nationalism, the Principle of the People's Rights, and the Principle of the People's Livelihood), were based on these ideas.[1]

As to the organization of the government during the process of revolution, Dr. Sun held that it should undergo three distinct stages:

> The first stage is a military government. After the outbreak of revolution all provinces will follow suit. . . . All soldiers and civilians should be under military rule. . . . All local government should be under the control of the military authority. . . . Each district should be ruled in this manner for a period of three years. . . . At the end of this period, the military rule will be replaced by a constitutional administration.
>
> The second stage is a provisional constitutional government. After each district has undergone the period of military rule, the central authority should grant the people self-government. . . . After six years, when the country has been pacified, the administration will be replaced by a formal constitutional government.
>
> The third stage is a constitutional government. After the provisional constitution has been put into practice by the whole nation for six years, a formal constitution should then be compiled and the military and the political power of the military government should cease functioning. The president and the congressmen should be chosen by public election to form a parliament. The political affairs of the whole nation should be conducted according to the constitution.[2]

Equipped with this political philosophy, Sun directed the revolutionary activities through the T'ung Meng Hui.

From 1906 to 1908 seven attempts were made to overthrow the Manchu regime by military strength: (1) The attempt at

P'ing-hsiang and Liu-yang, Hunan (1906). (2) The attempt at Chaochow and Huang-kang, Kwangtung in 1907. (3) The attempt at Huichow, Kwangtung in 1907. (4) The attempt at Anking, Anhwei in 1907. (5) The attempt at Ch'in-chou and Lien-chou, Kwangtung in 1907. (6) The attempt at Chen-nan-kuan, Kwangsi in 1907. (7) The attempt at Hokow, a frontier town in southeastern Yunnan in 1908. Of these seven attempts, all except the first and fourth were made entirely by members of the T'ung Meng Hui.[3] Although none of these revolutionary attempts were successful, they had a profound effect in accelerating the steadily increasing antipathy between the Manchus and Chinese.

At the time of these revolts, Dr. Sun encountered many difficulties. After leaving his exile in Tokyo, Dr. Sun moved his headquarters to Hanoi, Annam (Indochina). There were seven attempts in 1908 to overthrow the Manchu dynasty; all were failures and Dr. Sun was obliged to flee to Europe. From there he went to the United States. He did not return to China until the Manchu regime collapsed in 1911. The activities of the T'ung Meng Hui, however, were continuously carried out by Dr. Sun's devoted followers. During the last three years of the Manchu dynasty there occurred, along with several minor riots, the following attempts at revolution: (1) On November 19, 1908, Hsiung Ch'eng-chi started an uprising at Anking. (2) In February, 1910, the new army started a mutiny at Canton. (3) In March, 1910, Wang Ching-wei attempted to assassinate the regent Tsai-feng. (4) On April 27, 1911, seventy-two martyrs shed their blood for the revolution in an unsuccessful attempt at Huang-hua-kang—known as the Canton Uprising.

Of these four attempts, only that of Hsiung Ch'eng-chi was not planned by the T'ung Meng Hui. Although they were not successful, they did help to promote revolutionary ideas on a national scale. The Canton Uprising, in particular, paved the way for final success of the October revolution of 1911. It served to awaken the great majority of the Chinese people to the fact that all hope for China's future lay in the formation of a new, democratic republic.

The energetic efforts and revolutionary spirit of Dr. Sun and his faithful associates of the Kuomintang finally brought an end to the Manchu regime in 1911. A new republic was born. Dr. Sun was elected as the first President of the provisional government at Nanking, and assumed office on January 1, 1912.

According to Dr. Sun, the provisional government should be organized according to the revolutionary process, as had been determined by the T'ung Meng Hui in 1906.[4] It should be a strong military government, a government necessary for a nation seeking to change overnight from a monarchy to a republic. However, he could not convince his followers of this revolutionary process. Dr. Sun said:

> At the beginning of the first year of the Republic, I resolutely watched over the revolutionary process in order to achieve the goal of revolution and reconstruction . . . but most of my comrades did not agree with me. Even though I repeatedly explained matters to them and argued with them, it was of no avail. Most of them thought my ideas were too advanced or was it that the knowledge of my comrades was too limited? I could not help feeling disappointed. . . . For this reason I intended to retire.[5]

Dr. Sun resigned on February 23 of the same year in favor of Yuan Shih-kai who professed the same democratic ideals advocated by Dr. Sun and his party, the Kuomintang. The center of government was moved from Nanking to Peking. A provisional constitution of fifty-six articles was promulgated on March 11, 1912. The Kuomintang won the majority of seats in the Parliament.

So far as the form of government was concerned, it appeared to be democratic enough. Democracy, however, is more than a political system: it is a way of life. In its true sense democracy is a virtue akin to the medieval virtue of "justice" which must form the moral content and basic spirit of all truly democratic institutions. But Yuan Shih-kai could not rise to this height, he hated people with ability and integrity—such people were difficult to order around. In comparison with his basic jealousy, his usurpation of power was a lesser fault.[6]

Yuan ignored the constitution, dissolved the Parliament, and outlawed the Kuomintang. He even went so far as to declare a monarchy in 1915.[7] These outrages compelled Dr. Sun to resume revolutionary activities. Yuan's plot was short-lived. He died in 1916.

These circumstances profoundly disturbed the young Republic, yet it continued faithfully on with the perilous beginnings that mark every transition from authoritarian to democratic regimes. Dr. Sun established himself at Canton in 1917 with a view to overthrowing the government at Peking which was being ruled by the corrupted northern warlords after Yuan's death. Civil war was the order of the day.[8]

To fully understand the situation that China found herself in these revolutionary times, it is necessary to understand the general intellectual setting in which Dr. Sun was working. Many outside influences were creating the intellectual climate of the nation: missionary activity, trade and economic problems, foreign relations in general, and the scholastic broadening of the intellectual class.

The Intellectual Revival

WHEN WE CONSIDER the intellectual influence on the younger generation of Chinese at the turn of the present century, we must not minimize the role played by the Protestant missionaries, especially those from the United States. They entered China later than the Catholic missionaries, yet they made greater strides in their intellectual work.

It is true that the number of the Catholics reached 1,292,287 in 1910 when the Republic was about to be founded.[1] It is also true that at this time the missionaries in China were reenforced by others from different countries.[2] However, their activities were centered on the peasant rather than on the educated circles. Furthermore, the question of the rites remained an obstacle in the apostolate to the intellectual leaders.

Protestant missionaries were in a different and more favorable situation for very obvious reasons. At the beginning of the nineteenth century, when Catholic activity was more or less limited to the interior and its influence rather unimportant, Protestant missionaries began to work in China. The Chinese in those days did not have a high opinion of foreigners. They saw that in religious as well as in trade and political affairs, there was no real unity among them, and they interpreted the disharmony in terms of egoistic motives. But they did have a predilection for Americans. In fact, it was a period of outstanding Americanism. The Monroe Doctrine (1823) made it clear that the United States was opposed to any kind of aggressive policy. Again, China came into contact with America through missionary personalities. There was no evidence in their lives or works to lead one to suspect that their intentions were connected with anything other than altruism.

The first Protestant missionary who arrived in China in 1807 was Robert Morrison. Scottish by birth and an Englishman by culture, Morrison went to China by way of the United States, and with the blessing of the American government.[3] Thus, he was thought of and regarded as an American. Furthermore, he found most of his useful helpers in the Americans, such as Bridgeman and Abeel in 1830 and Samuel R. Brown in 1839. The Americans in those days seemed full of evangelistic fervor. The Chinese felt their efforts seemed childish at times, but thought their intensity of purpose admirable; and they considered their sincerity and ethical ideals beyond reproach.[4]

Under the able and energetic leadership of Morrison, the Protestant missionaries laid emphasis, from the very beginning, on the intellectual apostolate. They considered that among such a people as the Chinese, high attainments in learning were necessary to secure respect and influence. Three enterprises which did a great deal of good in this field were: the Morrison Educational Society, the Medical Missionary Association, and the Society for the Diffusion of Useful Knowledge among the Chinese.[5] The medical mission associated medicine with the propagation of religion. The cultural efforts resulted in the publication of numerous religious books of all types in Chinese. The scriptures were translated. The Western education of Chinese youth began. Americans saw the practical value of educational institutions and later they put an increasing portion of their time, effort, and money into establishing and staffing high schools and universities throughout China.

In carrying out their evangelical program, the Protestant missionaries devoted special attention to the Chinese overseas.[6] The economic interests of the Chinese overseas may lie elsewhere, but they centered their cultural sympathies always around the homeland. Thus, these Chinese offered a natural field of development for evangelical purposes. As they were held in high esteem by their relatives and friends on the Chinese mainland, they could exercise extensive influence on the Chinese mind as a whole. Protestant missionaries were able, in those days, to accomplish much because of their close association with the Chinese overseas. This long-ranged policy should be weighed carefully in view of the inaccessibility of the China mainland today.

As we have already indicated, most of the Protestant missionaries came from the United States. By nature, they were resourceful. Moreover, during the period between 1820 and 1844, most of them were receiving adequate training for the mission field.

Their mission method was that of "adaptation." Full of zeal and with a sense of the practical, they spared no effort in making full use of the laity who used to get out and knock on doors to let people know they were personally interested in their work and their lives. After they became friends, religious talk or discussion was introduced as a natural subject of conversation. Whether the people really understood or believed in what Protestantism could offer was another problem, but they deeply appreciated the sentiment and friendship embodied in these "visitations."

Last but not least, there were financial resources. As a result of the Boxer Uprising in 1900 China was made to pay an indemnity to foreign powers. In 1908 the American Congress by joint resoultion authorized President Roosevelt to reduce the United States' share of the Boxer Indemnity from $24,440,000 to $13,655,492.[7] This refund was made available for the education of Chinese students abroad, especially in the United States, and for the establishment of colleges and universities in China mostly under the aegis of the Protestant missionaries. Though the Chinese were always friendly to the Americans, it was only with the great drift of students toward America at this time that serious American influence resulted. The totality of that influence in the educational and cultural fields was Protestant.

But what of Catholic activities in the cultural field at this time? More Catholic missionaries arrived from abroad during this period.[8] They made many contributions toward forming the new and Christian China, but circumstances were such that their achievements in the educational field left much to be desired.

The first Catholic school in China, founded by the Jesuits, was St. Ignatius College in Shanghai in 1850. Another Jesuit institution, Aurora University of Shanghai, was established in 1903. The Hautes Etudes College of Tientsin (Kung Shang) was founded in 1923; and transformed into the University of Tsinku in 1948. It was directed by the Jesuits of the Province of Champagne. The Fu Jen University of Peiping was opened in 1926, at first under the direction of the Benedictines, later under the Society of the Divine Word (S.V.D.) Fathers. As late as 1949, 90 per cent of the students at this Catholic University were non-Catholics.[9]

This being the case, it was Protestant religion and "liberal" thought that predominantly influenced academic circles both before and after the Revolution of 1911. Latourette points out that "Christianity has exercised in the shaping of the new China an influence which it is impossible to measure accurately and yet is certainly very great. The new medical profession owes its foundation chiefly to Protestant missions, leadership in modern education—especially higher education—was long largely in Christian (Protestant) hands."[10]

Dr. Sun Yat-sen himself was brought up and educated in Protestant thought. In spite of this, he did not conform to its teachings; neither did he accept the thought current in Europe during the eighteenth and nineteenth centuries as the theoretic basis for Chinese revolutionary action. In fact, he condemned Rousseau's doctrine of the "natural rights of man" and the cult of individual liberty.[11] He advocated the middle path of rejuvenating China's traditional heritage in the light of Western civilization. However, Dr. Sun was unable, in the midst of political disturbances created mainly by Yuan Shih-kai, to check the rising currents of skepticism and positivism.

When Yuan Shih-kai, Sun's successor to the President of the young Republic, abused his leadership and attacked democratic ideals and institutions, the intellectuals reacted violently and began to insist that half-measure reform was no good for modern China. It should be a reform based entirely on the Western pattern, or no reform at all.

This political frustration occasioned the so-called language reform. According to a personal account of Dr. Hu Shih, the initiator of this movement, it all started by chance in the United

States. Hu wrote an article called "Some Tentative Suggestions for Chinese Language Reforms." This article also by chance was published in the January issue, 1917, of the *New Youth,* a magazine edited by Chen Tu-hsiu, the future founder of the Chinese Communist Party. Chen Tu-hsiu used it as an occasion to launch a violent assault against Chinese cultural values as a whole. The language reform, harmless as it may seem, actually assumed the momentum of a literary revolution; and was later known as the "Intellectual Revival."

The literary revolution was in full vigor after China's disappointments with the post-war settlements of Versailles. In spite of Woodrow Wilson's well-intentioned policy toward China,[12] the Treaty of Versailles completely ignored China's request for a reexamination of the foreign concessions in China especially in regard to the Shantung problem. Discontent flared into open revolt.

On May 4, 1919, fifteen thousand students from more than thirty schools and colleges paraded the streets of Peking denouncing the government, and general strikes were declared all over the country. This mass movement is also known in the history of China as the Student Movement of May the Fourth. The movement, partiotic from the start, marked itself by an intellectual interest in "humanistic learning." In essence, it was a revival of the rationalist neo-Confucianism philosophy of the seventeenth century. Modern China was full of "liberal" scholars who saw the merit of the Western scientific analytic technique, and tried to apply it in human knowledge. There is no doubt that they gave Chinese culture a new impetus.

In spite of its honest and energetic effort toward intellectual scholarship, this revival of "humanistic learning" was a sad performance. The intellectuals in China failed to see what modern Western scholars and philosophers like Maitland, Toynbee, Whitehead, Bergson (in his later years), Maritain and many others now see: the immense importance of the Christian Middle

Ages, even for the development of modern science. Science is a good thing, but *scientism* is an evil masquerading as an angel of light. They did not realize that America, for instance, would not have been half as democratic and prosperous as she is, were it not for the faith of the founding fathers and their quest for the kingdom of God and His justice.

As Frank J. Sheed says, "If there be no God, everything loses background."[13] Instead of pursuing knoweldge in accordance with the principles of natural law, men became slaves of skepticism and cynicism. This passage from Latourette outlines the effects of this "Intellectual Revival":

> Much of their (the intellectuals') scepticism was purely destructive. The old Confucian orthodoxy had passed and with it the intellectual unity and uniformity of the educated class. . . . Intellectually the young educated men had passed almost completely out of one world into another and were dominated by an enthusiasm for science—of a Western type. Socially old customs were going, here and there the family was showing signs of disintegration, the relations between the sexes were being revolutionized, and former moral standards were actively challenged. The nation had struck its tents and was on the march—but whither no one could foresee.[14]

The situation was aggravated by the introduction of foreign writers. To everyone in China, Columbia was *the* American university. John Dewey had made that quite clear. He was invited to lecture in China in 1919. The following year, Bertrand Russell was appointed professor of Philosophy at the Peking National University.[15] In spite of their good will and friendly attitude towards China, the influence they exerted on Chinese modern thought was devastating.

Dewey spoke at many public meetings in the principal cities of China. After his visit, progressive education was advocated and in 1922 a national educational policy called "the new school system" based entirely on Dewey's theory of "growth" and "felt-need" was formally adopted.

Bertrand Russell had even more destructive ideas to offer the Chinese than the Columbia University philosopher. He furnished ammunition for the attack against religion; he told his Chinese audience that what China needed most were those modern philosophies, such as evolution, agnosticism, atheism, and socialism that were flourishing in the Western world.[16] "Institutional religion," he said, "has 'murdered people,' suppressed invention and thought, and caused immeasurable sacrifice, including human sacrifice. As to individual religion, it restricts man's will, feelings and conduct, and thereby the free development of the individual. Morality is not improved by religion, for strong religious beliefs make one's behavior mechanical and one's attitude conservative."[17]

The intellectuals believed and preached with Russell that the China of tomorrow will need no religion, because (1) China must be modern and the modern world renounces religion; (2) China needs a rational approach in her reconstruction and religion is opposed to rationality; (3) China needs truth, initiative, equality, and freedom, all of which are alien to religion; (4) China will have none of the tolerance of religion; (5) China will overcome whatever difficulties she may encounter in her regeneration not through religion but through moral cultivation and atheistic training.[18] In this sense, religion is necessarily in opposition with science and should be abolished. There is no such thing as absolute unchangeable ethics. Ethics is relative to circumstances of time and space. Utility is the sole norm of morality.

Until the arrival of Dewey and his disciples, China had a precise philosophy of her own concerning the education of the young. Confident of their own established values in ethics, law, and culture, the old-fashioned teachers passed down these values to the young as part of their way of life. They held that these traditions were all one cultural heritage, and the more of it they learned the wiser and more mentally alert they would be. The philosophy of Dewey and Russell attacked this certitude.

One cannot deny weak and inadequate aspects in the traditional Chinese teaching methods, or that they demanded improvement. But instead of modernizing the old teaching methods, the new educators went further and denied all tradition. Today, the American public has come to realize the ill effects brought by the Dewey and neo-Dewey practice in educational theories.[19] Although in America much harm has been attributed to the worst aspects of this educational program, the general traditions of American life and learning were able to survive; and later, even to improve through some of the program's more valid suggestions. But in China the problem created by adapting this modern educational theory has caused severe damage; valuable tradition was already losing its strength in many areas when Dewey's influence was experienced in its most destructive form.

From Dewey's "modernistic" thought evolved two popular slogans: "Science is all" and "Democracy is everything." But how to attain this scientific development or how to make democracy work, nobody seemed to know or care. Nothing in a constructive way was done. Emphasis continued to be laid on negative and destructive attitudes.

In order to be "scientific" it was imperative to get rid of everything old, feudalistic, and reactionary. Confucius became the target, and his teachings were attacked long before the Communists began to suppress them a few years ago. From Darwin's *Origin of the Species,* the Chinese younger generation were given descriptions of fossil men, yet they found that the origin of man was as mystifying as ever. Today the Communist regime in China is carrying out, through political indoctrination, an intense study of the monkey as the origin of man. This is only a natural continuation of the Darwinian evolutionism which flourished in China more than a quarter of a century ago.[20]

In order to be "democratic," it was imperative to be free—free from everything foreign. Christianity was of foreign origin, therefore it was imperialistic by nature. Anti-feudalism, anti-imperialism and anti-Christianity became the dominant theme of this so-called "Intellectual Revival." It did undoubtedly lead the Chinese along a certain stretch in the path of progress, but eventually it led to an intellectual dead-end.

A generation arose "which knew not Joseph." It removed Confucius from the modern scene and attacked the greatest asset that the West could offer—the Christian religion. Now, science and democracy became no more than a "moon shadow in the lake." For science without a high and sound philosophy as its supreme guide becomes scientism; while democracy becomes illusory if it is not based on a true appreciation of the rights of the individual human personality.

A noted Chinese scholar has said something very pertinent to this intellectual movement:

> The Movement of May the Fourth claimed that China should have democracy and science. However, in order to attain this end China must, first of all, permeate her cultural values with a spirit basic to democracy and science. There are two possible ways of achieving this spiritual basis: (1) to free China's traditional values from self-imposed limitations, and elevate them to a higher spirit, and make them feel the necessity for a new knowledge and a new institution. But this was neither thought of nor understood by those who involved themselves in the movement; (2) to ignore altogether Chinese cultural heritage and accept Western civilization *in toto*. No matter whether such kind of approach is possible, the serious problem remains, for if this is done, China would have to take from the West the bad along with the good. And this would defeat the very purpose of renovating the original values. However, the policy which governed the Movement of May the Fourth inclined mostly to the second way. That the result was bound to be an evil one is, of course, clear. . . . The Movement of May the Fourth intended to reform Chinese culture, but it failed to understand the essence of Chinese culture. Therefore it did not know how to uplift it to a higher level and achieve what it had hoped for. Again, it wished to accept Western civilization, but it failed to see what are its merits and demerits. For this reason, what it had absorbed from the West was essentially superficial. Worse still, as it basically did not under-

stand the integrated nature of cultural values, everything relating to intellectual renovation was handled without any deep thinking. And this resulted in a spiritual vacuum.[21]

The gist of the "Intellectual Revival" comes then to this: Science was the new god. Dewey and Russell announced the new gospel. Confucius, Mencius, Lao Tzu, Buddha were outmoded. Unbelief was the new style. The ancient ethical system was removed in its entirety. Atheism was on the march and religion was a toy. The "old-fashioned" virtues were gone, though people were not too sure what the "new-fashioned" virtues were. So-called scientific thinking meant a complete wiping out of religious purpose and of religious faith in men's lives. It left a vacuum which prepared the way for an organized and philosophical materialism, in the shape of Communism, to come in and fill the void.

Modern China could assimilate and adopt what the West offered her; she certainly could not *become* the West—she could be changed, but not Westernized. Industrialization is necessary for modern China, but it cannot substitute for Chinese civilization. Heretofore the Chinese reform program has been in the hands of those who knew China, but did not know the West. The result was stagnation. Now she gave herself into the hands of those who knew the West, but unfortunately did not know China. The result was almost as damaging. China for centuries had yearned for an intellectual and spiritual salvation; but when she came into contact with most Westerners who claimed to be saviours, she became disgusted with their religion—she saw only the Deweys, not the Maritains.

Yen Fu, who, as we noted, had been responsible for acquainting the Chinese intellectuals with the Western philosophies of Spencer, Huxley and John Stuart Mill, expressed shortly after the First World War his people's growing disillusionment with the new experiment. "Western progress," he said, "has culminated in four achievements: to be selfish, to kill others, to feel little integrity and less shame."[22] These are serious accusations from such an ardent admirer of the modern West.

But the damage was done. The old civilization had been uprooted, and it was now impossible to restore it to its ancient form. At a spiritual impasse, China wandered in a chaotic region between East and West, between the past and the future; and China, "reformed and modernized," expressed her revolt in extreme nationalism. The "Intellectual Revival" which started with the driving force and patronage of the West ended in an anti-Western campaign. Foreign missionary activities, because of their connection with the "unequal treaties," were regarded as another phase of cultural aggression; and suspicion and opposition arose against missionaries and their institutions. Under the influence of Dewey's pragmatism and Russell's amoralism and anti-moralism, it was logical for the Chinese youth to be as impatient with the classic and Christian views of the Occident as they were with the classical culture of their country.

During this anti-Christian movement, the Catholic missionaries had an advantage. The movement was centered in intellectual circles and took place mostly in large cities, but the Catholic Church in China had confined her activities largely to the rural classes and the farmers, and it escaped, in some measure, the full force of the attack.

The foregoing events make it clear that modern China was at one time deprived of its ancient ethical tradition and prejudiced against the spiritual foundations of Western civilization.

The whole episode is reminiscent of the story of the man who, after learning that he had won a prize in a lottery, immediately burned his old clothes and dressed up to collect his winnings. He realized too late that he had left his winning ticket in the clothes he burned. Modern China was taught by these false philosophies to give up what was old before attaining the new. The result was cultural poverty, for the new could not grow without the native soil and indigenous fertilization. These words from the Apocalypse sum up most fittingly the whole tragic episode.

Because thou sayest: I am rich and made wealthy and have need of nothing: and knoweth not that thou art wretched and miserable and poor and blind and naked. I counsel thee to buy of me gold, fire tried, that thou mayest be made rich and mayest be clothed in white garments: and that the shame of thy nakedness may not appear. And anoint the eyes with eyesalve, that thou mayest see.[23]

Reminiscently, Dr. John C. H. Wu says:

With the overthrowing of the Ancient Régime, a disintegration of the ancient ethical system has set in. And up to the present, the Chinese youth are still living in an atmosphere of moral disintegration. The old philosophy of life is no longer a living force in the moulding of the young man's character, and no new philosophy of life has really taken root in the mind and soul of the youth. They seem to be wandering between two worlds, one dead, the other powerless to be born.[24]

In short, "They have sown the wind and they shall reap the whirlwind." The "Intellectual Revival" left China with nothing but a spiritual vacuum.

A *Spiritual Vacuum*

The danger of the spiritual vacuum in modern China's life was never overlooked by Dr. Sun Yat-sen. He knew the situation too well and realized that left to itself it would benefit only the followers of the materialistic philosophy of Marxism. International communism did, in fact, take advantage of the so-called language reform to supply Chinese youth with quantities of communist literature. Dr. John Wu writing on his childhood in China commented, "for a time, the names and doctrines of Marx and Lenin came into great vogue."[1]

After the Chinese Communist Party was formally established at Shanghai in 1921, the general trend towards "liberal" thought reached such a state that China seemed ready for a Communist rule. Dr. Sun sought help from the western world, especially from the United States. Unfortunately, no such help was forthcoming. Instead, Soviet Russia in 1919, after its Revolution, made a friendly gesture toward China.[2]

Chinese acceptance of Russian friendship at this time involved several factors. Most basic, however, was the psychological factor. China, as a modern nation, was struggling with its traditional poverty and a national economy based almost entirely on individual crafts. The West was far advanced in the industrial age, and it enjoyed a standard of living so high that it began to "look down" on the sensitive Oriental peoples. This gave the West an air of superiority which was often labelled "the white man's burden." At the same time, there were many things in Russia disliked by the Chinese. But Russia herself was economically undeveloped and could not assume a superior attitude. Indeed she knew from her own immediate experiences the needs of the so-called backward nations. This common knowledge of poverty and suffering fostered a genuine sense of brotherhood between the Russian and Chinese peoples. They were involved in the same struggle for survival. The Chinese knew that Russia, as a nation, could not be a trustworthy friend. However, between a genuine rascal and a sophisticated gentleman, they preferred association with the rascal than the gentleman. This explains why Dr. Sun Yat-sen later stated: "We have to fight together by uniting with all the peoples in the world who treat us as equals." At that time, only Russia seemed to treat China as an equal.

This being the case, Dr. Sun firmly believed that Russian friendship was necessary for China's revolution. He was also convinced that with Russia's help he could deter the Chinese Communists from creating internal troubles and sabotaging the National Revolution. Although Dr. Sun realized that Communism was something which could not be applied in China, he also knew the nation's most pressing need was to achieve national unification and to attain full independence. Soviet Russia's aid to the Kuomintang was meant to help it in this great task. The cooperation between the Kuomintang and the Russian Communist Party was precisely for the purpose of assuring successful completion of this revolutionary task. For these reasons, Dr. Sun adhered to his policy of alignment with Soviet Russia and the admission of Chinese Communists into the Kuomintang. It was against this intellectual and political background that Dr. Sun initiated and concluded the agreement of collaboration of the Chinese Communist Party and the Soviet Union through Adolf Joffe, a representative.

The basis for the collaboration was defined in the joint statement of Dr. Sun and Joffe issued on January 26, 1923. In this statement it was agreed by both parties that the Soviet system would not be introduced into China, and that the paramount problems for China were unification and national independence. Joffe reaffirmed the readiness of the Soviets to enter into negotiations with China by renunciation of the unequal treaties, and by settling the problem of the Chinese Eastern Railway at a later conference.[3]

Sun Yat-sen sent Chiang Kai-shek to Russia in the summer of 1923. When Chiang reached Moscow, Lenin was seriously ill; but Chiang had talks with Trotsky and other leaders. During his stay in Moscow, Chiang made a thorough investigation and study of the Soviet system. He was aware "of the deep dissimilarities between the Russian and the Chinese situation. He recognized that revolution in China must be a vastly different undertaking from its counterpart in Westernized Russia. . . . After staying in Russia for four months, Chiang returned in December to Canton, where he made an unfavorable report on certain aspects of the Soviets, but suggested a reorganization of the Kuomintang along the lines made by his observations in Russia."[4]

The Kuomintang was reorganized in January, 1924. A new revolutionary method was adopted so that the party would "become a powerful political organ with concrete platforms," and be able to use "the power to reconstruct the nation."[5] The *Three Principles of the People* were reaffirmed.

Of these three principles, that of nationalism *(min-tsu chu-i)* supports two aims: the liberation of China by the Chinese people; and the establishment of equal rights for all races living in China.

The principle of the people's rights *(min-ch'uan chu-i)* was recognized by the Kuomintang as supporting not only indirect rights but also the specific rights of election, referendum, and recall. The exercise of these rights is described in Sun's *Five Power Constitution,* which provides for the separation of powers: namely the legislative, judicial, administrative, examining, and supervisory powers. This system of government seeks to avoid the defects of other modern parliamentary governments and to correct the weaknesses of the traditional Chinese civil service examination system.

The principle of the livelihood of the people *(min-sheng chu-i)* comprises two major aims: equalization of landholdings and regulation of capital. To achieve economic equilibrium no monopoly in land ownership is permitted. The State must regulate the ownership, use, and purchase of land as well as tax levies on land. Such regulations implement the principle of equality in property rights. To prevent private capitalism from controlling the people's livelihood, the State will manage and control all banks, railroads, and ship lines, and all other large enterprises. With the regulation of landholding and the regulation of capital, the State will establish socialism on a secure foundation.[6]

These *Three Principles of the People* still serve as the political, economic and social programs carried out by the Republic of China in Taiwan.

After the Kuomintang was reorganized in 1924, Sun Yat-sen, the party leader, was more determined than ever to join hands with Russia. Soviet Russia, to support the Kuomintang, commissioned General Bluecher (Galens) and Michael Borodin to Canton. Both served as advisers to the Kuomintang and played an important part in China's political life. Relations between Sun Yat-sen and Soviet Russia became closer and closer. Although many of Sun's followers, including Chiang Kai-shek, were dubious of the wisdom of such a policy, nobody seemed able to change the situation. As Chiang Kai-shek puts it, "Though I became anti-Communist as a result of my visit (to Russia), I was overconfident too, and failed to settle the Communist problem in a fundamental manner."[7] Communist infiltration into the Kuomintang had begun.

Collaboration with the Soviets lasted for three years and proved to be a complete failure. "The period of ostensible Kuomintang-Communist collaboration," as W. W. Rostow says, "was marked by interminable if somewhat obscure communist maneuvers designed to seize and hold strategic posts in the Kuomintang structure and to develop independent popular support."[8]

It is generally thought that this conciliatory policy was, to a certain extent, responsible for inviting Communist penetration into the civic, political, and cultural life of China. But this does not tell the whole story. The truth is that Dr. Sun, when he entered into the agreement, was not entirely unaware of the Communist menace, especially in the intellectual field. The agreement assured cooperation between the two contracting parties, but the basis for this collaboration was the hope that the Chinese Communists would give up their allegiance to the Communist Party and pledge loyalty to the Kuomintang. This is clear in the following words by which Dr. Sun defined his position toward the Communists in the Kuomintang: "The Communists are joining our Party in order to work for the National Revolution. We are, therefore, bound to admit them. . . . If the Communists betray the Kuomintang, I will be the first to propose their expulsion."[9] Dr. Sun hoped to convert the Communists by his sincerity, and absorb them into his revolutionary program. Though he was struck by the underhanded methods used by Chen Tu-hsiu, leader of the Chinese Communist Party, and others with dual-party memberships, he still thought that they could not cause China any harm. Furthermore, Dr. Sun's policy of alignment with the Communists was based on a sincere desire for nationalism; he did not believe that Communism was applicable to China. Therefore, it is not so much the fault of Dr. Sun, whose wisdom and revolutionary efforts should be recognized, but the "Trojan Horse" tactic of the Communists which should be blamed.

The Soviet Union's treaty obligations were, as usual, shaped entirely by necessity or expediency or both, never by international ethics or interest in human welfare. Dr. Sun was a victim of Soviet treachery. Here is an excellent lesson for those who advocate co-existence with Communism.

Dr. Sun died in 1925. In his will he said, "The work of Revolution is not yet done." The responsibility of carrying on the revolution and unifying the country fell on his able and faithful disciple, Chiang Kai-shek, the future President of the Republic of China. He fully realized the difficulties ahead.

Unfinished Business

THE COMMUNIST threat was intensified following Dr. Sun's death, but Chiang Kai-shek, still the Generalissimo of the Revolutionary Army, was able to achieve the preliminary success of the National Revolution by 1927. Generalissimo Chiang immediately recognized the danger of the Communist conspiracy; he knew they planned to take advantage of the National Revolution and to turn it into a social revolution patterned on the Soviet model.

Turbulent conditions reigned in the young Republic. Communist-directed troubles and disorders were beyond calculation. It is impossible to achieve social reconstruction in a period of chaos, when the very ones who pledge themselves to peace and order betray that cause and deliberately foster chaos. Chiang Kai-shek courageously and wisely decided to "split" with the Communists, and end all collaboration. He purged the Kuomintang of the Communists and their sympathizers. Borodin and the other Russian advisers were sent back to Russia. Were Dr. Sun Yat-sen alive at the time, he would certainly have done the same thing.

The purge of 1927 saved China from the Soviet conspiracy, but began a series of wars which have not yet ended. The Communists remained independent of the National Government of the Republic of China, and their armies have fought it to this day.

Chiang Kai-shek has tried hard to tell the world the full truth about Soviet Russia and Communist conspiracy. As a result, he has been personally smeared and depicted as "dictator," "warmonger," "fascist."

Chiang Kai-shek has been proved consistently right in his anti-Communist crusade. As Dr. Hollington K. Tong, China's leading journalist and diplomat, said in July 1953, "During much of this sixteen year period, Chiang Kai-shek has been a controversial figure, abused and misunderstood by many of his own best wishers. The ordeal was inevitable for a man whose vision was so far ahead of his time. Today, the Free World appears to be catching up with him. . . . He has been wrong; but he has been right oftener than his contemporaries."[1]

For over three decades, Chiang has steered a straight course. He has the necessary knowledge and understanding. He was convinced from the very beginning that the greatest threat of Communism is not purely of a military nature; it lies in the spiritual realm. He traced the growth of Communism in China to the disintegration of the spirit:

After the Student Movement of May the Fourth, 1919, two currents of thought, ultra-individualistic liberalism and class-struggle communism, found their way into Chinese academic circles, and later became widespread in the country. On the whole, Chinese academic circles desired to effect a change in our culture, forgetting that it had certain elements which are immutable. With respect to different Western theories they imitated only their superficial aspects and never sought to understand their true significance in order to improve China's national life. The result was that a large number of our scholars and students adopted the superficialities and nonessentials of Western culture and lost their respect for and confidence in our own culture. . . . The result was only to make Chinese culture sink into a state of decay and disintegration. Under these circumstances Chinese scholars and politicians who misinterpreted liberalism and abused communism were disposed, openly or indirectly, intentionally or unintentionally, to take a foreign Power's interests with theirs. . . . Their propaganda and educational activities among the masses were conducted in this mental atmosphere, causing the people to regard as a matter of course the impairment of our national life. And what is worse, they were unaware that such impairment and endangering were furthered by their blindly following foreign "isms." This truly constituted the greatest crisis in the history of our culture and the most serious menace to the spirit of our people.[2]

To remedy the deteriorating situation and defeat Communism at its root, Chiang convincingly advocated at the outset of his rule, China's reform primarily on the spiritual level, through a genuine assimilation of Chinese culture with Christian principles. Thus, he pointed out:

From the facts of history we can see that our nation has the moral virtues of self-respect without self-conceit, and humility without self-abasement. The maxim, "Dignified and yet not proud, humble and yet not abject," truly expresses the moral spirit of our people. The attitude of the Chinese towards alien religions and philosophies is in fact based upon these innate qualities of character.

With respect to religion, China had for a long time her own philosophy of life which, as propounded by Confucius, elaborated by Mencius, and commended upon by scholars of the Han Dynasty, forms a sublime system in itself. . . . The introduction of Christianity into China at the end of Ming and the beginning of the Manchu dynasty further served to enrich Chinese philosophical thought. Indeed, the Chunghua (Chinese) nation is endowed with a great capacity for assimilation. Never has it, in regard to foreign religions and cultures, adopted an antipathetic attitude, a close-door policy. This accounts for the complete absence in China of religious wars which ravaged Europe in the Medieval Ages. Since the last century, Christianity has exerted salutary influence upon the development of scientific knowledge and the reform of social life in China.[3]

Nations, however, cannot be made to spring up suddenly from the earth by the words of a manifesto; they must rather mature gradually with the people so as to express better their aspirations and their practical experiences. China is no exception. Chiang Kai-shek indeed erected a framework of democracy copied on Western models, and an active program for the realization of Dr. Sun Yat-sen's political doctrine, but the civil wars absorbed his time and energy. He simply could not do the job alone.

In spite of these difficulties, Chiang, a Methodist himself, spared no effort in promoting all kinds of cooperation with religious activities. Marked progress was made in the relationship between New China and Christian churches.

Among the things which Chiang contributed to the growth of Christianity in China, I wish to single out the encouragement and help he gave Dr. John C. H. Wu, during World War II, to bring out a literary Chinese version of the New Testament. This version has been warmly received by the Chinese intellectuals, Christians and non-Christians alike. Dr. Wu tells us:

People may wonder how could President Chiang spare his busiest time during the war years to do the translation work. As a matter of fact, the draft was mine, but the President, in the course of three years, spent about one hour a day to read and revise the manuscript. Though he himself made a few drafts wherever necessary, he used to devote himself to the work of revision and correction. Wherever there was a doubt, or something to be improved in the manuscript, he signified it with a mark calling for further study. He simply could not do this without having drunk deep of the inner thought of the Holy Scriptures. . . . Indeed, the New Testament not only gives benefits to one's spiritual growth, but also throws light on the fundamental principles of political philosophy. I was most impressed that when the President revised the following passage in St. Mark he underlined it in a most sympathetic mood: "You know that those who are regarded as rulers among the Gentiles lord it over them, and their great men exercise authority over them. But it is not so among you. On the contrary, whoever wishes to become great shall be your servant; and whoever wishes to be first among you shall be the slave of all; for the Son of Man also has not come to be served but to serve, and to give his life as a ransom for many." (10, 42-45)[4]

Speaking of Chiang's spiritual life, Dr. Hollington K. Tong has this to say:

In all my acquaintance with public men, I have seldom met anyone of comparable position who has the deeply religious, almost austere attitude toward moral conduct that I have found in the Generalissimo. While he never wishes to exploit or discuss his religious life, those who work with him are frequently reminded of the part which religion plays in his daily life. Wherever he goes on his extensive travels, he always consecrates one room for his worship, to which he retires, regardless of the pressure of work, for at least a half hour in both morning and afternoon.[5]

Chiang's personal life may become even more religious now in Taiwan. This we gather from a dispatch by Richard Hughes, special Far East correspondent for *The Sunday Times of London* and published in the *New York Times* (magazine section), Sep. 28, 1958:

He allows nothing to interfere with his prayers and meditations morning and night. He neither reads nor writes English, but consults a Chinese edition of the Bible. . . . He lives a Spartan life, studies the Chinese classics, plods indefatigably back and forth through Old and New Testament alike, . . . fills his diary (which he has kept for three decades in war and peace, victory and defeat) with searching comment, opinion, self-reflection and self-criticism.

How Chiang became a Christian is a well-known story in China. His conversion may be compared to a Constantine-like decision in battle. In 1928, Chiang was trapped by his enemies near Kaifeng, being almost completely surrounded. In his desperate situation he prayed to God for deliverance, pledging that he would publicly acknowledge Jesus Christ as his Lord after the Almighty had delivered him. God did answer his prayer by sending a very heavy snowstorm, which was unusual at that time of year, so that his enemies could not advance. In the meantime, his reinforcement came from Nanking by rail, thereby not only saving his life but turning certain defeat into victory.

It is Chiang's attitude toward the Catholic Church rather than his religious life which concerns us here. My latest audience with the President in Taipei, Taiwan, in August 1956, revealed that he has an enduring interest in, and great esteem for, the Catholic Church. He praised highly, among other things, the heroic sacrifices sustained by the Catholic Church, clergy and laymen alike, on mainland China under Communist persecution. I discussed with him, in his private residence, how the Chinese version of the New Testament that was translated by Dr. John Wu with Chiang's personal collaboration could be made available to a wider Christian audience. Priests of various nationalities in Taiwan told me also that Catholic activities had benefited from Chiang's interest. Truly, with his unreserved cooperation since his coming to power in the 1920's, the Catholic Church has enjoyed a more fruitful time than she had ever experienced before in her long missionary history in China.

The appointment of the late Archbishop (Cardinal) Celso

Costantini by Pope Benedict XV in 1922 as the first Apostolic Delegate to China opened the way for a religious revival which was further encouraged by his successor, the late Archbishop Mario Zenin. Even more important, however, was the consecration of six Chinese bishops by Pope Pius XI in St. Peter's, Rome, in 1926.[6] The establishment of the Chinese Legation to the Vatican in 1942 was hailed especially in Catholic circles as the harbinger of a new era in the advancement of the Church in China. Thus, Chinese Catholics numbering more than three million were brought into direct communion with the Pope.

The controversy of rites was settled in 1939 by Pope Pius XII. In 1946, when the Holy See judged the Church of China mature —a status accorded the Church in the United States only in 1908—China was given a Hierarchy of nineteen Archbishops and seventy-nine Bishops. In the meantime, Bishop Thomas Tien of Tsiangtao was elevated to the cardinalate, the first Asian to be so honored.[7] With this close relationship between China and the Vatican the achievements of the Church in China attained a new height.

Efforts were made to promote the spiritual enlightenment and social welfare of the people. The Legion of Mary became a most active and effective apostolate of the laity. Catholic action, under the leadership of Lo Pa-hong, a great and saintly layman, was organized on a national scale. Along with these achievements was a steady growth of the native clergy.

A study of the number of Chinese priests and seminarians shows that great advance was made in establishing a native clergy capable of carrying on the Catholic work in China.

1865: 514,227 Catholic, 167 Chinese priests;
1 priest for 3,080 Catholics.
1900: 741,562 Catholics, 470 Chinese priests;
1 priest for 1,577 Catholics.
1948: 3,274,740 Catholics, 3,015 Chinese priests;
1 priest for 1,086 Catholics.

From the consecration in 1926 of the first six Chinese bishops until today, exactly sixty-six Chinese priests have been promoted to the episcopal dignity or to the functions of Apostolic Prefect.[8] When the Communists intensified their assault on the Church in 1949, the Chinese native clergy was already strong enough to accept the challenge.

In this regard, a special tribute must be paid to Father Vincent Lebbe (1877-1940). A Belgian by birth, Father Lebbe arrived in China in 1901 and worked there, with the exception of a few years exile in Europe, until his death in 1940. No missionary ever went to China with more devotion to the people or to the nation, and no missionary ever received such intense devotion and love from the Chinese people.[9] As Dom Pierre-Célestin Lou Tseng-tsiang says, "He was the soldier of the Papacy in China, always in the front line, obedient, humble, ascetic, tireless. . . . Following the example of Ricci, of Schall and of Verbiest, so as to give himself wholly to the country to which he burned to give the Gospel, Father Lebbe, in his turn, sought to become a Chinese citizen. He asked for and obtained naturalization."

That Father Lebbe loved wholeheartedly his adopted country and sought always to "win all to Christ" was apparent to all when he registered a protest against the non-Christian French Consul who tried to extend the French concession at Tientsin in 1916 in open violation of the territorial rights of China. This violation was actually embarrassing to the foreign missionaries.[10] However, Father Lebbe's intervention made it possible for the people to see him as a living challenge to the claim that Christianity brought foreign oppression.

In this act, Father Lebbe presented an integral Christianity, which demands devotion to the mission country as well as to God. This splendid example of true Catholicity was manfully repeated by the Vicar Apostolic of Shanghai, Bishop Auguste Haouissée, S.J. who, scarcely three weeks after the Japanese invasion in 1937, issued his pastoral letter urging the Chinese people to carry out their duty of patriotism.[11]

Father Lebbe sought to Christianize China by first giving China to the Chinese and then bringing the Chinese to Christ. In this respect, his letter to the Vicar Apostolic of Ningpo was proved by subsequent events to be a very useful instrument. It gave a striking picture of the religious situation and provided Pope Benedict XV with adequate background to publish in 1919 the Encyclical *Maximum Illud* which called on missionaries to prepare a native hierarchy. His audience with Cardinal Van Rossum, the eminent Prefect of Propaganda, through Cardinal Mercier, proved later to be a part of Divine Providence which guided Pope Pius XI in his decision to consecrate six Chinese Bishops in 1926.[12]

A description of Father Lebbe's life in China would be incomplete without mentioning his part in the development of a strong native clergy. Immediately after the consecration of six Chinese Bishops in Rome, he founded, with his able associates, Father Anthony Cotta, Father Abbé Boland, and Father Raymond J. de Jaegher, the Society of Auxiliary Missionaries (S.A.M.).[13] They placed themselves entirely at the service of Chinese bishops—a magnificent example of true detachment, of apostolic zeal, and of devotion to China and the Chinese, which is now being followed by numerous foreign missionaries including several religious dignitaries in Taiwan.[14]

Besides S.A.M., Father Lebbe founded three other societies. They are the "Little Brothers of St. John the Baptist" for men (1927), the "Theresians" ("Sisters of the Little Flower") for women (1929), and International Catholic Auxiliaries in 1937 (generally known as A.F.I. which stands for *Auxiliaries Feminines Internationals*). The "Little Brothers," with the personal example of Father Lebbe, worked as stretcher-bearers and medical aides on the battlefield during the war with the Japanese. Here they showed the Chinese people the true nature of Catholicism and how deeply Catholicism had been absorbed into the very soul of China. A wonderful Chinese Catholic patriotism was evident in their selfless service and devotion to the sick and wounded.

For this, the Chinese people were grateful. This sentiment we gather from the letter addressed to Pope Pius XII by President Chiang Kai-shek right after World War II—a letter which I was honored to present to His Holiness in person in October, 1945, and which read as follows:[15]

September 1, 1945

Your Holiness Pope Pius XII:

It was with a sense of consolation and gratitude that I received Your Holiness' letter of August 12th brought to me by His Excellency Bishop Paul Yu-pin. From the present sacrifice suffered by the whole world, we have once more witnessed the truth that right makes might and justice is eternal. During the eight-year-long struggle against the Japanese invasion, it was gratifying to note that the Catholics in China, under Your Holiness' spiritual inspiration, have persistently rendered their invaluable service to the national cause. As Your Holiness very rightly pointed out, China has suffered most from this war; her need for the establishment of permanent peace is greater than that of any other nation. I am fully convinced that the future great task of reconstruction should proceed directly from human efforts but ultimately from the Providence of God. I sincerely hope that Your Holiness may from time to time give me all the necessary encouragement and guidance relating to what China may be able to contribute to and work for the peace and welfare of humankind.

I hereby authorize Dr. Kwang-tsien Sih, Chargé d'Affaires with Ministerial rank of the Chinese Embassy in Italy to bring to Your Holiness this personal letter and my autographed photo and convey also my personal highest and warmest respects.

(signed) Chiang Kai-shek

Father Lebbe's humble spirit, apostolic zeal and Catholic charity served, in a word, to foster and intensify the love of the Chinese clergy for the foreign missionaries. This was borne out by the fact that the Communists, who could in later days exercise the "divide-and-rule" policy among the people on the mainland, failed to drive any wedge between the foreign missionaries and the native clergy.

This question will be discussed later on. For the moment, let it suffice to note that along with his genuine cooperation with the Church, Chiang Kai-shek initiated in 1933 the *New Life Movement.* It was fundamentally a moral reform of social customs and habits based on the Confucian ethics.[16] A stocktaking of his moral reform highlighted certain significant things; one spectacular result of the *New Life Movement* was the renewed impetus which it gave to the national crusade for opium suppression—an evil prevalent in China since the Opium War.

The growth of the *New Life Movement* revealed Chiang Kai-shek as the most dynamic force for national regeneration that modern China has produced. He brought into public service the ideal of abnegation of personal interests. By living a noble, energetic life he set an example that has inspired the whole nation. This influence upon the Chinese of will and fortitude was later to be shown in their resistance to the Japanese invaders.

In spite of all its accomplishments and noble purposes, the movement was not a success. It was unable to transform the people and the nation on the moral level which was its original intention. The movement was promoted under Chiang's direct surveillance. While this constituted a strength in the effect, it also was the cause of the movement's weakness. As it assumed openly a political character, the result, as generally happens in such cases where no separation of political and moral orders is assumed, tended to emphasize the external rather than the internal. If moral action is performed and judged externally or is backed by police measures, at the precise moment it begins to succeed, it fails. There is actually no such thing as a moral reform that is not held voluntarily through a spontaneous inner conviction. To be real, it must be alive in the hearts of the people themselves. This explains why this movement, good as it was in every respect, could not achieve the desired success.

The real physical handicap for the national progress rested, however, with the Sino-Japanese War in 1937 which signified the start of World War II. Before this Sino-Japanese War started, China had devoted great efforts toward the development of constitutional democracy outlined by Dr. Sun Yat-sen. The new Civil Code, an adaptation of the best of Western legal science to the needs of a renovated China, was promulgated in May 1931. The first draft of the Constitution, under the chairmanship of Dr. Sun Fo, son of Dr. Sun Yat-sen, and the vice-chairmanship of Dr. John C. H. Wu, was completed in 1933, and it was promulgated on May 5, 1936. A feature of the Constitution is a bill of fundamental liberties and rights of the people, which can be limited only by "laws imperative for safeguarding national security, averting a national crisis, or maintaining peace and order." With the war just beginning, this Constitution was not given a chance to work.

The years of hostilities lasted until the end of World War II, and the national life as a whole suffered a great setback. Still in all, remarkable achievements were made, especially in the fields of education and communication, which were under the direction of Chen Li-fu, Minister of Education, and Chang Kia-ngau, Minister of Communications.[17] The famous Burma Road, chief artery into China during World War II, was completed under enormous difficulties. So far as education was concerned, a unified system of higher learning with long-range vision based on national need and aspirations was inaugurated for the first time in China's modern history. Fundamental and free education for all the children of school age was carried out on a nation-wide basis, including the border regions.

Hitherto, China's higher education had been largely in the hands of foreign missionaries. Their motives were good. However, their outlook was limited by national and missionary backgrounds. Thus, each institution had its own policy and curriculum in accordance with the need, not of China, but of the particular missionary group associated with the establishment. With the new reform, a more liberal and realistic approach was made toward all kinds of studies, humanistic and scientific. For instance, Dr. Tsung Dao Lee and Dr. Chen Ning Yang, who were awarded the Nobel Prize for their discovery of "nonconservation of parity," which has been hailed as a triumph for modern science that ranks with the basic discoveries of Albert Einstein, received their basic scientific training during this period. Further, this new policy in the educational field helped to permeate the Chinese people with a new spirit of self-confidence—a spirit which proved to be vital throughout the course of national resistance against the invasion from Japan.

The Folly of Co-existence

In the autumn of 1937, Japan invaded China, and the Chinese government resisted with all available force. In the Winter, Shanghai fell, and in a moment of extreme urgency, the government was compelled once again to cooperate with the Communists. This was the second effort of co-existence. The first took place in 1923.

Once again the Communists promised to abandon the policy of armed insurrection against the National Government and to stop their program of land confiscation. They promised to give up their propaganda warfare, to strive for the realization of the three principles of Dr. Sun, to abolish the autonomous Soviet governments in the border regions of Shensi-Kansu-Ninghsia and Shansi-Hopei-Chahar, and to reorganize those governments as local organs of the National Government. They also agreed to reorganize their armies as national revolutionary armies subject to the command of Chiang Kai-shek.[1]

The Kuomintang, as the party in power, agreed to assume responsibility for the Communist armies, to assign them particular areas of operation, and to subsidize them financially. Further, it bore all responsibility for the functions of government: local order, economic welfare, and military resistance against the Japanese. The Communists, as an opposition with armed forces, played their own game. They started to sabotage and undermine the National Government as soon as the collaboration began. They stirred the troubled waters yet more and increased their strength in every field.

Mao Tse-tung, leader of the Chinese Communist party, professed agreement with the principles of the Kuomintang, but he would never abandon his Communist ideals. He defined his policy as "70 per cent self-development, 20 per cent compromise, and 10 per cent fighting the Japanese." He wanted first to achieve equality with the Kuomintang and then to take away from the Kuomintang its leading position.[2] This is exactly what the Chinese National Government experienced as a result of its co-existence with the Communists for the second time.

Militarily, the Communist Army, in the course of eight years' war against Japan, increased from a numerical strength of 25,000 men to more than 3,000,000 men.[3] Politically, it extended the "liberated area" from a few counties to nineteen provinces containing 94,500,000.[4] In the economic field, long years of war-attrition made it possible for the Communist Party to further its propaganda for peace at all costs. The Japanese invasion had actually helped the Communists to achieve their intrigues. As recently as 1957, Mao Tse-tung told us:

The Japanese attack (on China in the Nineteen Thirties) was a bad thing because it meant war. But, on the other hand, it resulted in good because the struggle against Japanese aggression made it possible to mobilize the whole nation around the Communist party which led the struggle, and ultimately made for the Communist victory.[5]

The Communists did not lead the struggle. They did not have to. They simply made use of the struggle to further their trickery —to create a "government" within the government, to expand an "army" within the country, and to fight a "war" within the international war. This has made it possible for them to complete their fundamental strategy of armed expansion and to exploit, with the help of Soviet Russia, the revolutionary situation to the full. Herrymon Maurer writes, "Without a defined strategy of attack, without material Russian help, and without Russian counsel in exploiting a revolutionary situation, the Chinese Communists could not have come to power. The war had given the party great opportunity for growth and for the perfection of its fundamental strategy of armed expansion; the Russian capture of Manchuria gave it supplies and a vast operating base. As for the revolutionary situation, it developed along a psychological pattern that resembled in many respects the Russian Revolution—and, indeed, the episode of nihilistic creation of confusion described in Dostoyevsky's *The Possessed.*"[6]

In his book, *Soviet Russia in China: A Summing Up at Seventy,* President Chiang Kai-shek tells the behind-the-scene story of how China succumbed to Communism, mainly through Soviet intrigue. All that we should know about the evil and treacherous character of the Chinese Communists is there. How the Reds repeatedly sabotaged "co-existence" is also there. Speaking of this work, George K. C. Yeh, Chinese Ambassador to the United States, wrote (*Life,* June 24, 1957):

Chiang Kai-shek is the only chief of State who, after falling victim to Soviet aggression, has re-established an effective government and made it the nucleus of a powerful opposition to Communism. He is the only leader of a major people who can tell, step by step, how the Russian Communists seized control under the cover of what is now called "peaceful co-existence."

However, Chiang does not say anything in connection with the Western powers, particularly the United States, which may, consciously or unconsciously, have contributed in certain ways to the rise of Communism in China, during and after World War II. This is quite natural for Chiang. By nature and culture, he personifies China at its best. Restrained, tolerant, modest and humble, he will not say anything which would or could hurt his friends and allies. A Chinese proverb goes, "When your front tooth is knocked off, it is better to swallow it without murmuring." Chiang could not have written this book without tears. His painful experience may be compared to the sea, for the sea is vast in extent and all bitter to the taste. If the free world in this struggle against Communism can really and truly take Chiang's words to heart—there will be still much joy for the anxious world.

This book is about China, not about American policy. But we wish to note here, even very briefly, some of the facts which should be made clear to all who are concerned with the relations between China and the United States, especially during the period China had to face the external enemy (Japan) and the internal foe (the Communists) at one and the same time.

First of all, we can never minimize the injury inflicted upon China by General Joseph Stilwell's policy toward the Communists. General Stilwell was assigned to China by the United States to direct military operations against the Japanese in northern Burma. He was sincere and a good soldier. The Chinese were all appreciative of his services. However, General Stilwell was influenced by Communist propaganda. He mistakenly believed that the Chinese Communists were "agrarian reformers" and elements of a "patriotic democratic party." He did not recognize their real nature and often overestimated their ability and utility against the Japanese. Worse still, he sought to re-equip the Communist forces, even at the expense of the administrative integrity of the National government. On this, Harold M. Vinacke made a fair comment:

> Communists were themselves conducting a war within a war, not having honestly subordinated themselves to either the political or the military authority of the National government. The Stilwell policy, however, could only have disturbed the existing status, and, as viewed by the Kuomintang, to the advantage of the Communists.[7]

When the controversial Stilwell policy reached a crisis in 1944,[8] Henry A. Wallace was sent to China to review the case. His mission, which was to improve Chinese-American relations, resulted in further deterioration. Wallace's effort centered around two aims: to get the Soviet Union and China together with a view to avoiding eventual conflict, and to persuade the Chinese government to settle with the Communists. The first attempt led the United States to Yalta, while the second paved the way for General George C. Marshall's mediation mission to China.[9]

The Yalta agreement was signed on February 11, 1945. China was not represented at the discussions, but China's sovereignty in Outer Mongolia and administrative integrity in Manchuria were sacrificed in return for Soviet Russia's entry into the war against Japan. As we see it now, China, under Chiang's leadership, took up the fight against Japan primarily for the defense of the rights in Manchuria. However, after fourteen years' struggle (since the Mukden Incident of September 18, 1931), China won the war, but lost Manchuria to Soviet Russia.[10] Dr. Tingfu F. Tsiang, Chinese Permanent Delegate to the United Nations, remarked: "It was under such psychological conditions that my government yielded to the pressure of the government of the United States in accepting the substance of the Yalta Agreement. Today we must pronounce the Yalta Agreement a great mistake. Without the Yalta Agreement the whole history of China and Korea in the post-war period would have been different and happier."[11]

Not long after the conclusion of the Yalta agreement, General Marshall was sent to China. He arrived there in December 1945. His mediation effort in China was carried out with all good intentions, though he did not realize the adverse effects that would be created.

The main points which Marshall was to realize were: to effect a truce, particularly in North China, and to form a coalition government including the Chinese Communists.[12] The position of the United States was that of a third party trying to mediate in the conflict between the Kuomintang and the Chinese Communists in the interest of China's own unity. However, the Chinese Communists thought differently and acted differently. They simply took advantage of the American mediation to gain time for military operations against the National forces. Harold M. Vinacke observes:

> The truce itself, as far as it was actually enforced, proved to have been of advantage to the Communists rather than to the Kuomintang when full scale civil war broke out in the first half of 1947, following recognition of the failure of American mediation efforts. When the truce began, the National Government armies had the initiative and were on the offensive. The activity of the truce terms in applying the terms of the agreement prevented the Nationalist armies from attaining their objectives and from wiping out large bodies of Communist troops. The period of the truce gave the Communists the necessary time to recover, and in their turn to assume the offensive.[13]

The Senate Judiciary Committee's report on American China policy indicates how accurate this observation was:

> At the end of 1945 when General Marshall left for China, the balance of power was with the Chinese Nationalists and remained so until at least June, 1946. Chiang's divisions were chasing the Communists northward, and the prospect of victory by Nationalist China was at its highest. . . . When the Chinese government did not effect coalition, by the summer of 1946 United States military assistance to China was brought to an end. . . . Admiral Cooke testified that while he was in China in 1946, in charge of United States naval forces, General Marshall said to him that the United States had armed the Chinese, but then was disarming them. While this process of disarming China was under way and while the source of ammunition of the Chinese Nationalists was drying up, the Communists were arming themselves with Japanese arms which were turned over to them by the conquering Soviet army in Manchuria.[14]

Conservative estimates of this Japanese military stockpile appraise it sufficient to supply a million men for ten years of fighting! This is the price that China had to pay for the third try of co-existence with the Communists. Her first attempt to co-exist with the Reds was in 1923. Co-existence brought conspiracy, which was thwarted by Chiang Kai-Shek through his courageous purge of 1927. The second time China had to co-exist with the Reds was from 1938 to 1941; this time to form a united front against Japan. As a result, the Communists grew to the powerful position that made it possible for them to undermine the National Government. Beginning in 1942, they even engaged in open rebellion against the National forces.

Chiang succeeded in turning the tide of the Communist conspiracy in 1927. He could have reversed the trends in the 1940's, were it not for a third try of co-existence forced by American influence.

This third attempt at co-existence resulted in the systematic deterioration of the Chinese Government and, above all, Chiang Kai-shek, as the leader of China. We should mark the year 1942. It was the year following Pearl Harbor.

People often wonder why Chiang Kai-shek was hailed as a

hero by China's allies in general and Soviet Russia in particular when he suffered great defeat during the first part of the war against Japan, and was later defamed as a "die-hard and reactionary Fascist" especially by Soviet Russia when he staunchly resisted after the Pearl Harbor attack in December 1941. The reason is very simple. Before Pearl Harbor, Soviet Russia wanted a strong China to fight against Japan, her enemy in the East. Through such fighting the Chinese Communists could benefit by gaining a breathing space for their long-range plans, and also recover their military strength at a time when they were being desperately chased by the National forces. That is why Chiang was worshipped as an international hero when he first took up arms against Japan.

After Pearl Harbor, the situation was vastly different. The fate of Japan was sealed. The Kremlin predicted well enough that the Pacific War would be won in any case without the use of Chiang Kai-shek. As. Dr. Tien-fong Cheng notes, "After Pearl Harbor Stalin no longer cared whether China would continue her war against Japan and the Soviet relations with China became exceedingly cool."[15] It was, in fact, more than cool: it was hostile. From that time on, Soviet Russia carried out an organized propaganda campaign against China in general, and Chiang in particular. As a result, the world, especially the United States, began to lose confidence in Chiang's efficiency, his integrity, his military judgment, and they began to consider his government corrupt.

What had happened? What earthquake of history had suddenly created such a change in the evaluation of Chiang and his government? Both before and after Pearl Harbor, Chiang remained the same. Chiang was not changed, but Moscow's tactics were different. The central aim of America's Chinese policy remained the same, but Russia's propaganda against Chiang had influenced American diplomats' view toward him in an adverse way. "Although it was American policy to support the National Government," as Harold M. Vinacke puts it, "the method of expression of policy actually served to weaken it."[16] With the help of the Senate Committee's document, we now understand that Soviet Russia's grand strategy towards the conquest of China was achieved largely "through (1) the efforts of American Foreign Service officers in the field, 1943-44; (2) the Henry A. Wallace mission; and (3) the directive to General Marshall and its implementation."[17]

It seems to me that no one has expressed a more fair and objective view on American China policy than Dr. John Leighton Stuart, American Ambassador to China until 1952:

> Notwithstanding the weakness and shortcomings of the National Government—which I have freely affirmed in my story—that government had after all been brought into existence through a revolutionary enthusiasm inspired by American democratic ideas. Throughout the years, it had been under attack from dissident elements in China, especially the Communists, and had been under the pressure of diplomatic and armed assaults from without, especially from Japan. There had been no period in which it could devote itself under circumstances of peace and security to problems of reform and the "people's livelihood. . . ."
>
> The National Government had counted on assistance from the United States greater in amount and different in kind from that which it received. Some of the aid promised was so long in reaching China that it did no good. The National Government had not envisioned a Yalta Agreement turning over vital rights in Manchuria to the Soviet Union and thus also to the Chinese Communists and paving the way for Communist victory in China. Nor did that government—or others—expect that the Soviet Government would so soon repudiate its agreement of August 15, 1945, promising material and moral aid to the National Government only. The aberrant and contradictory policies of the United States Government during the period between the end of World War II and the beginning of the Communist attack in Korea in 1950 served to weaken rather than to strengthen the National Government at a time when it desperately needed sympathetic understanding and assistance.[18]

This was precisely what Walter S. Robertson had in mind when he wrote on October 8, 1949, with regard to the State Department's *United States Relations with China, 1944-1949,* usually known as the *White Paper on China:*

In justice to ourselves as well as to whatever friends we may have left in Asia it would seem to be imperative that we clarify our objectives and pursue them with fidelity. Chiang Kai-shek has now been made the official scapegoat not only for China's sins but for ours as well. His back is hardly enough to bear such a burden. . . . In my opinion, at least, it can be fairly demonstrated that the confused and confusing inconsistencies of our own vacillating policy, however well-meaning it may have been, contributed directly and indirectly to the debacle which engulfed him and his Government, our ally, and brought to power the Communists, our long-avowed enemies.[19]

Stuart and Robertson were not alone. Similar views have been expressed by General Albert O. Wedemeyer, General Claire L. Chennault and the then Secretary of Defense James Forrestal in his diaries concerning the Far East.[20]

To say this, is not to say that we can entirely blame the West, especially the United States, for the China tangle. The Chinese themselves cannot disclaim responsibility for the loss of the mainland. The Chinese Government committed a number of mistakes. For instance, the currency reform plan whereby gold dollar certificates were issued in August 1948 resulted in further deterioration of the currency. This caused nation-wide demoralization, especially among the armed forces. Most serious, however, is the failure to counter the Communist offensive on psychological and ideological levels. President Chiang Kai-shek tells us:

Admittedly, many factors have contributed toward our defeat. The mortal blows to our anti-Communist struggle, however, did not come from administrative failures alone. The mortal blows had come from serious defects in organization and technique and serious errors in policy and strategy, and, above all, from the weakening in our national spirit at the time when it was most needed.[21]

Communism feeds on human poverty, social disorder, political disturbances, and public discontent. However, it results even more from spiritual instability or ideological hunger or both.

In the book *Social Orientation,* Rev. William A. Nolan, S.J. points out that people became communist "for two main reasons: (1) a distorted sense of injustice to oneself or others; (2) excessive ambitions."[22] In the case of China this is true for a limited number of agitators and politicians who based their motives mainly on self-interest, but not true for the large masses.

The masses were then experiencing a vacuum, brought about by the disintegration of the Chinese culture—a culture which had kept them as a vital, integrated society for centuries. This culture failed partly from within. It was also corrupted from without through the influence of Western industrial civilization with its philosophies of rationalism, empiricism and liberalism. These philosophies are "broken cisterns that can hold no water."[23] They do not fit China. They led China into further decline until, as a matter of natural course, she was plunged into the whirlpool of atheistic materialism.

Dr. Sun Yat-sen, as we noted before, tried to chart the course and to eliminate the menace of Communism politically by absorbing its elements into the Kuomintang. He had an intense desire to convert the Chinese Communists, but the flame of that desire died in the ashes of bitter disillusionment. President Chiang Kai-shek's *New Life Movement* was started in 1933. It aimed at a moral revival of the whole nation. But it achieved, as we also indicated, only limited ends.[24] Nor were the Christian churches in a position to do much after having suffered so greatly from the long years of war-attrition.

The general spiritual hunger and poverty which sprang directly from the literary movement of 1919 was further intensified. It was not confusion; it was chaos. When World War II came to a close, the thirst for a new philosophy, a new imagination, and a new hope were more acute than ever before. At this moment, the Chinese Communists who were then being depicted by some Westerners as harmless "agrarian reformers" poured into the vacuum a flood of propaganda. For better or worse, the Chinese people accepted, by default, the Communists' "pie in the sky" promises.

Analyzing the mistakes that were responsible for the defeat in China's struggle against Communism, Chiang Kai-shek attributes the basic reason to the collapse of the national spirit:

> When the war ended the Communists resorted to armed insurrection. They did everything to nullify all reconstruction projects, to hinder the Government's program of demobilization, to disrupt the nation's economic life and to upset its social order. They spread national defeatism at a time when the people were weary after the long war. Finally the general public became so confused and bewildered that all that they asked was peace at any cost, however transient it might turn out to be. This was the basic reason for the tragic reverse which China suffered in her war against Communism.[25]

It was the psychological warfare and organized propaganda launched by the Communists that made the people lose their will to fight and their confidence in the Government's policy of resisting by force. Through a complete process of deceit and fraud, the Communists usurped the mainland. But for Free China, under the continued leadership of President Chiang Kai-shek, it is still unfinished business.

"For several decades," write Fathers J. A. Lefeuvre and Y. E. Roguin, "the rationalistic influence of the West coupled with the adoption of foreign customs were undermining the intellectual, moral and social foundations of China. Dewey's philosophy and that of an agnostic science had prepared the way for the dialectical materialism that was to follow."[26] It is clear that the basic reason for the loss of the mainland to the Reds was the great confusion in the realm of ideas. Now we realize this. We must also realize that agnostic science leads to a political tyranny which often must be resisted in silence until the day of action arrives.

This lesson should be learned by other Asian nations. Already

India begins to experience profound disorder of a spiritual nature. The famous Benares Hindu University was recently closed because of student unrest. Prime Minister Nehru himself, a declared Marxian socialist, acknowledged that the essential reason for this rising chaos was that the ancient ideals had been shattered and new values had not been established. He found a conspicuous vacuum in the minds of the younger generation.[27]

India still has an opportunity to save itself. But China is already experiencing the final penalty for trying to substitute agnostic science for sacred traditions. That is one lesson. The other lesson is that a sacred tradition unable to cope with modern problems must be supplanted with a sacred tradition that can cope with these problems. The sacred tradition that is now needed in Asia is Christianity. It has proved itself in the West. It can prove itself in the East if only it is given the opportunity.

Part Four

HISTORY IN THE MAKING

"Drop down dew, ye heavens, from above:
and let the clouds rain the just. Let
the earth be opened and bud forth a
saviour: and let justice spring up
together."

—*Isaiah* 45, 8

Silent Thunder

In 1949, the Chinese mainland was captured by the Communists. Millions of Chinese surrendered to their iron system. Even the "Strange Song," once popular with the Communists when they were not yet in control of the mainland, was banned when they rose to power. It had been used as propaganda against the National Government. Now the people used it as a convenient expression of inner revolt against their new masters. In spite of Communist prohibition, they still sing it in secret. It goes:

> Few strange things happened in past years,
> But many strange things happened this year.
> The moon rises in the west,
> And the sun sets in the east.
> What a strange thing!
> The tiger entered the house in the middle
>   of the night.
> I asked him what he came for, and he said
>   he came to protect the lambs.
> I entered the city early in the morning and
>   saw dogs biting men.
> The dogs were allowed to bark but the men
>   were not allowed to talk.
> Men beg for rice from rats,
> And scholars have become robbers.
> The larks weep and the owls laugh.
> Even the little ghosts in the Temple of the
>   City Gods sing in daytime.[1]

Today the Curtain is drawn. All doors are closed—silently closed. However, nothing has ever been so noisy as the silence which now enfolds the land. Silence is only another higher and more intense form of speech. It beats upon the inner mind, then reverberates in the heart. The silence of truth speaks louder than the tongues of men. Everyone knows that something is wrong. Here are three impressions by various observers on the aspects of Chinese life under Communist domination.

A Hongkong observer summarizes the mainland mood as follows:

On one point all reports agree. The "People's Government" has enslaved the people to a point where fear is the spirit of the times. No one dares speak in public for fear that it will be reported. No one dares laugh or even smile, lest it be reported and investigated. No one dares associate with others, lest by that association reasons for accusations and persecution be begotten. In fact, no one dares think freely, for one's thought might filter through one's eyes and be discovered by the Government. It is said that the people of the "People's Government" have become cold, silent, and filled with fear. They are a people who have forgotten to laugh.[2]

Raja Hutheesing, a journalist from India, records a visit to a Shanghai nursery school early in 1952:

In the classroom [the children] were being taught the five loves: love of fatherland, love of the people, love of labor, love of science, and care of public property. There was no love for parents or family, and these little children sorely missed it. They clung to the visitors and wanted to be fondled and kissed. Some had tears in their eyes as they were picked up and patted. I knew then what cruelty meant. I saw it again and again elsewhere, in the clusters of small children that flock around us, the faces of men and women who wanted a little affection. There are no friendly faces in the New China. Those who lived for years in China spoke repeatedly of the Chinese smiling in the midst of poverty, but now the faces are set and grim.[3]

A similar picture of the effects of Communism in China was given by a French journalist in the *Manchester Guardian*:

A formerly shrill, noisy, infinitely amusing nation has become silent, bored, and gloomy. . . . The Chinese are now an almost silent people. . . . The most surprising disappearance is that of intelligent people. Previously, most intelligent men, quick-witted, subtle, and extremely well-informed, were encountered in China. Now they seem to have disappeared into thin air.[4]

This was confirmed by Grey O'Dwyer in his *Impression of an Australian University Student in [Red] China* (London: Free China Association, 1957). O'Dwyer was one of the eight Australian students, representing the National Union of Australian University Students, who visited Red China from January 28 to February 22, 1957, at the invitation of the Chinese Communist "All-China Students' Federation." Throughout 5,000 miles of travel in Communist China, nowhere did the Australian student see a single cheerful Chinese. "There is no happy character as the women pass the hours in the food queue, no groups of smiling people passing the time in idle conversation on the streets and all of these showed up in marked contrast to what we had seen in Hong Kong, and to what I believe, is or was, a normal Chinese characteristic."

Similar observations have been made by several foreign observers such as Hitoshi Wada (a Japanese journalist), E. Stuart Kirby (professor of economics of the Hong Kong University), James Cameron, Peter Schmid (a Swiss reporter), and George S. Gale, author of *No Flies in China,* who accompanied the Attlee mission to Red China in 1954, and Dennis Bloodworth of *The London Observer*. We have an eye-witness account by Father Henry van Straelen, S.V.D. when he visited Shanghai on May 25, 1958:

Shanghai left me with two distinct impressions. First, that of the grim monotony of Red China life. There seemed to be an invisible indescribable pressure which you could sense everywhere. We sometimes speak of guided economies: I would describe the new China (at least Shanghai) as a place where human life in all its phases is minutely directed in every detail. A sinister and mysterious power has drained the life of the soul from these teeming millions who sweat and bleed under this oppressive regimentation. There seems hardly a single human function left to the free choice of the individual.

In Shanghai I sensed a total disappearance of any difference between physical, biological, intellectual or psychological activities. All the life functions of the masses were minutely regulated, and whether it was manual labor, marriage, birth, recreation or any other area of life, the specific functions became almost identical functions moving on the same human or rather dehumanized level. There was no evidence anywhere of individuality, variety, private initiative. There are not seven million souls in Shanghai. There is one gigantic soul which is incessantly flogged and driven forward by some mysterious power. The beaten and weary people in Shanghai have a look of sad resignation. Dressed in their blue over-alls, these millions shuffle along bent under the weight of oppression. . . . They are spiritually starved. No smiles, no laughter, nothing but hopeless resignation.[5]

It is sufficiently evident that the silence which fear imposes does not mean agreement. Actually, the silence warns of approaching rebellion.

Communists proceeded to consolidate their iron rule on the mainland by four means: mental reorientation, requisition of foodstuffs, collection of taxes, and land reform. The first is the most fundamental.

Mental reorientation is, of course, the process of "brainwashing" by which the Chinese Communists seek to reshape the thoughts of the people, and make them conform to their dictates. They are attempting to remake the whole of human knowledge to fit their beliefs.

The ethics of Communism is based on materialistic belief. Its theory is that moral standards grow out of economic conditions. "All moral theories are the product in the last analysis of the economic stage which society has reached at a particular epoch."[6] Morality, as consonant with the law of Heaven reflected in conscience, is denied. It is not the moral nature of man but economics which rules human life. This being so, the Chinese Communists must repudiate the moral order expressed in the Confucian tradition and experience.

However, the Chinese, moulded in the ancient system of ethics, lay more emphasis on moral values than on economic factors in their thoughts and actions. Therefore, the impact of Communism in China, as in any other country, should be considered in its relation to human values even more than in its relation to political conditions. It is well known that Communism has been making a violent assault on Chinese traditions, and that a great conflict between the two is in process.

Chinese traditions are now being put to a test the like of which has never been known in the past. The Communists are trying to establish a new order by introducing a totally new way of life with new standards of cultural and moral values. They have even gone so far as to introduce a twenty-six-letter Latin alphabet, replacing ideographic characters; this amounts to an attack on China's cultural past.[7] This new order denounces all Confucian, Taoist and Buddhist ideas as "poison," just as it falsely condemns Christianity for duping the poor.

In order to destroy Confucianism, the Communists have launched a violent assault against the books which contain the finest traditions of the Chinese people.[8] To replace them, they have translated and printed in Chinese, within the last six years, 12,400 different Russian books—with a circulation of two hundred million copies.[9]

Communists teach that the Party is the supreme power to which the individual must submit himself in an absolute way. So long as the demands of the Party line are met, the debasement of the individual is of no consequence. The Reds realize only too well that anyone in China with a moral code will not easily accept these teachings which are in direct opposition to the traditional way of thinking.

With a view to replacing the Chinese system of thought, the Communists are trying very hard to fortify the "New Culture" program. Professor E. Stuart Kirby of the Hong Kong University, commenting upon this farce, says:

> There were Russian songs with Chinese words, Russian dancing in Chinese costumes; great Russia called the tune, and set the step. . . . A common culture, at the lowest common denominator, was being established in this fashion, all the way from Leipzig to Hanoi. Much of the literary effort was on the same lines.[10]

That this almost incredible situation truly exists in the land of Confucius was confirmed by another personal report, that of Robert Guillain of *Le Monde*. After a two-month visit there, he said:

> In Communist China thinking is absolutely forbidden. To be a good citizen under the Red Regime is not to think but only to repeat what he has been told. . . . The whole Communist system is such that it is impossible for anyone to say anything different. The average Chinese on the mainland has literally turned into a non-thinking man, a speaking apparatus.[11]

But the people are still Chinese; the Confucian tradition and its ethical values have roots deep in the past. They do not exist in man's head alone—they are in his heart and blood. Long-established custom and habits formed by the Confucian tradition constitute the Chinese way of life. The Chinese have chosen the Confucian heritage as their weapon of resistance. It becomes increasingly evident that the present tyranny has reached its height, yet it has also reached its limit. We do not know what the future will bring in the external order, but we can say with certainty that in trying to eradicate what they call "undesirable influence," the Communists have assumed a task full of unsurmountable difficulties.

Red China seeks to overcome the difficulties through the enforcement of law—law, as the Reds know it, and want to know it. Mainland China has been, in effect, a lawless land since the Reds took power in 1949. All old laws were abolished while new civil and criminal codes have not yet been enacted. The only important law passed by the Communist regime is the Marriage Law.[12] It is a calculated design for the furtherance of police rule, and attempts to revise the basis of Chinese society by an attack on the family system, a system deeply rooted in the Confucian tradition.[13] Under this new law, a woman may be forced to divorce her mate or to wed against her will for the good of the Party. Her mate may set her aside on grounds of "ideological incompatibility." She has to work to help increase production, and her children are taken away from her to be cared for and moulded according to Red standards of education. Commenting on this legislation, Peggy Durden, a freelance writer who has reported on the Far East for many years, observes:

> While eradicating real abuses, this legislation had motivations more central to Peiping's purposes than humanitarianism. Giving women half of the family property, letting them break marriages, leave homes, husbands, parents, in-laws, and ancestral tablets, and perform men's jobs (locomotive driver, steel chainmen and busybody, cooperative head, petty official, Cabinet Minister, even General) demolished a key pillar of the family . . . and thereby weakened the entire family structure.[14]

What is the result? The result can be told in two ways. It works among the Communists themselves, but fails with the masses. For instance, in Kwangsi, Communists reported, "many women are marrying and divorcing at will and even become absolute romanticists! Cadres have in some cases married and divorced eight times within a year. The number of children born out of wedlock has greatly increased. . . . Everywhere there are monstrous phenomena of the Three Plenties; plenty of divorce, plenty of infanticides, and plenty of female suicide."[15]

The fact that this Marriage Law has not achieved its original aim among the masses is revealed by the Communist persistent campaigns to implement this legislation. We refer here to an article "Mao and Marriage" published by the Communist magazine *China Youth*. It was reproduced by the *New York Times* (magazine section) on September 14, 1958. In it we find that in Red China marital life is replaced by Party loyalty. The Party is the marriage broker. The love of a man and a woman is supplanted by obeisance to the Party machine. Political maturity, not love, is considered the decisive factor in choosing a mate. The Party has the final say in marriage. Such kind of love-making and lovelorn, Communist style, has never been heard of by the Chinese. It is totally alien to China's established ethics, culture and tradition. How then could it work?

The marriage ceremony of traditional China was perhaps the most solemn in Chinese social life. In China the good wishes of friends at the marriage were often expressed in such phrases as "May you grow old together and live to see grey hairs on each other's head!" "May you see your children and grandchildren fill your hall!" "This union is made by Heaven!" "May you always love each other like a pair of mandarin ducks!" A Chinese proverb runs: "So long as husband and wife love each other, what if they are beggars together?" Marital life in old China was meant to be a life-long romance. This concept may not be generally kept by the Chinese of the young generation since their minds have been influenced by the modern romantic notions of the West. Yet the ancient Chinese culture still has a powerful effect upon marriage and family life in China.

For the same reason, the Communist drive for birth control has proved to be a complete failure. Dennis Bloodworth of *The London Observer* reported in the *New York Herald Tribinue* of September 22, 1958 that this nation-wide birth control campaign inaugurated in Red China in 1956 "had in fact lost its initial impetus and was, if anything, being quietly slowed down.

. . . 'The idea was never very successful,' a Peking Communist told me frankly. 'It is not being dropped, but it will not be pursued whole-heartedly. There was a lot of old-fashioned superstitious prejudice.' " This is what the Communists have told us. What they do not say is that the Chinese, by nature and culture, love to have many children and an active family life; that they consider childlessness a shameful curse;[16] that the Chinese have a tradition coming down from Mencius: "There are three things which are unfilial, and to have no posterity is the greatest of them."[17] To destroy this age-old Chinese family system neither "brain-washing" nor any other political means is enough. A completely new cultural formation would be necessary, and it is very doubtful if the Communists are really capable of imposing a new culture so diametrically opposed to the traditional culture of the Chinese people.

The Communist attack on Taoism is no less harsh than on Confucianism. Unlike the Confucian system, Taoism assumed an external structure and had organized societies.[18] Here is a striking picture of what has happened to Taoist organizations in the last few years:

> During 1950 and 1951 the campaign against Taoist societies in China was ruthless and merciless. Their members were executed as counter-revolutionaries. At the end of a vicious drive against the Taoists in 1953, P'eng Chen (the Mayor of Peking) reported to the Government Council that more than "4,000,000 duped members had withdrawn from these reactionary sects and societies," and the battle was essentially won. Yet in 1954 reports of resistance led by "reactionary Taoist sects" continued to appear in the Communist press. Communist figures on the size of the sects being eliminated, however, have grown gradually smaller over the past five years. It is probable that Taoism will soon cease to have any importance in China.[19]

But it is not this external form of Taoism that we are concerned with. Rather it is its philosophy which is impressed deeply in the minds of the people. The Taoist system of thought noted for its philosophical detachment and love for personal freedom has national as well as individual application. The Chinese, as a people with Taoist traditions, would no more dream of getting involved in the affairs of other nations than they would as individuals involve themselves in the affairs of their neighbors. An illustration of this fact is found in the following statement made by Walter S. Robertson, United States Assistant Secretary for Far Eastern Affairs:

> Recently, 14,000 Chinese prisoners of war in Korea (more than 95 per cent of the total amount), by choosing to forsake the ties of family and community in order to live under a truly Chinese flag, exposed the fraudulence of the claims of the authorities in Peiping to speak with the voice of China. The passionate determination of so many soldiers from their command not to return to Communist rule clearly came as a great shock to those authorities. It did not surprise us in the least. There has never been any question in our minds as to how the Chinese people would choose if given the choice between a government rooted in Chinese tradition and one that has made of China a handmaiden of an alien imperialism. It is because of what we know of the Chinese people's ability to endure the most malignant fortune without being crushed by it or surrendering to it that we have no doubt of the outcome of China's present travail.[20]

In this passage, Mr. Robertson spoke of the political significance inherent in this heroic event. Actually, he gave a beautiful picture of the under-current of the Taoist spirit working effectively in the depths of the Chinese soul. It is a spirit which has made the Chinese stubbornly defend personal freedom, and strongly averse to the dominant note of Communist policy—aggression.

Buddhism, noted for its theory of resignation and asceticism, was not immune from the Communist oppression. Mr. Richard L. Walker, in his book *China Under Communism,* has written the following about their persecution:

Undoubtedly the Buddhist faith has suffered much oppression under the Communists, and it has for the most part been forced to suffer in silence. . . . During the Land Reform the lands of a large percentage of Buddhist monasteries were seized and redistributed, and many monks were classified as landlords. Buddhist temples were often selected for . . . executions in the countryside. Temples and shrines in both city and country have been converted into workers' "cultural palaces." In the larger cities, the devout Buddhists were found mainly among the older people; the Communists have succeeded in preventing new converts from among the masses.[21]

Are the followers of Buddhism in China sitting helplessly in the tide of Communist outrages? To show its firm resistance to Communism, even before the mainland was entirely engulfed by the evil force, let Father Raymond J. de Jaegher speak of his personal experience:

When I was in Peiping in 1948, representatives of all the Buddhist organizations which had gone underground visited me in secret to see if there was not a possibility of their uniting to fight Communism. We talked for a long time, and they told me of their determination to keep alive and to fight Communism. At that meeting there was a devout and courageous Buddhist who is crusading throughout Red China today, encouraging other Buddhists, lighting their hopes, strengthening their hands. Actually, the philosophy of Buddhism, unchanged for centuries, is today, by force of circumstances, undergoing a profound change, turning from its ancient, contemplative mysticism to a dynamic philosophy of active resistance to Communism. I am sure that the Communists never anticipated that a religion which stressed pacifism and resignation could, when threatened with extinction, transform itself into a hard knot of rebellion. But that is precisely what happened. Buddhism underground is a vital, powerful, fighting force against all Communist doctrine and practice.[22]

In the light of the above account of the Communist attack on China's traditional thought, we are sure that there is no lack of trouble inside Red China. Oppressive measures are severe.

"Foreign specialists, carefully sifting reports from refugees and other sources, estimate that, since October 1949, *at least 20 million Chinese* have been 'deprived of existence.' This does not include 23 million who are believed to be held in forced-labor camps."[23]

The brutal conditions under which these forced-labor camps operate was pointed out by Prof. Karl Wittfogel, one of America's foremost authorities on Far Eastern affairs. In an article published by the United States Information Agency in August 1956, he writes: "Not all who enter the Chinese Communist prisons or corrective labor camps are fortunate enough to leave. There is ample evidence that the death rate in prisons and camps has been high. How high it is hard to guess."

In his eyewitness account, "The True Story of Red China," Mr. Lucian Taire tells of purges bloodier than Russia's, of slave-labor camps that have sprouted in every province of China.[24] In no previous war, revolution or holocaust, from Tamerlane to Hitler, have so many people been destroyed in so short a period.[25] The iron rule which has long been in effect in Soviet Russia has been literally copied by the Chinese Communists. In fact, Red China's national policy and almost its very existence are based on close ties with the Soviet Union and on a strong and undivided Communist bloc.

For several years there has been quite a bit of wishful talking and wishful thinking about the possibility of a "Chinese Tito" who might emerge at the head of the Communist regime in Peiping. Presumably it would be Mao Tse-tung. However, Peiping's unqualified devotion to Moscow has been the theme song of all the Communist Chinese-Russian meetings for almost a decade. There will be no straying from the international party line. There will be no "Chinese Tito." After the Yugoslav congress in Ljubljana in April 1958 took issue with official Soviet doctrine, *Jenmin Jihpao* (People's Daily), official organ of the Chinese Communist party, developed the Peiping attack on

Titoism or "revisionism"—Communist jargon for any deviation from the Moscow-dictated line. Yang Tsien-tseng, Communist theoretician and member of the Central Committee, also declared that there will be no "revisionist" wandering and that Communist China had vowed to help crush "Titoism."[26]

This had been said long before by Mao himself. In November 1957 during his visit to Moscow for the 40th anniversary of the Bolshevik Revolution, Mao stated: "The Socialism camp must have a head, and that head is the Soviet Union. Communist workers must have a head, and that head is the Soviet Union." It is difficult to see how there could be a successful Chinese "deviationist" unless some Chinese leaders wish to "deviate" in the first place. The condemnation of Titoism by the Chinese Communist leaders shows clearly enough that no deviation of any kind is contemplated. The only difference between the Soviet and Chinese Communist attacks on Yugoslav Communist doctrine is that Peiping's tone has been more violent than that of Moscow.

One cannot rule out the discord between Peiping and Moscow, especially on foreign policy. Yet any discord is overshadowed by the fact that the Moscow-Peiping axis works for a common program—to sovietize the whole world—and has a common enemy, the United States. Economically, politically, and militarily, Peiping depends upon Moscow. Communist China has the advantage of being closer to events in Asia. It has, therefore, a more important role to play there. But this does not mean that Peiping can pursue its goals independently of Moscow: still less against it. Red China's activities in Asia have always been confined to the broad strategy formulated by Moscow. Red China fought in Korea; she is still causing disturbances in Indo-China. In doing so, she makes her contribution to the global aggression directed by the Kremlin. In order to fulfill this international role in Asia, the Chinese Reds must assume an exceedingly heavy economic and military burden, one far beyond the capacity of China's resources. Hence there is continual trouble and restlessness among the people, and this results in inner-political conflicts among the Reds themselves. A repressive terror is the order of the day.

There have been no executions, no spectacular public trials in the crackdown on the critics of the regime. It has been done "new style," as in Russia, with demotion and degradation. A province-to-province Communist party purge is under way, and Chekiang, Huan, Anhwei, Sinkiang, and even Chinghai have been effected.[27] The Communist governor of Chinghai province, Sun Tso-pin, a member of the Chinese Communist party for approximately 30 years, was accused of sabotaging party unity and aiding anti-Communists.[28] High ranking generals and officials have lost their positions. Party leaders have been purged. Spies are set on agents, and agents are planted on spies.[29] "Who will guard the guard?" This is the question that tears at the whole fabric of totalitarian control. There is no end to Red China's internal troubles.

Crossed Fingers

THE ROOT OF Red China's troubles, we know, is economic. No matter where the Communist leaders look today, they have their fingers crossed. Immediately after they took power in 1949, the Chinese Communists, following Soviet precepts, embarked on a program of rapid industrialization and forced collectivization of agriculture. The brutality of the change produced acute tension, and its speed and scope caused a population relocation problem. Peasants driven off the farms converged on the cities but could not find work because of a shortage of plants and materials.

Economic strain is first found in the acute shortage of consumer goods. The stringent situation with regard to food and certain other basic necessities on the China mainland is reflected in severe rationing regulations. Cereals, cooking oils, pork, and cotton cloth are distributed only in absolute minimal amounts. Peiping has been able to curtail a large-scale exodus of peasants from the grim conditions on the farms to the cities only by measures that prevent rural dwellers from travelling anywhere without prior official approval.

The general desire of the peasants to leave the countryside for the cities is an indication that conditions are better in urban areas. Even in population centers, however, the shortage is severe. Two reporters assigned by the Communist Hinhua News Agency to study the situation of city consumers in June 1957 tell us: "Upon entering Taiyuan (a city 250 miles southwest of Peiping with a population of about 1,000,000) one is bound to see customers in long lines before grain stores, cake shops, bathhouses, barber shops, photo shops and food departments in department stores. Shorter queues may have about a dozen persons but the longer ones are made of scores, even hundreds of persons. In some cases a person may not be able to get what he wants after having spent several days in these queues."[1] Such economic distress, of course, is not limited to one city alone. Everywhere we see the marks of strain.

The chief of Peiping's 1958 mottoes for nation-wide observance is "Work and Economize as Never Before." According to this drive, women must "watch the boiling pot so not a spoonful of food boils over; measure each daily ration carefully; eat less; grind water chestnuts or chaff to mix with flour; substitute potatoes and vegetables for bread and rice; serve liquid foods in summer and periods of slackened work."[2] The Chinese grain is rice. Now sweet potatoes are used as a substitute for rice. This has led the people to coin a saying: "Sweet potatoes and noodles are the rice of socialism."

Famine has further complicated the totalitarian regime. The Western newspapers are now saying that bad as the present situation it is better than it was in former times. This is not true. Even Mao Tse-tung himself denies this. Mao acknowledged that poverty prevails in mainland China and he praised it as "a good thing." "Apart from their other characteristics, China's 600,000,000 people are first of all poor and secondly white (politically pure)."[3] This is borne out by available evidence.

According to the United Press dispatch from Hong Kong dated March 12, 1954, the Communists admitted that "at least 200,000,000 persons in China do not have enough food." It was one of the rare instances where the Reds divulged any concrete figure about the food shortage among China's half-billion population. Reports of a severe food shortage were still coming in as late as June 1957. In the eastern Hopeh province alone, 15,000,000 persons were facing starvation as a result of this famine. The failure adequately to distribute emergency food in a famine-stricken area in Kwangsi province had caused the death of 550 persons. These are the figures made known to the public by the Reds themselves.

In July, 1957, William Kimmond of the Canadian newspaper, *Global Mail*, of Toronto, toured Red China for ten weeks; upon his arrival from Canton in South China he told the press in Hong Kong that the living standard on the mainland was "incredibly poor." He stated that nearly 200,000,000 people on the Chinese mainland "do not have enough to eat."

It was generally known that the people, before the Red Rule, had food—lots of food. They were not fine foods, but there was enough—cheap and sufficient. Now, why is food so short? The land in China is unchanged. Natural conditions there remain the same. The people know how to farm because China has a long agricultural tradition, but now about one third of the Chinese population is demanding relief.

Hunger and famine are certainly not strangers to China, but in the past they have stemmed from acts of God, from natural calamities. Man-made famine, however, is something different. The Communist regime dares not admit that its whole system of state-controlled economy has been wrong. Export of foodstuffs to Soviet Russia in exchange for military equipment is one factor. Since 1953, Red China has exported to Russia more than 2,000,000 tons of foodstuffs each year. More serious, however, is the farmers' lack of material incentive for the collective system.

So far more than 95 per cent of China's peasants have been forced into collective or cooperative farms, under a firm and false belief that this would work wonders in agricultural output. Its effect has been just the opposite.[4] The reason is simple. All the farmers have a deep dissatisfaction toward, and an inner revolt against, the Communist system. By enforcing the land-pooling "cooperatives" this system kills the Chinese spirit entirely.[5]

Wolf Ladejinsky, a noted expert on agricultural problems, pointed out in his article "Carrot and Stick in Rural China"[6]: "The collectives created many problems. For peasants used to working in family groups, a collective farm is a new and confusing experience." Tillman Durden of the *New York Times,* in his dispatch from Hong Kong, Jan. 7, 1958, said the same thing: "The slow growth of agriculture had several causes. One undoubtedly was collectivization. The collective farm system, begun on a nation-wide basis in 1956, was still operating badly in 1957." The situation in 1958 became even worse. In the article "Deep Challenge to Chinese Communists," Peggy Durden wrote in June, 1958:

In the past two years the Communists have wrecked the economic foundation of the family. More than 95 per cent of China's peasants have joined cooperatives. Not the household head, or family council, but the state, party, and collective own the land and tools, decide when and what the family members sow and reap, when and how much and what they have to wear and eat. A man has no precious bit of land or hoard of cash to leave his sons or give to help them get ahead. Anyway, since a manual laborer is theoretically already at the peak of Communist society, the very idea of "getting ahead" is selfish, bourgeois, rightist and even counter-revolutionary.[7]

The farm population clearly dislike collectivization and reflect this aversion in indifference to production. The peasants hate collective farming. They are more interested in enjoying a full family life than in theoretically owning a share in the cooperative farm. It is not the material things that concern the Chinese most. They have known poverty and physical hardship. Yet they have had spiritual solace. Now collectivization has destroyed the most precious thing that they possess. Red China boasts much about its reconstruction works in industrial and technical fields. Some of the Westerners who have had access to Red China on conducted tours seem to have no end of admiration for these material accomplishments. This, however, is not the feeling of the Chinese. First of all, all these reconstruction works, no matter how attractive they may look, are largely for military purposes. They have scarcely anything to do with the welfare of the common people. But even if they did bring material benefits to the people, these benefits could not be weighed against spiritual values. Hardship means nothing to them when cultural and traditional heritage is at stake. This was borne out when more than one million Chinese refugees fled from the mainland to Hong Kong, preferring physical suffering, and possible death if caught, to Communist rule.

In 1956, I visited Hong Kong twice, and found that about one third of these one million Chinese refugees were sleeping in the open air. They could only make an attempt to keep themselves warm at night by covering themselves with ragged, dirty sacking, worn-out blankets, or old cotton quilts. Although winter is short in Hong Kong, many refugees died on the streets from cold and hunger. Those refugees who could afford it rented a sleeping place in the city. It was a common practice for four to five persons to sleep at the same time on a bed no more than two and one-half feet wide. Many sleeping places were rented on an eight-hour basis, three shifts a day; that is, three persons utilized the same sleeping place on a rotation basis, each of them paying one-third of the rent for the privilege of "resting" himself for eight hours.

Most of these refugees had to survive a hard struggle for bare subsistence. They had to grab what food they could find, and their meals consisted mainly of crumbs discarded by restaurant cooks. Some help has been extended to them by a number of religious agencies and the Free China Relief Association (FCRA) with the limited means at its command. But they have not received any large-scale relief from the greater international agencies.

I myself travelled the length and breadth of the refugees' quarters. Without murmuring they endure hunger, exposure, sickness, hardships and miseries. Never did I hear anyone of them complain. I once made an inquiry as to whether they thought it worthwhile to suffer so much for the sake of victory over Communism. Invariably their reply was: "Of course, it is worthwhile; we do not mind the sacrifices." They consider it their duty to sacrifice, in order that their tradition and human values might survive. The price they have paid for their freedom is indeed high; they remain however the "window of the free world." This reflects, in a measure at least, the general feeling of the people behind the Bamboo Curtain, although they cannot communicate directly with the outside world. No matter how great the privation yet in store for the Chinese people in their struggle against Communism, they are spiritually undefeated and will remain so.

An even more impressive instance showing the Chinese rejection of Communist rule bears recalling. In 1954 when Chiang

Kai-shek's forces were impelled to evacuate from the Tachen Island group of offshore islands, the local population was given an American-supervised choice of whether to stay on under Communist rule or go to Taiwan (Formosa). Nineteen persons chose to stay and 18,505 persons chose to go to Taiwan.

The more we think of the continuing flow of refugees fleeing out of south China to Hong Kong and to other parts of the Free World, the more we are convinced that Lenin was right in saying: "Refugees are people who vote with their feet." Being unable to modify their regime by the ballot, the oppressed Chinese have no alternative to a geographical change.

Of course, not everybody can flee. Those who remain there, however, still continue their resistance, silently but firmly. This is especially true of the intellectual classes. Chou En-lai, Chinese Communist Premier, once complained that only 45 per cent of China's intellectuals were "progressive," 40 per cent were "middle-of-the-road elements," while a little over 10 per cent were "backward elements."[8] Evidently more than half of the intellectuals in China remain to be "educated."[9]

This is certainly true, especially as regards the difficulty between the Communists and the Chinese scholars. At a press conference held in Taipei, Taiwan, on August 16, 1957, Education Minister Chang Chi-yun of Free China, 1954-1958, stated on the basis of authentic information gathered from behind the Bamboo Curtain: "The people who suffer most on the Chinese mainland are former famous professors. They have been doing their best to keep up the spirit and moral courage of the former Chinese scholars. They would never willingly submit to the Communists and they lead a lonesome and isolated life. They do not write to, or call on, their friends. Nor would they talk much to each other. There is no longer such a thing as a 'friend.' They only want to live for the day when the Chinese Government forces counter-attack the mainland."

In the West many observers fear that the young people of

China who know only the Communist system will be easily indoctrinated with their ideals. But this is not so; they are not suddenly all atheists. Christianity is losing some of its flock that is too weak to withstand the pressures, yet great numbers remain faithful. Even those who have given in externally remain true in their hearts—a grave concern to the Reds.

The education of Chinese youth is raising problems for the Communists. According to a report made public by the Communists themselves, during the scholastic year 1954-1955 there were 144,000 withdrawals in the middle schools (about 4 per cent of all students), and 2,900,000 in the primary schools (about 5 per cent of the total).[10]

There can be many explanations for this resentful attitude toward education. The most common pretext used by the parents for such withdrawals is that they need the young people as farm helpers. Although this may be true to a degree, the significant aspect of the matter is that by doing this, the youth are made immune from Communist education and indoctrination. In June 1956 the Minister of Education of the Red regime reported that 78 per cent of the population are still illiterate, that 52 per cent of the children of school age are not going to school at all.[11] Worse still, newspapers in Red China reflect sharp discontent among university students. In one university, critics branded Communists as a "Fascist privileged class."[12] We realize that Communist youth, once regarded as the backbone of the new system, become increasingly uncooperative, and insistent on less interference with their lives.

Growing dissensions and discontents are even more evident among the masses. Chinese workers and peasants are human, with the same aspirations as human beings anywhere else. Their interests have been sacrificed to the pitiless drive to build up military power.[13] But they have no love for this system of compulsion and, above all, starvation. Peasants now are resisting collectivized farming with deliberate slaughter of livestock and with sit-down strikes.[14] Disgruntled workers, their wages outpaced by a runaway inflation, are staging strikes and sabotage. Both in their body and soul there is an acute hunger. In short, they have become increasingly restless.

Revolt is not limited to inner passive feelings alone. The Communists themselves admit that anti-Communist guerrilla forces are found in no less than 16 provinces.[15] The regime is kept busy crushing intermittent revolt. This gives the lie to the Red-inspired theme that the Peiping regime is an effective control of mainland China and its 600,000,000 inhabitants. Anyone who has read and analyzed newspapers from mainland China cannot fail to note that Peiping has found it difficult to extinguish the flames of resistance to its rule. Tung Pi-wu, President of Red China's Supreme Court, told the Communist Congress in July 1957 that during the past year Red China's courts handled 1,000,000 cases of "corruption, theft, assault, public disturbances" and other crimes, most of them involving peasants.[16] Communist *Ching Hai Jih Pao,* published in Chinghai province in western China, reported on August 20, 1957, that part of the province was in a state of anarchy because of anti-Communist uprisings.[17] Even Prime Minister Jawaharal Nehru of India indicated as late as October 1958, upon his return from a two-week trip to Bhutan through Tibet, that conditions inside Tibet were not "fully normal"—a typical Oriental understatement reported in the *New York Times* of October 3, 1958.

Tension between the armed forces and civilians is also a matter of serious concern for the Red regime. This we gather from the fact that Communist China has ordered the immediate launching of a propaganda campaign to counter hostilities to "the People's Liberation Army." The Communist regime publicly states that "there is serious tension between political factions in the Army, and between the Army and the civilian population."[18] It further concedes that "brutality and torture had been used on drafted soldiers who did not respond to Communist political indoctrination."[19]

The Reds have long believed that their philosophy, which denies dignity and importance to the individual, could be drilled into people's minds and would cause them to accept their position as servants of the state. But this simply does not impress the Chinese people whose basic aspirations for individual recognition run too deep to be changed, even by a constant barrage of propaganda. As Lieut. General Chiang Ching-kuo observes: "When the Communists came into power on the mainland, it was the people who were afraid of the regime for the first few years. But conditions have changed. Now it is the Communist regime that is afraid of the people."[20]

What the Chinese Reds fear most is the silent and passive resistance, especially among the intellectuals. They can use force to crush physical opposition, which is visible. But they cannot reach the minds of the intellectuals, invisible but deadly dangerous. This led to Mao Tse-tung's two now famous speeches in February and March, 1957, as first reported in the *New York Times,* in a story filed by its reporter, Sydney Gruson.[21] The speeches marked themselves with the slogan, "Let a hundred flowers bloom, let a hundred schools of thought contend." It was Mao's public invitation to the people granting "free criticism" and "free speech."

Subsequent political developments proved that two essential motives underlined Mao's policy: (1) as many of the elements which precipitated the Hungarian revolution are present in Communist China, the new Mao line was primarily designed to prevent a Hungarian-type disaster in his own realm,[22] (2) Mao merely used the slogan of "bloom-and-contend" in order to discover what people were against the regime and to seek for better implementation of his totalitarian rule.

How sharp are the horns of the dilemma on which the Chinese Communists find themselves is clearly shown in Mao's first speech. Mao himself admitted that contradictions could, and did, exist between the Government and the people, even in a Communist country. He also conceded that up until 1954 his forces executed 800,000 persons and claimed that since then "we are no longer using methods of terror." Mass murder in Red China, as in all Communist nations, is not news. Mao's figure of 800,000 is only a small fraction of the number of persons actually liquidated in the Chinese Communists' effort to consolidate their power.[23] But even if Mao's words are taken at face value they imply that Red China has been obliged to massacre four-fifths of a million persons to stay in power and that by 1954 it had found terror inadequate and even self-defeating.

In the speeches Mao bade the nation engage in free criticism to resolve contradictions in society and to bring to light defects in the Communist party and Government. Secretary of State John Foster Dulles seemed prophetic in saying, shortly after Mao's two speeches had been made available to the world, that the Maoist slogan of "bloom-and-contend" was a Communist plot of purging dissidents. "It is suggested in some quarters that the purpose of the speech (Mao's) was merely to allow some of these different flowers to stick their heads above the ground so that they could then be cut off."[24]

After Mao's speeches had been made known to the public, the response quickly broadened into a movement that involved the whole population and the regime at all levels. Professors, students, journalists, managers of state enterprises, officials and scientists let off pent-up resentment in an outcry against lack of freedom, bureaucratic bungling, Communist party monopoly on jobs and power, Soviet influence and injustices at earlier liquidation of groups and individuals. One of the most serious and most effective demonstrations against the Communist regime has been displayed in the form of student "strikes." Dr. Hu Shih, Representative of China, told the United Nations General Assembly on September 26, 1957: "On the evening of May 4, 1957, 8,000 students gathered at a commemoration meeting, at which 19 student leaders made fiery speeches openly attacking the Communist regime for suppressing freedom and democracy in the schools and in the country. From that evening on, the wall-newspapers of Peking University became an open forum of the free opinion of the students. . . . As one of the student leaders put it, 'The call is for the mobilization of an army of one million youths to fight Communism, to oppose the so-called revolution, and to overthrow the real enemies of the people. We must fight for democracy, for freedom, and for the rights of man.' . . . The most serious case of student rioting took place in the industrial city of Hanyang in Central China. Nearly a thousand students of the First Middle School of Hanyang went on strike on June 12, and demonstrated in the streets, shouting anti-Communist slogans and hoisting anti-Communist banners. . . . The official Communist report said that the instigators of the Hanyang riots had called them 'the Hungarian events in miniature.' "

So vocal and clear did this nation-wide opposition become that the Red regime felt it necessary to clamp down on those who had made themselves enemies of the regime. A great "anti-Rightist" or "counter-criticism" struggle, also called the *cheng feng* (rectification) movement, ensued. It marked a sharp repudiation of the "free-criticism" line and occupied the entire last half of 1957.

The Reds claimed that this rectification movement would be carried out "as gently as the spring rains." Subsequent events proved that it was a terrible "hurricane!" The first two victims of this campaign were Chu An-ping, editor-in-chief of the Peiping *Kwang Min Jih Pao,* and Professor Ke Chi-pei of the Communist People's University.[25] In June 1957 the "counter-criticism campaign" was in full swing in the cities of Shanghai, Tientsin, Peiping, Canton, Wuhan, Anshan, and other places. Numerous outspoken intellectuals have been punished for "crossing the permissible limits of discussion."[26] In an atmosphere of police-state pressure many intellectuals were impelled to confess their errors and begged absolution and forgiveness.

Even Chiang Ping-chih (alias Ting Ling), winner of the Stalin prize for her literary works back in 1951, and her associate, Chen Chi-hsia, were attacked by the Communist union of Chinese writers on charges of "Rightist conspiracy." According to the *New York Times* of January 9, 1958, she was reported to have been expelled from the Communist party after twenty-six years of membership. It was said that she, along with many "distinguished professors" was hard at work on a new job: "scrubbing floors at the Peking headquarters of the Writers' Union."[27]

The intellectuals who had received their higher education in the United States and who were assailed as "Rightist counter-revolutionaries" included Tseng Chao-lun, Ph.D. from the Boston Massachusetts Institute of Technology; Wu Chin-chao, Ph.D. from the University of Chicago; Fei Hsiao-tung, graduate of the University of Chicago and author of "Earthbound China"; Chien Tuan-sheng, Ph.D. from Harvard University; and Pan Kwang-tan, Ph.D. from Harvard University. Lo Lung-chi, the Red Minister of the Timber Industry now branded as an "arch-Rightist," holds a doctorate degree from New York's Columbia University. What began as an officially sponsored and encouraged movement of free criticism and free-speech has been turned into a tough nation-wide ideological persecution.[28]

This "anti-Rightist" or rectification movement cut off only the "noxious weeds" emerging with the "hundred flowers." It could not reach those who had remained silent and had not spoken "freely." Another Communist drive called "give-your-heart-to-the-party" was started in early Spring 1958. It was to force the intellectuals to speak out again, and to make them pledge their "whole heart" to the Chinese Communist party. This, however, gave another opportunity for the intellectuals to express their open resentment against Communism, fully realizing the risks involved; in consequence, more professors, students, and intellectuals are persecuted. Among them, the most prominent one is Fung Yu-lan, author of the well-known study *A History of Chinese Philosophy* translated by Derk Boode. In his public confession published in the June 1958 issue of the *Cheng Ming* monthly, Fung admitted that he had not completely accepted Communist leadership and in 135 instances he had "contradicted" the teachings of Marxist-Leninist doctrine. For all his pledges, the Communists still considered that he had not yet given his "whole heart" to the party.

Along with these oppressive measures, the Reds then embarked on a "back-to-the-land" movement. This campaign was a convenient weapon for Communist leaders. Dissident intellectuals, university presidents and professors, and students, all of whom had created "troubles" for the regime could be moved to the countryside where they would have few opportunities to agitate. According to Peiping *People's Daily* of Nov. 11, 1957, more than 3 million students had been sent to provincial areas as "permanent farm workers." Accompanying them were teachers who "volunteered" to work with their hands. Two universities in Peiping alone contributed 700 teachers and staff workers.[29]

Indoctrination, rectification, incessant campaigns of terror have swept Communist China since 1949. What is the result? The result has been increasing resistance which has caused a moral-political crisis, not only among the people but also among the party members themselves and among the military forces. This is borne out by public statements of the Reds themselves.

Lo Jui-ching, Public Security Chief, spoke of the "anti-revolutionary struggle" over the Peking radio on January 4, 1958. He referred to "socialist ideological education" being specially given to party and state officials in Peking at that time and told why. Here are a few excerpts from his talk:

The nationwide, internal movement for the suppression of counter-revolutionaries was victoriously launched among more than 18 million workers and other personnel between June, 1955 and October, 1957. Tremendous achievements were made in this two and a half-year intense struggle, unprecedented in the history of our Party both in intensity and tensiveness and in great accomplishments and rich experiences.

First, during the movement more than 100,000 counter-revolutionaries and other bad elements were discovered. Some 5,000 had infiltrated the party and more than 3,000 had infiltrated the Young Communist League. Some 220 of the most heinous counter-revolutionaries were unmasked within state central organs.

Also discovered were many cases of political sabotage and destruction. More than 3,600 spies were hidden under various cloaks.[30]

Liu Shao-chi, No. 2 man in Red China, announced in a major policy address broadcast over the radio in May 1958, that "the Chinese Communist army is to be rectified."[31] Such rectification means self-criticism, confession of errors and purge aimed at assuring political reliability.

In the midst of these internal troubles, the Reds struck in April 1958 still another blow against the basic formation of Chinese social life. They embarked on a program of organizing peasants into "people's communes." Under the regulations for a full-fledged commune, a few thousand to ten thousand peasant households merge their farm collectives into an organization that takes over all collective property as well as the small plots, tools, livestock and fowls the peasants have been permitted to keep individually up to now. Instead of splitting up the income of the collectives as heretofore, the peasants go on a fixed wage system.[32] Family and individual household living virtually disappears. The commune members eat in central mess halls and live in communal housing. Nurseries take care of the children and the women do full-time work in the fields along with the men. Each commune is ruled by a party committee that controls everything from food distribution to funerals. Organized into work brigades, the commune members mostly have no set jobs. They can be shunted on a day-to-day basis from farm work to military or industrial duties. Ultimately, private property is to be utterly abolished. Already the most "advanced" communes have compelled the peasants to tear down their houses and use the salvaged brick, tile and timber to build communal barracks. In the communes everything is carried out in the way of discipline and conformity. The members live and work collectively. Instead of turning to his wife when his trousers need mending, the good commune member now takes his problem to the "sewing brigade." The result, according to a Communist report reproduced in *Time* of Oct. 20, 1958, "is that twenty million women in seven provinces now find themselves 'freed' to contribute the family pots and pans to a scrap-metal drive and turn their attention from housework to such progressive tasks as 'road building, tree planting and ditch digging.' " The life that faces Red China's peasantry in the communes is regimented beyond the dreams of ancient Sparta. These communes will give the regime more direct control over the populace and will enable it to channel able-bodied persons into the militia to build up its military potential. This formation demonstrates the Red regime's most determined attempt yet to reduce human beings to the status of ants. It is of such an inhuman nature that news concerning the development of these communes shocked the Communist leaders themselves in the eastern European nations. We read in a *New York Times* news report of Oct. 21, 1958, that a joke is now heard in Warsaw that says: "Thank God for the Soviet Union. We are lucky to have a buffer state between us and the Chinese."

In this respect, it is significant for us to note the views expressed by *News Chronicle* in London which is known for its "liberal" thinking. In addition to a front-page article entitled "Mao's Land of Slaves" dated Nov. 25, 1958, it expressed a very critical view on Red China's communes in the editorial which reads:

The inhumanity of the Chinese Commune plan is matched by its ambition. Never before has there been so ruthless a revolution on such a colossal scale. More than ten times as many people as live in Britain are having their whole lives transformed at the diction of a handful of men in Peking. To raise the standard of living of the Chinese people is a great aim. But the means adopted will ensure that the miseries of flood and famine will be replaced by a tyranny as savage and even more complete than Russia endured under Stalin. The core of every human society has been the family, and in the great Chinese civilization of the past the family was accorded a special place of honor. This is to be swept away. From cradle to grave the Chinese is to be a tool of the State. As a child he will be allowed to see his parents only one day a fortnight. When he dies he will be buried in a communal graveyard so that the Chinese devotion to the family tomb can be obliterated. He will have no property and eventually no wages. His long day of toil will be ended by compulsory military training. The Commune's main relaxation will be Nuremberg-style rallies, at which praise for the regime will be mingled with ferocious denunciation of "deviationists." In short, the Chinese are to be slaves.

How far the Chinese Communists can go with this new system, we do not know. What we already know is that with more than 95 per cent of the peasants organized into cooperatives the Reds still could not achieve their objectives because the cooperatives killed the family spirit. How, then, can they expect to succeed with this new organization which aims at a more radical destruction of the family? Stalin's forced collectivization of Russian agriculture in the 1930's—a program less radical than the establishment of the Chinese communes—was achieved only at the cost of more than ten million Russian lives. Whether Mao can succeed without resistance on a similar scale in China remains to be seen. A *Hsinhua* (New China) *News Agency* dispatch from Peiping on September 23, 1958, said that "10,000 communes had been set up so far, incorporating more than 30 per cent of the country's 500,000,000 peasants." But at the same time it was reported that Peiping had given out orders to the cadres advising them "not to be too hasty in setting up communes."[33] Most probably, this new system, like the birth-control campaign, must be slowed down because it has already invited serious opposition from the peasants.

According to a report made by Earnest Hoberecht from Asia and published in the *Evening Bulletin,* Philadelphia, on December 18, 1958, "Competent students of Chinese affairs in Manila, Singapore, Bangkok, Taipei, Macao and Hong Kong told me these troubles could even include open revolt—on a scale much larger than anything the Communists are experiencing and putting down with force right now." We do not know all the reasons for the present unrest or for Mao's resignation announced by the Peiping radio on December 17, 1958, but we do know that resistance to the new communes is one of the main factors involved.

The major factor in the problem of China is the will of the people, particularly the farmers, who constitute 80 per cent of the population. Dynasties and rulers come and go; their fate is always tied to the determination of the people themselves. Indeed, the tragedy in Red China, as elsewhere in the Communist world, is that freedom itself is the enemy. Freedom is something that can be suppressed, but it cannot be destroyed. It is basically indestructible. What, then, will be the alternative for the Communists? Can they modify their own program to the extent of granting even a minimum of freedom? This, obviously, is impossible. We have already seen what happened to the "hundred flowers." We cannot imagine that a government based only on terror can survive. The Communist grip on the mainland, no matter how effective and tight it may be, can only have a very limited duration.

Now people's freedom is greatly restricted. But these restrictions can also affect the future of the Reds. Prior to Communist rule, the people were not well organized. Now, the Communist regime has organized them, first into cooperatives, and now into communes. In former times, they were without arms and leadership. Now, with the communes they have been armed; with the "back-to-the-land" movement they can seek leadership from the "undesirable" professors and students who have been sent to the countryside as "permanent farm workers." Under these circumstances we wonder whether all these Communist authoritarian measures, which seem advantageous to the regime now, may not turn out to be disadvantageous later. The "Strange Song" provided a clue to such development. If we look into Chinese history, sudden revolts and mass uprisings of the people have not been rare. In fact, most of the seemingly powerful authoritarian regimes were short-lived ones.[34]

Those who know Chinese history well will remember such national heroes as Yao Fei (1102-1141), Wen Tien-hsiang (1236-1281), Fang Hsiao-ju (1357-1402), and Shih K'ê-fa (1604-1645). They exemplified, through supreme sacrifices, and unfailing vigor, their courage and integrity in the defense of national honor from foreign encroachment. Wen Tien-hsiang's *Cheng Chi K'e* (The Song of the Spirit of Moral Supremacy) champions natural justice. In a superb manner, the author himself taught the Chinese how to die martyrs to the cause of justice and human dignity.[35] In spite of its pantheist taint, his work still serves as a living force in the hearts of the Chinese people who are engaged in a life-or-death struggle against the injustice and the tyranny of an authoritarian regime.

Generally speaking, the Chinese people are not so adventurous as Westerners. The general tenor of Chinese life is philosophical, passive and conciliatory. It is not conciliatory, however, in matters concerning the ethical and moral bases of human society and family life. The average Chinese can be dangerous and unpredictable once he effectively loses long-preserved composure, no matter what philosophy he believes in. In the words of Mencius, the famous Confucian thinker, "When men are subdued by force, they do not submit in their minds, but only because their strength is inadequate."[36] The Chinese may be compared to the bamboo, which grows straight. It bends in the wind, but always straightens itself again. Many things have changed with the rise of Communist tyranny in these dark days, but not the Chinese character.

We all know Communism has within its corrupt self the seeds of its own destruction. But the argument is often proposed that the Soviet government, with more than forty years of brutality and suppression, still maintains itself in Russia. How can we expect that the Chinese Red regime will be overthrown from within? Here the essential fact to note is fairly simple. The Chinese Communist leaders, like Stalin before them, realize that they cannot finance national industrialization without brutally depressing the standard of living. However, the situation in China is more grim than that in Russia. The standard of living in China cannot be further depressed without starvation. Anything can happen if men's stomachs have nothing to digest. Then they will not think with the head, but with the belly. Furthermore, the Chinese people are enjoying some of the conditions favorable to their revolt that were not present in Russia. (1) The people on the Chinese mainland, in spite of all Communist restrictions are not completely isolated. Through the holes of the Bamboo Curtain, they are still able to get much information from the outside world. This is important for a revolutionary movement. (2) Russia is able to adjust her domestic policy according to circumstances. Not so Red China. Communist China is subservient to Moscow. She has to consider the interest of Soviet Russia first, then the welfare of her own people. This gives added pressure to the revolutionary mood. (3) Unlike the Russian people, the Chinese people have a powerful and sturdy ally in Free China with its temporary base in Taiwan. Taiwan enjoys today the best government in modern Chinese history, and is progressing rapidly on all fronts, political, cultural, and economic. Although the Joint Statement by President Chiang Kai-shek and Secretary of State Dulles, reported in the *New York Times* of October 24, 1958, stated that Free China agreed to renounce the use of force as the foundation of its sacred mission to return to the mainland, it still represents the hope of the Chinese people for an eventual restoration to freedom. While there is such a hope, the Reds will never feel secure and safe within. (4) Communism is, after all, a product of the West. It is basically against the temper and mentality of the Chinese people. Family life in China occupies an even more important place than in Soviet society. Chinese Communism has now assumed a more radical form than the Russian variety. It must and will encounter greater resistance from the Chinese people. The Chinese have always been taught to practice self-control, but self-control has limitations. Lily Abegg shows his keen insight of the Oriental mentality when he writes: "An East Asian is able to keep control of himself for a long while, but once the fetters are broken he becomes unpredictable and mostly knows nothing of what he is saying or doing. All the grievances, the anger and dissatisfaction he has bottled up over months or perhaps years, are suddenly let loose."[37] A similar observation was made by Joseph Alsop when he predicted an eventual revolt of the Chinese on the mainland: "At the risk of an unusual accusation of over-optimism, this reporter would venture the opinion that they (the Chinese) will not suffer and submit. They are more vital, tougher and more dynamic than the Russians. Their history shows that they are somewhat like camels—capable of bearing enormous burdens but also capable of sudden, unshakable, unmanageable resistance when the burdens grow unbearable."[38] *Tai Chi Ch'üan,* the representative type of boxing in China, teaches that the greater the strength of your opponent, the worse and more dangerous it is for him. The Chinese are playing, for the present at least, *Tai Chi Ch'üan* with the Communists. They are not to oppose force with force; they try to control their opponent's strength and to bring about the collapse of their enemy through his own strength and by means of his own efforts!

Need we then wonder why there is disquiet and silent revolt in Communist China, why the search for scapegoats has started in full fury, why Communist policy has pursued a steady course in its campaign to extinguish faith in anything but Communism?

This is, indeed, a dark moment in Chinese history. But it is not without hope. Confucianism was made precisely for such a time. It understands the need for revitalization. It teaches also that final triumph belongs to those who suffer bravely. As Bernard of Clairvaux (1091-1153) says rightly: "Our trials are wings that carry us to God."

Wings to God

THE COMMUNIST persecution of Christian churches in China shocks every reasonable person. One cannot read the many books revealing the tragedy of Christianity in China without a sorrowful heart. The Red regime argues, as does every Soviet satellite, that there is freedom to worship in Communist China, and likewise freedom not to worship. It is contended that religion is forcibly opposed only when it works openly against the State. But though this is proposed as truth (and believed by some to be the truth), this is not, and cannot be the case.

According to their own stated views, Communists believe that to succeed in their conquest of the world they must discredit religion and break its hold on the minds of men. Karl Marx, in his Manifesto of the Communist Party, published in February 1848 stated, "Communism abolishes eternal truths, it abolishes all religion and all morality." Communists believe, as Marx preached, that to further Communism they must have no respect for human life. Therefore, people have no rights as individuals, they are merely cells in a society based on materialism and moulded by economic considerations not spiritual needs. In a word, man was made not for God, but for the State. History is nothing more than an articulation of the theory of economic determinism. "It is vital to the whole system (of Communism)," as Frank Sheed puts it, "that this life should be the only life and that there should be no Supreme Being."[1] How then, could Communism co-exist with religion?

In reality, Communism, as a materialistic philosophy, cannot tolerate competition for men's minds by a spiritual force. Deep within, it *fears* religion for it sees in it an eternal force which has faced other tyrannies through the centuries and outlasted them to emerge victor in the struggle for men's loyalty. It is only too natural and logical for Communism to intensify, in every way, its offensive against religion.

As the Communist magazine *China Youth* admitted to its readers, religious believers offer a special problem to brainwashers: "People can break any idol, but this won't wash the divinity off the brain of religious followers. This must be done through persuasion and education . . . constant atheistic propaganda."[2] From this basic point of view, current events in China show that it is not China alone who is on trial, but all humanity.

The Communist plan to destroy Christian churches met stubborn opposition from foreign and Chinese Catholics alike. As a result, the Catholic Church, its hierarchy, clergy and lay members, has been the object of a particularly vicious persecution.

The records of the Church of China tell of men and women and young children who died for their Faith with all the fervour of the early Roman martyrs.[3] As we noted in previous chapters, Christianity was persecuted in China during the controversy of the rites, in the Taiping Rebellion, and during the Boxer Uprising, chiefly because of misunderstanding. The more violent assaults came from the anger of local leaders against foreigners in general. Never have the people of China opposed Christianity because of the doctrine it brought. But now, Communism, a force totally alien to the Chinese tradition, acts differently.

Communism attacks Christianity directly for its religious doctrine and its defense of human rights. "Communism has come to the conclusion," as Albert Galters points out in his careful analysis of the Communist tactics and techniques used against Roman Catholicism, "that it will never succeed in destroying religion with brutal force; open persecution will never suppress the faith but only destroy its public and exterior manifestations. The Communists do not want this. They do not want a church in the catacombs which would escape the Communist Party's and government's control. They want a Communist-controlled church that may be active, with administration of the sacraments and even large church attendances."[4] China provides a typical example of how the Communists seek to destroy the Church from within by promoting a state-directed and state-controlled ecclesiastical organization.

The moment the Communists gained control of the mainland, they used "patriotism" as a smoke screen to initiate the "Three Independences Movement": (1) Independence in supporting religion (financial); (2) Independence in propagating religion (no foreign missionaries); (3) Independence in governing religion (no foreign Pope). The people were called upon to sign their names in support of these three "independences." By this plan the Communists hoped to divide the Church, and thus corrupt it from within. On the other hand, the so-called independent churches would be creatures of the State and be used or suppressed as convenience and the Party line dictated.

There was actually nothing wrong with the first point regarding financial independence. The Church would be very happy if it were possible for all her churches throughout the world to be supported by the native Christians themselves. The Communist drive was simply to force the foreign missions to give up property holdings without any compensation whatsoever.

Schools, colleges, and hospitals previously maintained by foreign contributions were taken over by the State.

In carrying out the second point, concerning the independence of propagating the Faith, the Communists have persistently been removing the foreign missionaries.[5] This is no place to describe the suffering sustained by these missionaries in the hands of the Communists. It is enough to reproduce here a letter written by a group of Chinese Catholics to Pandit Nehru's sister during her visit to Red China in 1952. It describes the state of the Chinese prisons, in which hundreds of Catholics, missionaries, native priests and laymen, are incarcerated:

> . . . It is not part of our present intention to give details of the religious persecution which is at present raging in China. It is well known that, with the exception of a few large cities, the freedom of worship laid down in the Constitution is nothing but a mockery. . . . In this letter we want to draw special attention to the fate of the Christian prisoners who were herded into the jails in their hundreds, on the pretext of having committed crimes against their country, although their real crime lay in their religious convictions. They were arrested at any hour of the day or night, in the streets or in their homes, often without a formal charge. . . . The dungeons and cells of these prisons are so overcrowded that the unfortunate inmates cannot always stretch themselves out full length, and have to take it in turn to go to sleep. In these cells, which are like ice in winter and like ovens in summer, the prisoners have to sit motionless on the ground from dawn to dusk. It is an offence even to shut their eyes, and anyone who falls asleep is awakened by an angry roar from the guard. For days or weeks or months, the monotony of this regime is only broken by the interrogations.
>
> At these sessions, the prisoner has to face his malignant judges, seeking to trap him with every question, alone, without the help of a counsel. He has only his memory to help him recall what he has said on previous occasions, for he is not allowed to note down his replies or details of the questions, and if he has to make a written deposition, he may not take a copy of it.
>
> If his responses are considered insufficient or insolent, or if he refuses to speak altogether, he is kept standing at attention for hours or days. Chains and manacles are loaded on to his

hands and feet, causing them to swell up immediately; thus pinioned to the wall of his cell like a wild animal, he has to remain until he begs for mercy and consents to speak.

This is the truth about the prisons of China, which you were not allowed to see during your visit.[6]

This was 1952. When we read the reports made public by the two Jesuit priests, Rev. John Houle and Rev. Charles McCarthy, who had been forced out of Red China by the Communists in June 1957, we know that the cruelty imposed on the foreign missionaries has become more severe than ever before.

The greatest danger that confronted the Church, however, was the third point. It planned for a complete separation of the Church from the spiritual supremacy of the Holy See. To maintain the unity of the Church the Catholic people and missionaries in China are, thank God, as a whole ready for martyrdom. They cherish no false hopes about Communism in China. They betray no tendency to become victims of fear and reprisal.[7]

The Communist movement for the independence of the Church from "foreign control" started with propaganda aimed at the Papal Internuncio to China, Archbishop Antonio Riberi. The first called upon to make a public denunciation was a Chinese priest, Father John Tung. Father Tung had been sent to Europe to study for the priesthood by Archbishop Paul Yupin. He was ordained by the Archbishop at Fribourg, Switzerland, during World War II as a diocesan priest of the Archdiocese of Nanking. When the Communists took over the mainland he was at Chungking. On June 2, 1951, Father Tung was asked to address a large regimented audience of Catholics assembled at Chungking. He was instructed by the Communists to call for the expulsion of the Papal Internuncio and to rally the Catholics to the Communist-sponsored Independent Church. Instead of being their tool and a traitor to his priesthood he flaunted them and chose death.

Reproduced here, in part, is the inspiring speech Father Tung made on this solemn occasion. It represents one of the most beautiful compositions in defense of Catholic doctrine that have ever been written, and, in a certain way, anticipated the encyclical *ad sinarum gentem* issued by Pope Pius XII on October 7, 1954, urging Chinese Catholics to resist attempts to enlist their support for a schismatic church in China.

... Gentlemen, I have only one soul and I cannot divide it; I have a body which can be divided. It is best, it seems, to offer my soul to God and to the Holy Church; and my body to my country. If she is pleased with it, I do not refuse it to her. Good materialists, who deny the existence of the soul, cannot but be satisfied with the offering of my body only. I believe that if the State and the Church could collaborate, the movement for a Triple Autonomy, conformable to Catholic principles, would result both for the State and for the Church! ...

I beseech the authorities to accept my sacrifice and not to show me any sort of indulgence. And above all, if it happens that I weaken, I beseech them not to tolerate this weakness. Are not the weak the scourge of society? Therefore, to prevent myself against all weakness, I take this opportunity, while I am perfectly lucid, to solemnly declare that I disvow them and declare them right now null and void. ...

Suppose, that under the effect of I know not what fear, I go against my conscience, talk contrary to my own opinions, sign what I disapprove of, then I deliberately deceive the authorities; and if I say in secret that I made a mistake because I was forced, I equally deceive the Hierarchy. Would not such conduct sow discord between the Government and the Church? If I strangle the voice of my conscience, deny my God, leave the Church and cheat the Government, I am nothing more than an opportunist and a coward. I would then become only one of those persons in whom nobody can have confidence, whose life has no value for anyone. Who then would want to have me, who would want to help me? I would only be a miserable outcast deserving of all punishments from the authorities in this world and eternal punishment in the next from divine justice.

It is true that I am a Catholic. But this does not prevent me from having a very great admiration for the Communists. They believe neither in God nor in the soul, still less in heaven or hell. It is my conviction that they are mistaken. However, they have more than one quality which compels admiration, shakes my own indolence and brings me to recall vividly the millions of martyrs of our Church during the course of 2,000 years. These martyrs are the ones who urge me to beseech God, day and night, to forgive my numerous sins and grant me the unparalleled gift of martyrdom. . . .

I do not content myself with admiring the unshakable courage of the Communists, and thank them for their noble intention of trying to win the Christians. I still have a great desire. It is to offer them the Catholic Church which is so dear to me, in order to bring them to God and make them our brothers in the faith. Do not say I am a fool who prattles crazy things, and do not believe that I lack sincerity! I dare say that Communists, who have a high ideal, would be made good Catholics completely devoted to their faith and would surpass a thousand times a Catholic such as I am, when the day dawns that they really know the Catholic Church. I also ask God that in the Communist Party there may be found many Sauls to become Pauls, who will far surpass the poor priest that I am. It is my most fervent prayer. To this end, I spare myself no sacrifice, praying with hope that the earthly life which I offer today might bring the conversion of future generation. . . .

I am a Catholic; I love my country but I also love my Church. I categorically disapprove of anything that is in opposition to the laws of my country or to the laws of my Church, and above all I strongly refuse anything that could breed discord. But if the Church and the Government cannot achieve an accord, all Chinese Catholics, sooner or later, will have only to die. Why not then immediately offer my life to hasten the mutual understanding of both parties? If my offering is not accepted, the only reason is that understanding is not wanted, that peace is rejected. I hardly believe the Government will permit itself to be drawn irrevocably into demanding the death of the 3,700,000 Chinese Catholics. . . .[8]

Father Tung was arrested on July 3, 1951, and nothing has been heard of him since. But his inspiration spread, and in August of the same year, another Chinese priest, Father Beda Chang, was imprisoned. Prior to his forced resignation as Principal of St. Ignatius College, Shanghai,[9] Father Chang had been picked by the Reds to become the leader of the "Independent Church." They had taken him into custody, given him living quarters, and treated him royally in an effort to win his "good will." When this failed, they went to the other extreme, threw him in prison, maltreating him until he died. If the Shanghai Catholic population was ignorant of how Father Chang died, at least they knew why he died!

When the death of Father Chang was made known, it struck no fear in the hearts of the Catholics. On the contrary, it fanned up such religious enthusiasm that in haste police were called from the neighboring cities to prevent a rebellion.[10]

The martyrdom of these two Chinese priests, Father John Tung and Father Beda Chang, raised spiritual resistance and was a national sermon *par excellence*. The persecution however continues.

It is impossible here to tell of all the priests, monks, and nuns—several hundred in all—who have been martyred by the Communists, or have died as a result of ill-treatment at their hands. Suffice it to note that in the same year (1951) nineteen native priests made their sacrifices through prison maltreatment or execution. They were from all parts of China. Father Matthew Su, diocesan priest, died in a prison in Wuhu, Father Peter Sun, C.M. was buried alive in Peiping, Father Joseph Chang executed in Sichang, Father Stanislau Chang was killed in Tientsin, Father Andrew Chao burned to death in Kirin. To them we have to add Father Joseph Seng, second to Father McGrath in the national organization of the Legion of Mary, and head of the Shanghai Branch, Father Michael Chang, Father Vincent Shih of the Trappe of Yangkiaping, Father Albert Wei, Cistercian, and Father You of the Chengtu Trappe. They were arrested and imprisoned around the same time. They chose death for their faith and deserve a place in the martyrology of China for their devotion to the true Church.[11]

After the Communists failed to establish an "Independent Church," they began another religious movement, parallel with the rectification movement in July 1957. This movement was a schismatic effort designated as the "Patriotic Association of Chinese Catholics." It was vigorously opposed by Bishop Wang Wen-pin of the Nanchung Diocese in Szechuan Province and Bishop Chao Cheng-shen of the Hopei Diocese. At a meeting in Peiping on August 2, 1957, they openly declared that the rejection of Vatican ties "will kill the soul of the Church." Many other priests, including Bishop Dominic Teng (Teng Yi-ming), S.J., Apostolic Administrator of the Canton Diocese, 76-year-old Bishop Joseph Hu, C.M. of Taichow who had been arrested once before in September 1955 and then released, Father Paul Su, Apostolic Administrator of the Wenchow (Yungkia) Diocese, Father John Wang, Apostolic Administrator of the Ningpo Diocese, and Father James Liu of the Nanchang Diocese in Kiangsi, were all against this Communist-controlled body. For this, they were either publicly accused of "crimes" or sentenced to prison terms ranging from ten to twenty years.[12]

Following the arrest and accusation of these native priests, the Peiping regime sent its agents to almost every mainland province to found branches of this "Patriotic Association of Chinese Catholics." Ever since October 1957, all adult Catholics on the mainland have been forced to undergo six hours of daily "brainwashing" under the direction of the "Patriotic Association." The six-hour "study" period is usually divided into early morning and late evening sessions. In the morning session, an agent from the religious affairs bureau of the Chinese Communist state council harangues at length on the "successes" of the Communist anti-rightists campaign, the five-year-plans and the land reform, and then darkly warns that numerous "counter-revolutionaries" among the Catholics must be uncovered. The evening "study" is usually given over to discussion of the need "to sever political and economic ties with the Vatican" and to the thesis, "religious belief may not be used as a pretext to reject the leadership of the Communist Party."

Special pressures were laid on priests, religious, and especially on Bishops by the Communists. They realized that without the support of the hierarchy the indoctrination of Chinese Catholics would be exceedingly difficult. To get an insight into the fearless resistance to this Communist oppression, we reproduce here a few passages from a letter written by a Chinese priest under Communist tyranny:

(During these "indoctrination courses,") we are advised that this Patriotic Association is purely political and has no bearing on religion. It is an organization for Catholics and priests are free to join in.

As time went on, the discussions became heated. The Director of Religious and Cultural Administration and his associates are always there. At these sessions he pounds the table, shouts, yells and screams at the stalling tactics employed by the assembled priests and laity. . . .

That the government has no intention whatsoever of interfering in matters strictly religious is their "line." It is repeated over and over again. Then each of us is called in turn to express his opinion on this matter. The Patriotic Association is purely political, they insist.

However, there are lots of difficulties and hesitations on this point. The encyclicals are dragged out, discussed and criticized. What is, and what is not, political or religious matter in these documents? In no time there is an uproar, with everyone shouting, banging the table, stamping on the floor and the Director of Religion threatening to call in the police if order is not restored immediately.

There have repeatedly been tumultuous scenes during discussions on this point. . . . At times one feels like jumping on the table and crying out aloud "Long live the Pope!" An inward upsurge of loyalty in face of the tumultuous onslaught makes one feel that now is the time to be a valiant soldier of Christ ready for the holocaust. . . .

(The Reds) pretend not to force or impose it on us. They insist, repeat, insist again and again always on the same statement wearying us out, breaking us down until unable to hold out any longer one is finally prepared to say "well, have it your way." . . . But they won't accept it in this way. They want us to concede as if we proposed it; as if we were finally convinced of what they have said and submit to their statements as to our own self-imposed directives! . . .

> No one wants this Patriotic Association; no one wants Communism—anyone or anything connected with it. But we are here on the horns of a terrible dilemma. Open resistance is of no avail. What are we to do? Try to save what we can, for the love of God, our neighbor and our Catholic faith.[13]

Now, the fight is on. Chang Chih-yi, deputy head of the united front department of the Chinese Communist party central committee wrote in this year's first issue of the Communist bimonthly *Philosophical Research* under the title of "Political Cooperation of Atheists and Theists," that "speaking in general, a great number of religious people still show suspicion of, or antagonism to, socialism and the Communist Party. . . . There are still people who even publicly manifest their determination not to sever relations with imperialism, particularly with the Vatican."[14] As a matter of fact, Rev. Chang Tseng-kuo of Kirin province was reported by the Communists to have declared in an address delivered before 4,100 Catholic Chinese delegates attending a regional Catholic conference held in Peiping: "We should not cooperate with the people's government! Kneel down and pray, then stand up and fight!" Reporting on the proceedings of the conference, the Chinese Communist Peiping radio quoted another priest, Rev. Fan Hsiu-yen of Hopei province, as having said: "What they (Communists) say is not what they think. Communist thinking is sinful." The majority of the Catholic delegates, went on the Red radio, were shocked by Wang Ko-jo's "reactionary rightist" statement. As Apostolic Vicar of Loshan, Szechuan province, Father Wang Ko-jo was reported to have urged immediate uprising "to eliminate the leadership of the Communist Party and to return to capitalism."[15]

Seeing how little success they were achieving with the Catholic people and their priests, the Communists made another desperate move aiming at the creation of a subservient hierarchy. In August 1958 we learned that in April of the same year the Communists had forced a Bishop of the Puchi Diocese near

Hankow, after two weeks of torture, into consecrating as bishops two priests, known as Yuan Wen-hua of Wuchang and Yu Kwang-ching of Hankow, selected by the Reds.[16] This was officially condemned as illicit by an encyclical letter *Ad Apostolorum Principis* (to the Prince of the Apostles) bearing the date of June 29, the Feast of Saints Peter and Paul, 1958. In the absence of the normal sources of private and newspaper correspondence free from Communist censors, we do not know what had happened there, and whether or not the unfortunate men involved had been mentally tortured beyond the limits of responsibility as in the case of many missionary victims. What we do know for certain is: (1) the number of priests who after persecution joined the "Patriotic Church" is insignificant, (2) the same is true of the laity, (3) the vast majority of Catholic people refuse to attend a "patriotic church," (4) twenty-five Chinese bishops are suffering or have suffered the horror of Communist prisons rather than join the "Patriotic Church," (5) as late as May 1958 three priests, Msgr. Odoricus Liu, Vicar General of Hankow, Rev. Peter Alcantara, Rev. James Wu, and the layman, Anthony Yang, were sentenced in Hankow to prison terms from ten to twenty years, because they had refused to have anything to do with the "Communist-controlled Church."[17] We should mark the place Hankow. It was the same place where the Communist-dictated consecrations had been held.

In the nature of things, Chinese priests found themselves in a more dangerous position than missionaries from foreign countries. Imprisoned foreign missionaries might hope for leniency because they are foreigners. They generally had the possibility of ending their prison terms with expulsion. Chinese priests, on the other hand, can only expect the worst possible treatment. They have nothing to look forward to except a life of suffering or death from exhaustion or execution.

These startling facts make a lie of the Communists' contention that they are only against foreign missionaries and really are not against religion itself. They likewise bring to light the heroic stand and the martyrdom of the Chinese priests who provided their motherland with that blood of martyrs which is the seed of future Christians. In the words of the Gospel, "Amen, amen, I say to you, unless the grain of wheat falling into the ground die, itself remaineth alone. But if it die, it bringeth forth much fruit."[18]

When the time comes to write a full history of the Church in China under the Reds, it will be a glorious history. The time has not yet come, for even now it is dangerous to mention names and places that would be used by the persecutors.

The Church In Torment

AFTER THE Communists' failure to win over the native clergy, the martrydom of the Church in China began. The Legion of Mary rose splendidly to the occasion. It became a fortress that could not be conquered.

According to the eyewitness account of Joseph M. C. Kung, "the Communists used every possible method, including murder and jailing, to subdue those who resisted them. They imprisoned groups of outstanding Catholics who had kept in touch with the Church authorities. But the more they killed, the more converts were baptized. After many arrests, the Communists attempted to nullify the work of the Catholic action groups by mixing a few turncoats in with them. The Church in turn strengthened herself by forming a Youth Front which included numerous active groups of the Legion of Mary. The Youth Front and the Legion of Mary then collaborated openly in the defense of the Church. They became, as it were, a bulwark protecting and inspiring the Catholic youth in China."[1] The Reds realized this, and consequently organized an all-out attack on the youth, especially the Legion of Mary.

With their natural reverence towards motherhood, the devotion of Chinese Christians to the Blessed Mother is instinctive. "Through her," as Very Rev. William A. Donaghy, S.J. puts it, "He was pleased to give us every good."[2] The Legion of Mary seems to have been assigned by Providence the special mission of getting the Church in China over this critical period. First to the Legionaries is personal sanctification; then effective Catholic action. God still has special work for the Chinese Legionaries. For this they are granted special graces. The fervent lovers of Our Lady in China make every effort to attain the heights of Divine Love.

Their heroism amazed even the enemies. Their leaders took special vows: never to miss a meeting, to accept every job for the Legion, never to flee on account of prison or death. Seventy of these Legionaries in Shanghai had already died for the Faith by the end of 1953.[3]

Chinese Legionaries remained spiritually dynamic. They requested days of retreat; helped organize novenas of sermons before the greater feasts; visited the sick, brought couples to have their marriages rectified; kept a friendly watch on those who were wavering or being worked on by dangerous influences. They explained to those who needed it, that religion and patriotism are not the same thing, but are not opposed to each other. They listened to talks and carried the message of others. Their enthusiasm was contagious. They were the leaven wherewith the whole mass became leavened.[4] In this way the "Independent Church" movement became a sorry fiasco.

This explains why most of the more dramatic instances which brought the courage of Catholics to the notice of the public were the cases of persecuted Legionaries. Stories got around of how Legionaries went to police stations with their little bags prepared to stay, but not to yield; of how some of them sat there fingering their rosaries while the police talked, threatened and attempted to indoctrinate them for hours; of how one after another went through the same ordeal (and some many times), without yielding, consistently winning a moral victory. People who never before gave a second thought to the Catholic Church now became interested not only in the Legion, but also in the Church. They were fellow travellers now; all were being persecuted; and they admired those who dared resist.[5]

If we speak of the external structure of the Church in Red China, it has suffered great loss, especially in the educational field.[6] But the totalitarian force has taught Catholic youth in a somewhat negative way to live completely dedicated lives, something they could hardly have learned so well and fully from books. We read:

> In schools and at home, in the jobs, in their neighborhood gatherings, in general meetings and small discussion groups, they are relentlessly forced to declare and reveal themselves and they do it uncompromisingly and with courage, bringing everything back to the one foundation of religion. . . . Even though deprived of their pastors by exile, prison or house arrest and often even deprived of their churches, they will put together enough money to rent a hall or room and obtain a priest who has been forced to live at home or with a family for the Sunday Mass. They have devised ingenious ways of receiving the Sacraments from imprisoned priests or those in hiding. Wherever the Catholic lay people have shown any weakness or wavering it is not a choice of open apostasy but rather of temporarily submitting until they can find a way out. They would prefer to choose open martyrdom. Actually there are many lay Catholic heroes and martyrs but we don't receive the same detailed information on them that we do on the priests and religious.[7]

Numerous instances can be cited to attest to the courageous defense of the Faith by the laity. One suffices:

On the night of June 15, 1953, the police raided the homes of six priests, several pastors and the Jesuit Fathers at Zikawei (Shanghai). Several Jesuits were immediately taken to jail; others were put under home arrest. Thousands of Catholics gathered at the square of Zikawei and knelt to say the rosary opposite the house where these priests were under Communists' guard. The people ignored the machine guns which were pointed at them. Still more and more Catholics gathered, their voices reciting the rosary in louder and louder unison with the prayers of the imprisoned priests. What a magnificent scene it was: soldiers, machine guns, priests under guard, people and the rosary![8]

Sometimes when a layman makes his supreme sacrifice, his heroic act is hardly recognized as martrydom. His imprisonment and execution by the Communists are always on political or civil grounds. Truly, sanctity demands a hidden life. "To decline consolation from any creature is a sign of great purity and internal trust in God."[9]

The Church in Red China is still living; it is growing stronger in secret in the silent hearts of the people. Despite all the methods used by the Communists, there were very, very few instances of betrayal of the Faith. This was manifested in the arrest of Bishop Ignatius Kung, his Vicar General, Msgr. Silvester Tsu, and more than 1,400 of the clergy and the faithful in Shanghai on September 8 and September 24, 1955.[10] This Communist attempt to destroy the Church proved to be another self-defeating design.[11]

The Communists failed in trying to have an "Independent" or "Reformed" church through their attack on the Papacy. They also failed to destroy the Legion of Mary and have admitted unwillingly that this cannot be done.[12] "In their attack upon the Church in China," Archbishop Pollio, P.I.M.E., of Kaifeng, observes, "the Communists have made a serious tactical error. They asked the people to condemn first the Pope and then the Blessed Virgin. It was a bad mistake. The Chinese Catholics love both. The Legion of Mary particularly has had a very long-lasting effect upon the youth. I am convinced that the faith will never fail among these Catholics."[13] A similar observation was made to me by Bishop Donaghy, M.M. of Kiangmen, Kwangsi.[14]

Thus, whatever the dangers that lie ahead, the Christians in Red China, with God's grace, hold fast to their faith. Their faith may not, in its liturgical and outward manifestations, be that with which the man of the West is familiar. But it is their faith, a faith that has brought them through many crises in their long past. As Father Mark Tennien says: "Their (Chinese Christians') lot will be hard, but no one under Communism will have an easy lot. Subtle and constant pressure will continue in order to force the Church into subservience to the Communist state. Just how well the faithful can resist, and how much the Communists in China can harm and bleed the Church, only God knows. Looking back across the centuries, we see that tyrants and puppets and blasphemers are a flash that quickly passes. For the present, Chinese Christians must pass through a dark night, but dawn has always come to give surcease from tyranny."[15]

By heroic examples, especially of the native clergy, Chinese Catholic youth have learned, intuitively if not through clearly rational processes, that the essence of Christian life is dependent not on time or tradition, but on persecution and the Cross. An imprisoned and returned missionary points out:

> We have seen the Church in China, truly the Church and truly Chinese, and we know that she cannot die. The blood of the martyrs is the seed of the Church and our Catholic youth have understood that it is their blood, their lives that count. There is no narrow nationalism in their attitude; they are too Catholic for that. . . . They claim the right of suffering for Christ themselves in their own land, and in that, as in the depth of their Catholic living, it is clear that even in these young souls, the Church in China has reached maturity and achieved her birthright.[16]

Indeed, the courage of the Catholics is sometimes more evident among children. They are often capable of great heroism. In one village a little girl of twelve took advantage of the presence of a missionary who was on a visit and went to Communion. She was savagely beaten by her schoolmistress, a thoroughly disreputable woman, for missing class. As a protest against this brutality, the next day the whole class went to mass, although they were predominantly heathen.[17]

The story about Little Mei is even more inspiring.

Little Mei was only three when the Communists began their reign of terror in the village where she lived, in April 1951. The Catholics were dragged out of their houses in the middle of the night and taken to prison to be interrogated. Several months later Mei's mother was arrested, and under pressure from the police, repudiated her faith. In order to prove her patriotism, she agreed to speak at a meeting held against "the imperialism of the Catholic Church." The archbishop of the place was already in prison, and the purpose of this meeting was to whip up the crowd into approving the arrest of the other missionaries.

Mei was restless while her mother spoke, and pushed away the sweet that was offered to her. Suddenly she heard her mother say:

> I have a little daughter of three who is a very intelligent child. Mei might have been another Saint Thérèse of the Child Jesus, but we are too poor and have never been accorded this honor. It is time to do away with the imperialism of the archbishop and the missionaries.

All at once Mei slipped away from the grasp of her neighbors and ran towards the scene, crying: "Mommy, Mommy, I want to go home! I want to go home!" At home, she said to her mother: "Mommy, didn't we promise God to be faithful to the Pope and our bishops? Why do you want to go to Hell?" Shortly after this, Mei's mother went to church to confess her mistake and on her return found a policeman in the house, who had guessed her change of heart. It was Mei who said to him: "Do you think we are afraid to go to prison for our faith?"

The same evening the mother and child were put in prison. Mei was not idle during her six months in prison. As she was allowed to circulate freely around the prison, she carried the hosts which had been consecrated by the missionaries in one part of the building to the prisoners in another. The child was quick to seize on the one moment when the guard's attention was distracted, and pass the Sacred Host.

When Mei and her mother were released, Catholics all over the town flocked to see the child who had showed such remarkable courage for her age. The missionaries were so impressed by the answers which she gave to their questions that they decided to allow her to make her first Communion, although she was only just four years old. Back at home, Mei continued to display courage and presence of mind. She twice repulsed apostates from the "Reformed" church, and once, when one of the men wanted to speak with her mother, she barred the way and exclaimed: "You are a traitor to our faith. If you want to go to Hell, go there, but leave us in peace. You cannot enter." The man had to go away without saying anything, and Mei said to her mother: "You see, Mommy, I am not afraid, because I have received the sacrament of Confirmation and I am a soldier of Christ. I fear nothing."[18]

We cannot continue to cite here such inspiring stories which would fill several volumes. In short, the faith of Chinese Catholic youth, like that of the early Christians, is such that they look upon death as a door to happiness. Whether it is because they are not so much in love as we are with the world, especially the world under Communist rule, and with worldly things, or that they look forward to heaven with more eagerness than we do, is something that no one can state certainly. Perhaps it is a little of both. "According to the multitudes of my sorrows in my heart, thy comforts have given joy to my soul."[19] The Chinese faithful must have realized what a supreme privilege it is to be a Christian and to die for Christ. In the words of Dr. John Wu, "In the trials of St. Eusebius, the governor said, 'These Christians are a hardened race, it seems to them more desirable to die than to live.' The fact is that they see what the world cannot see. The same story is being repeated in China. The stories of our contemporary martyrs like Beda Chang, John Tung, Bishop Francis Ford, and many others will form a glorious chapter in the history of Christianity."[20]

On the other hand, the Church is making gains among the Chinese abroad who can exercise extensive influence upon the minds and lives of the people behind the Curtain. They represent a force which cannot easily be measured by statistical methods. As Rev. Jean Monsterleet notes it, "However dim the chances of the conversion of China at the moment may be, one unexpected result of the expulsion of the missionaries has been the active evangelization of the Chinese abroad. The Church in China is bearing fruit on foreign soil among the twelve million Chinese who live outside their own country. In Europe and America the former missionaries are spreading the truth about Communism. When the doors of China open again, there will doubtless be numerous volunteers to enter and continue the apostleship and at their side will be the five or six hundred Chinese seminarists who are even now preparing themselves in exile for their future mission."[21]

All in all, religion will survive in China. And that is something of tremendous importance. The Communists, despite their ruthless oppressions, have not liquidated religion. Nor will they. Every religious manifestation or service is a sharp sting in the flesh of the Peiping atheists who keep saying that God is dead. But God is not dead—not dead even in Soviet Russia which experiences its forty-first year of religious persecution since the Bolshevik revolution.[22] It must confound the Chinese Communists, and occasion them no end of exasperation to know that after several years of materialistic indoctrination, millions of Chinese still cling to their faith, still recite their creed, still lift their hearts to God in prayer. For them, God lives. Every relic, every crucifix, every domed tower, every pagoda silhouetted against the Chinese skyline is a symbol of those imponderable of the spirit by which the mighty are cast down.

At the present time, it is as if the Chinese Church, in silence and in torment, was lifted high upon the Cross, from where, with Christ, it will bring salvation to the whole world. St. Peter might have been writing to the Chinese of the trials and tribulations they are undergoing today. It is only through their endurance that we understand his words:

> You are a chosen generation, a kingly priesthood, a holy nation, a purchased people: that you may declare his virtues who hath called you out of darkness into his marvellous light.[23]

The people who have sustained bloody persecution so steadfastly and still have their faith are the kind of people who will surely cause Communism to break up. As surely as light follows darkness, the problems created in such people by the forced maintenance of power will somehow in the end destroy that power.

The Chinese Are Chinese

SOME MAY ASK, "What has made it possible for the Chinese people to survive the Communist oppression, and what is their assurance of final triumph?"

As we have stated, the Chinese people have drawn their cultural strength from Confucian, Taoist, and Buddhist traditions.

The charm of Chinese life is largely due to its emphasis on moral and spiritual values, and to the Chinese, civilization can never be measured merely by material progress. The material world becomes unreal and rather childish if it is deprived of its moral basis; and this is why the Chinese sometimes laugh at things which the West considers urgent and why they do not become excited about many things which the West believes are important. How many Chinamen have been called "lazy" by Westerners when in reality they are simply detached in their outlook.

With this philosophy of life, the Chinese learn how to remain calm and unmoved whether they are praised or blamed. They possess certain inborn qualities which serve very well as an antitoxin to the Communist disease. By nature, they hate regimentation, or any kind of control which runs counter to the natural expression of their life and thought.

One quality of the Chinese mind stands out above the others, and that is a certain calm disposition flowing spontaneously from an inner harmony of soul. This inner harmony rests on atonement with the cosmic harmony of the Universe. Whether the Chinese is Confucianist, Taoist, or Buddhist, this feeling of unity with Nature forms, as it were, the inarticulate substratum of his soul. The typical Chinese regards himself as a microcosm, and he feels at home in the macrocosm. Thus, he intuitively tends toward serenity of soul and aspires to a life of natural tranquillity. As Lily Abegg puts it, "It is the East Asian feeling of oneness with the world and life which creates this frame of mind: the inner calm, philosophic resignation, the joy in the outside world, together with humility in the face of the inexplicable and the eternal, cheerful industriousness and activity, joy in material things and indifference to their loss or destruction. It is the feeling that man is never isolated, for he forms a community with the living and the dead, with the spirit of the universe and with nature, in which gods, spirits and demons still move and have their being as in ancient times."[1]

To this context belongs the Chinese attempt to seek moderation in every thought and act. But what does moderation mean? Moderation is neither mediocrity nor compromise. It is a poise or inner firmness that immediately counters any inbalance that may arise, and restores equilibrium, harmony, proportion. Self-mastery is of key importance to the development of moderation. One disciplined to moderation attains a personal integration within, and an adjustment of social forces without. The Chinese ideal of moderation is to strike a balance between, or to overcome one's conflicts, thereby achieving a reposeful and harmonious maturity. This establishes the natural basis on which a truly free and happy life can flourish.

Moderation is, then, not something theoretical. It is a living force, concretely expressed in the ordinary way of life. For instance, the Chinese have developed a set of *kuei chu* ("the rule of the square and compass") to measure every action and guide every feeling, to limit every motion. The imposition of these outward disciplines should be accompanied, in private, by a freedom which manifests itself in dress, at the table, and on all social occasions. On the other hand, when one rests, he is taught not to relax without a style. Chinese chairs are usually made in stiff and straight forms. One should rest on them in a perpendicular line. Therefore, it is not a full rest at all. Certainly one is not supposed to put his feet up on anything. All educated Chinese, except those who have lived a long time abroad, move with dignity; they detest the hasty. Even the porter in China adopts a graceful way of moving in lively fashion and with excellent balance. Hardship and ease are felt by the whole psyche. Strain and relaxation must go hand in hand. In some activities one should slow down; in others one should definitely speed up; to be able to change one's pace and to preserve a spiritual balance is the essence of moderation.

Human life moves, therefore, in a relaxed mood on the line of least strain. This enables one to avoid extremes. The ideal is to find oneself in a natural well-balanced state. This balance is a dynamic pulsation of life in all its activities. It is not something static. Its inner norm is the natural law, so splendidly described by Mencius. The Chinese are keenly aware of the natural impulses of the human heart. There is consistent reference in Chinese writings to the immediate compassion that arises in every human heart at the sight of a child about to fall into a well and to the human instinct to save the child. On the Chinese awareness of such immediate norms of goodness and evil in human actions they built up their entire philosophy of life. With a similar immediacy in their knowledge of man they recognized that amid all the manifold activities of life there was need of a masterful sense of control, of poise, of moderation. This same philosophy of life led them to see that moderation must, in the practical order, rest on a sense of confidence in the cosmic order and ultimately on the higher Providence of *T'ien,* Heaven Itself.

While this is the traditional Chinese way of life, the Communist way of life is exactly the opposite. The Chinese are at peace within themselves, with the social order, with the universe and with God. The Communists are at war within themselves, with the social order, with the natural order of things and with God.

If one is honest and a Communist, he is not Chinese. If one is Chinese and a Communist, he is not honest. If one is Chinese and honest, he cannot be a Communist. This means, in fact, that the seeds of the destruction of the Red regime lie, not in the shifts of policies or of external factors, but rather in its essentially false relationship to the Chinese people themselves.

In theory and in practice, Communism is so anti-moral and anti-human that it is necessarily opposed to the Chinese ideal of moderation as a way of life. When the very sense of moderation is lost, the survival of the Chinese spirit is in peril.

Moderation is not passive. Nor is it neutral. Moderation is constructive and positive. It resists and counteracts everything going to extremes. It favors and defends everything following the middle course. If the regime is too severe, the only way to pursue moderation is to take up appropriate resistance. That more than twenty million Chinese have died under Communist tyranny is enough to show the true force of moderation practiced by Chinese on the mainland. For moderation, fortitude, vigor, and sacrifice are one.

Moderation, though a good moral virtue and sufficient in the past, is now inadequate in the face of Communist aggression. In dealing with Communism the Chinese need something more than moderation on merely moral and natural grounds. Only with a stronger spiritual power can they hope to strengthen their natural gifts and to counter this wicked force. This cannot be done without a truly religious life. "The sorrows of hell encompassed me: and the snares of death prevented me. In my affliction I called upon the Lord."[2]

Under Communist oppression, the indifference long accorded to religion, when natural wisdom was thought to be enough as a way of life, has been revealed as a source of weakness.

In this respect, I wish to quote a statement made by Dr. Chang Chi-yun, who is non-Christian, yet has expressed a most Christian view:

All natural philosophies have their limitations. No matter how highly endowed, they cannot find what they do not seek; and they cannot seek what only faith can seek, if they have not the faith. Therefore, we must seek the divine source which transcends reason and goes beyond human knowledge. This being true, the moral teachings of Confucius can be very well supplemented and fulfilled by the spirituality of Christ. In fact, Confucius himself anticipated such a fulfillment when he remarked: "If a man in the morning embraces the law of Heaven, then he may die in the same evening without regret." (*Analects* 4, 8) This spirit of free acceptance leaves ample room for the Chinese to pursue the supernatural faith which is nothing more than giving the soul to God. When we come across the words of St. Paul that "through many tribulations we must enter the kingdom of God," (*Acts* 14, 21) we cannot help but reflect a Chinese proverb which says: "Suffering and sanctity are synonymous."[3]

Truly, every culture is man-made, and hence subject to all the weaknesses of man. Man is a creature whose perfection is found only in the spiritual realm. The same is true with the Chinese.

The descendants of the Chinese civilization everywhere still possess the ancestral virtues. These virtues may be generally hidden under the cloak of degeneration. But this degeneration is often superficial. It comes chiefly from idleness, lack of vitality and spiritual discipline. A new impetus is needed, a new challenge which will evoke a reassertion of ancient vigor and creative activity. The Christian West has brought this to China. Rapid progress is found, particularly at the present time, in the regions where Chinese Christians have resided.

In Taiwan, for instance, conversions are numerous. The Church there, with the blessing of Cardinal Tien and under the enlightened directives of the Hierarchy,[4] is proceeding with vigor and reaching great numbers. The large staff of experienced personnel, the encouraging results of the last few years, the open-minded friendliness of the people and the cooperative spirit of the civil authorities, including the Ministry of Education,[5] all combine to expand the hope of an abundant harvest these coming years. This was revealed to me on my most recent journey to the East.

I visited Taiwan in August and September, 1956. There I made a special trip to the interior of the island with particular interest in the Church activities. What impressed me most was the religious zeal of the common people. I saw this most vividly on my visit to a church at Kao-hsiung under the pastoral care of Father Thomas J. Smith, C.M. It was late in the evening, at a time when in China every one usually is retiring for the night. However, when I arrived at the church it was practically impossible for me to get in. A crowd of people were lined up at the entrance waiting for their turn to be called for religious instructions! In another place called Si-chia in the suburban area of Kao-hsiung there was a little chapel which can accommodate at most thirty people. I went there on a Sunday morning and found the chapel packed to its full capacity. About one hundred people stood in the courtyard. Still more, two to three hundred people were standing on the street outside the chapel. They were all attending the Mass. It was a hot day; the temperature hit 102! Only the spiritual refreshment in their souls had made it possible for these people to endure the physical heat.

Because of this religious zeal the number of Catholics has increased from 20,112 to 80,661 over a short period of five years (1951-1956).[6] According to a report issued by *Worldmission Fides Service* of November 28, 1958, as of June 30, 1957, the number of Catholics in Taiwan reached 114,805 in addition to 73,407 Catechumens. Numerically speaking, the figure is not surprising. But the rate of increase and, above all, the fact that many of the new Catholics are intellectual converts, is really quite significant in recent Chinese history.[7]

There is also a blossoming of the faith in Hong Kong—a harvest such as never before has occurred there. It is reported that, on the average, about one thousand Chinese, many of them intellectuals, are received monthly into the Church. The colony is now the scene of a great renaissance of the faith.[8] This fact was confirmed by the Bishop of Hong Kong, Bishop Lawrence Bianchi, when I met him there in December 1955. "The number of converts is limited only by the number of people available to instruct them," he said.

The number of the newly converted faithful on the mainland of China we do not know. What we do know for certain is that Communists themselves have helped the Christian cause by making people aware of the reality of the Devil, for their brutality is certainly not human. According to reports gathered from refugees and expelled missionaries, we learn that those Chinese priests who are still free to move about are unable to cope with the ever growing need of these hapless souls. In a word, the whole population is favorably disposed. Persecution has drawn attention to the Church, and has won for it the sympathy of numerous sections of the population. Overseas Chinese also, many of them potential leaders of China in coming years, are increasingly inclined toward the Church.

Thus China is once more resurging, full of vitality and bristling with new ideas. Conservative aged China is again youthful. Her eyes are filled with new vision, her heart with new hopes. This is what makes it possible for her to stand firm for freedom against Communist materialism, and to play an historic role in a confused world. "Just as preparation for so many centuries conquered the ancient medieval world for Christ," as Pie-Raymond Régamery, O.P. writes, "so let us hope that if today God is making use of the probability of catastrophe and so strengthening our souls for the spirit's warfare, it is for the sake of harvest mightier still."[9] How significant then is China's present trial, if its effect is to raise enough minds and hearts to the vision and love of things divine.

A shift is coming. The Chinese remain Chinese. A Communist unbalance has come into their life. This unbalance cannot remain. A new balance on a more sublime plan must be, and will be established.

The present situation in China, therefore, may be summed up in the following manner: (1) The Chinese people, with their deeply rooted cultural heritage, will never accept a Communist rule which tramples ruthlessly upon all human dignity and upon the most elementary rights of man. The philosophy of moderation with its roots in the natural law convinces them that Communism, like everything in the world, will sooner or later revert to its opposite after it reaches a certain extreme. (2) In the absence of armed uprising, the silent and passive resistance of the people places a severe strain on the entire Communist system and threatens its disintegration. (3) In suffering and trials, the Chinese people have been prepared for a more full and perfect religious life. (4) With the mainland sealed off by the Bamboo Curtain, the seeding ground for the Church in China is in Taiwan, Hong Kong, and Southeast Asia.[10] As soon as access to the mainland is available, the new Christians in Taiwan and elsewhere will be a strong nucleus in apostolic work among the Chinese population. (5) Missionaries and Chinese priests forced out from the mainland are available not only for the present urgent work among the free Chinese, but also for establishing a new, dynamic, long-range spiritual program for the future. All this marks an historic turning point in the whole development of modern China.

The Turning Point

THE IMPLACABLE challenge of Communism may, by a paradox, be actually beneficial to China, because the very weight of its tyranny is impelling the people to re-examine their own consciences, to correct abuses where they exist, to bring what they actually do into accord with their traditional beliefs.

However, just as China's present misfortunes were not all created by China herself, so her salvation will not be hers alone. In other words, China's turning point cannot be isolated from the world's. We are facing today an impasse in China. This situation is a part of that larger impasse that we designate with the title of the Cold War. What we witness in this area of the Far

East is a decisive phase in the worldwide struggle between Democratic freedom and Communist tyranny. The threat is not even primarily to China; it is a threat to the entire free world.

This was made clear to us in President Eisenhower's State of the Union Message to Congress, Jan. 9, 1958, when he said: "What makes the Soviet threat unique in history is its all-inclusiveness. Every human activity is pressed into service as a weapon of expansion. Trade, economic development, military power, arts, science, education, the whole world of ideas—all are harnessed to this same chariot of expansion. The Soviets are, in short, waging total cold war. The only answer to a regime that wages total cold war is to wage total peace."

But what are the specific ways in which this total struggle for peace can be carried out?

First of all, we must establish a genuine and dynamic leadership. Communist leaders have their minds and hearts set on ultimate world leadership, whereas the free nations have their minds on almost everything else. Communism, as concept, program, organization, action and method, works on all fronts, at all levels, in all activities, but always with a real unified policy and purpose. This is not the case with the free world. A bit of policy here and some aid there will never be adequate to counteract this unified Communist pressure, a pressure which manifests itself most seriously in Asia, with Red China as the major threat.

Herein lies the challenge confronting the free nations in general, and the United States in particular. In fact, this challenge is in that very field in which the United States is best fitted to respond.

Since the Open Door Policy toward China in the 1900's and the Washington Conference of 1921-1922 safeguarding China's unity, the United States has long been respected by almost every country in Asia as a power which is great, but which seeks no self-interest or territorial expansion. In fact, the American Revolution has long taught the Asian peoples that "all men," not merely Americans, are born *in principle* not merely free but also democratically equal before the law and have the inalienable right to such democratic freedom and equality. Thus, America's good will is well recognized: its prestige is high. In recent years there have been some isolated incidents which could be interpreted as ill feelings toward America. Yet we must not let the trivial obscure what is essential, and what is essential is, that a strong friendship for America exists, and provides the basis for a widespread democratic leadership throughout the entire Eastern world.

Secondly, we need a many-sided but unified strategy. Communism in Asia, as elsewhere, has one persistent and consistent policy, that of ultimate political domination. To achieve this end, it varies the role according to circumstances. It exercises direct control in Red China, North Korea, North Viet Nam. It uses military pressure on Taiwan, South Korea, South Viet Nam. It applies silent but all-pervading pressures leading to future political, economic and military control on Burma, Laos, Cambodia, India, Malaya, and Indonesia. Its most powerful instruments, however, are the intelligent and active Communist agents throughout the area.[1]

What are our counter-measures? Often, when we deal with the same problems, our projects are fragmentary or even contradictory. To make up this deficiency, we must formulate a flexible but consistent plan. It should be founded on the realization that the central problem of Asia is the Communist domination of the Chinese mainland. There are many places in Asia where we must fight against Communism. But we must keep foremost in mind the need to eliminate and destroy the Communist rule of Red China, which may be more properly called Soviet China. Everything depends on this.

Finally, in order to win the total peace, we must think and act with a creative vision. Western colonialism is dead in Asia. That means that a struggle *against* something is past. Now comes the time of a struggle *for* something—for the formation of a new Asia. What is it to be?

Communism has its own ideas about the future shape of Asia. For the present, it seeks to establish order through disorder, to achieve conquest through divide-and-rule, to foster hate through disguised appeal for human fraternity. However, the Asians recognize the deceit. They do not like it. Nevertheless, they may choose the Communist way as a feasible alternative simply because there is nothing else to be chosen. The fact that Communism has made headway in Asia is not because it is wanted; it is because there is no alternative.

Herein lies the urgent need of a creative vision shared by both Asia and the West. The various nations in Asia yearn for a new expression of their native life. They realize the need for a new education, a new economy, a new social order, new forms of government, and, above all, a new spirituality which will revitalize their ancient religious and humanist heritage. They realize that they must have assistance from the West. Their choice is between the Russian Communist West and the Democratic Christian West. They desire to be associated with this Democratic Christian West, but the vision of a new order of national and international life that we present to them must be as clear and vivid, as entrancing and inspiring as the vision offered by the Communists. But we must not only present a vision. We must assist with all our resources in the realization of this vision. This is the positive element in our association with Asia.

We must also recognize that Communism as an ideology is a product of the West, not of the East. The West, because of its Christian culture, was and is able to offer some kind of resistance to the Communist ideology; but the East, which had already given up many of its finest moral traditions, is most vulnerable—China is a typical example. Nevertheless, Chinese culture, as Dr. Hollington K. Tong stated in his address at the Commencement Exercises of Seton Hall University (June 8, 1957), "has provided a favorable soil for the acceptance of the Christian faith by both Chinese and other Asians. Christianity to the Orientals is looked upon as a form of culture closely similar to their own." Christian thought has firm foundations in the Far East. The need now is to work toward the union of the spiritual traditions of the East and the West, with Christianity supplying the leadership.

We are behind Russia in the effort to win the hearts and minds of the Asian peoples, but not because Soviet Russia is superior to us in thought or ideals. We have the best ideals in the world, but we have not shown sufficient ability to make these ideals effective in the world of reality.

Will time favor us or our enemy? This depends on our ability to bring a spiritual message to Asia. Now, the Western world has an excellent opportunity for getting closer to the Eastern world whose soul is in agony. Now more than ever, the most effective apostolate is by example rather than by word. Tradition must live; faith must work. Because of the Communist threat, the world is more and more insistent on a moral order. This moral order, as Emerson put it, "lies at the center of nature and radiates to the circumference." Only a center based on Christian principles is able to shake the morals of world Communism. And only the relentless aggression of Communism, apparently, will make Christians the world over face the situation with the needed vision, restraint, responsibility and courage. As Father Martin D'Arcy, S.J. puts it, "Christianity has become familiar to the West, and familiarity has bred, if not contempt, indifference. One hope is that this very indifference has been accompanied with so much ignorance, that the truth of the Christian faith can be stated as to startle and inspire, and there is also the unique feature of the Christian faith that its riches are such as never to be exhausted."[2]

In the Eastern world, China, as one notable example, has

begun to know the Church. Her destiny is with Christianity, because the Chinese people have been prepared for Christ by the natural gifts China has received.

Thus, we of today are witnessing an important movement in the historical development of Christianity. Whether Christian influence will mold China, or whether she will remain under Communism, depends not only on China but also on Christians in the West. As Archbishop Paul Yu-pin said as early as 1945, "China is like the helpless paralytic at the pool of Bethsaida. The angel has come and stirred the waters. All is ready for the saving. The poor man looks longingly toward the pool, but when Christ approaches him, the plaints of years still lingers on his lips: 'I have no one to put me into the pool.' The laborers are few—how terribly few!"[3] These words were pronounced more than ten years ago. They remain a challenge to the Christian world to this day.

This is the time for us to prove to the world that Christianity is more than theology. We must demonstrate to the Communists that Christianity is adequate for the spiritual needs of man, that it solves our cultural and social problems. We should let the world know not by empty words but by exemplary living that Christianity is superior to Communism.

What Can We Do?

WHAT PROGRAM is best for the Christian world in relation to China which remains now, as in the past, the central country of the entire Asia continent? Of course, we should prefer not to talk of war under modern conditions—it is unthinkable. But let us think in positive terms of political, economic, social, and, above all, moral strength.

Politically speaking, we should, first of all, remember the importance of Taiwan. The government of the Republic of China in Taiwan occupies a unique position because it is the only government in Asia which offers the alternative of a non-Communist focus for the loyalty of the Chinese. Free China is a powerful beacon of hope, not only to those under Communist tyranny on the mainland, but also to the Chinese people scattered through Southeast Asia. Traditionally, these peoples have looked, not only to the governments where they live, but also to the Chinese government for guidance and assistance. The Chinese in the Philippines, for example, look to the Ambassador of the Republic of China in Manila, and the Chinese in Indonesia, which recognized Red China, look to the Communist Ambassador, for special aid in all that concerns their welfare.[1]

There is, of course, a fundamental difference between the Communist policy and the policy of Free China. The former seeks to utilize the overseas Chinese as subversive agents to spearhead the aggressive designs of the Russian imperialists on Southeast Asia, while the latter promotes only the legitimate interests of these Chinese and the welfare of the communities where they reside. Thus the continued existence of Free China is imperative to commend and to strengthen the allegiance to the free world of these powerful minorities scattered throughout Southeast Asia.

The essential reason why tension and unrest are more evident in Hong Kong, Malaya, and Singapore than elsewhere in the area, is because of Great Britain's recognition of Red China. This recognition has given the Communists a convenient and powerful instrument for bringing about their evil ends in these localities. When the Earl of Home, British Secretary for Commonwealth Affairs, spoke out strongly against the menace of

Chinese Communists to Southeast Asia,[2] he must have regretted that his country should have recognized Red China in the first place. This we gather from his observation that "relations between Britain and Peiping have not been exactly cordial."[3] In fact, when Britain made the hasty recognition of the Red regime in 1950, Sir Winston Churchill said that it was "not to confer a compliment but to secure a convenience." Recognition saved none of Britain's 840 million dollars in investments in China; and instead of an exchange of Ambassadors, Britain has had to be content with a chargé d'affaires who got a humiliating run-around in the waiting rooms of the Peiping bureaucracy.

The Kelly resolutions of the United States Congress, opposing the recognition and United Nations membership of the Peiping regime, which passed the House of Representatives, 391 to 0, and the Senate, 86 to 0, marked political wisdom at its best. Free China's armed forces on Taiwan of some six hundred thousand men, trained and equipped by the United States, is a powerful deterrent to the Communist overt aggression in Korea, Viet Nam, and elsewhere in Asia. If Taiwan should fall to the Communists, Japan, the Philippines, and all of Southeast Asia would be seriously threatened. Thus, the defense of Taiwan is not only for the benefit of Free China itself, but also for the safe-guarding of the security from Communist aggression of the free world as a whole. As Walter S. Robertson puts it most clearly:

Let no one say we are denying representation of 600,000,000 Chinese. The defiant Marxist imposters in Peiping come no closer to representing the true interests, aspirations and will of the Chinese people than William Z. Foster (leader emeritus of the United States Communists) comes to representing the will and aspirations of the American people. . . . The National Government (of China) is a symbol, the only rallying point in the world for non-Communist Chinese, the only alternative to Communism for millions of Chinese on the mainland and throughout Southeast Asia. If the National Government should be liquidated, some 12,000,000 overseas Chinese would automatically become citizens of Red China and potential cells of infiltration and subversion against the governments of the countries where they reside.[4]

This is precisely what Secretary of State, John Foster Dulles, emphatically reiterated in July 1957, "the United States determination to give no comfort to Communist China diplomatically, commercially or culturally."[5] This attitude was reaffirmed by a Department of State statement of policy regarding nonrecognition of the Chinese Communist regime as sent to all United States Embassies (*New York Times,* August 10, 1958). It rules out the "two Chinas" concept which is opposed by both Peiping and Taipei, and would be bitterly resented by the Chinese people as an attempt to split their country. It emphasizes also that continued United States recognition and support of the Republic of China enables it to challenge the claims of the Chinese Communists to represent the Chinese people and keeps alive the hopes of those Chinese who are determined eventually to free their country of Communist rule. In the effort to block Communist influence in Asia, the withholding of diplomatic recognition is an important factor.

As a matter of fact, the Communist propaganda infiltration into Southeast Asia has already assumed full force even without diplomatic recognition. Therefore, withholding diplomatic recognition from Red China meets only one phase of the problem. The other phase is the invisible expansion and organized subversion in Southeast Asia, which are mainly responsible for the area's instability.

As the Communist invasion is invisible, the opposition must also be invisible. This is a struggle of a new type, to be waged with new weapons. Communism cannot match us in the export of machines and manufactured goods. She proposes to beat us with her ideas and her "religion."

Basically, the Communist appeal rests on four things that the

Asian peoples want. They are peace, good living, self-government, and their human dignity. These are things which only the free world can help the Asian peoples to gain. However, the Communists have persistently disguised their falsified appeals by trying to identify Western culture with Western domination. Asian peoples realize this. They need no help in understanding what is actually behind the Communist propaganda. However, they are very much concerned about one thing, that is, their human dignity.

Needless to say, all the less-privileged regions in Asia need economic assistance. The Asian peoples realize well enough that only the democratic West, with the tremendous resources of the United States, can offer such help. In accepting any economic aid from the West, however, they are conscious of one essential point; that is, whether or not the retention of their self-respect is involved—this I learned from my own personal experience.

In October 1957, I attended, as a representative of the Chinese Catholics, the Second World Congress for the Lay Apostolate held in Rome and was honored to chair the Workshop on culture (in the English language) and "The Asian Day." Almost all the delegates from Asia stressed that economic aid would be conducive to mutual understanding and cooperation insofar as it would be inspired by that true charity that has regard for the self-respect of the recipient. "Material comfort is no substitute for human dignity" was the general cry.

Orientals have long been taught by popular axiom: "A gentleman should starve to death rather than accept survival without honor." Soviet Russia succeeded in winning the Chinese friendship in the nineteen-twenties because of her disguised sympathy for weak and less-developed countries; she is still practicing these tactics in Asia.

The success of Communism in Asia lies, in fact, not in its respect for human dignity, but in its constant encouragement of Asian peoples to stand up against the West whenever their human pride or self-respect is at stake. The Communists rely not upon the strength of these nations, but upon their weakness. Thus, to be against the Communists is not enough. Positive human and democratic values must be supported if man's loyalties are to be won and inspired to action. No counteraction can be affirmatively successful unless it is based on a thorough, spiritual understanding of the situation as it really exists in Southeast Asia.

Is our program able to meet this spiritual approach? Do we truly understand the systems of thought and belief of the Asian peoples? Only by a genuine understanding based on high principles which is in complete harmony with native cultural aspirations can we resist Communist ideas. This requires the work especially of Christian missionaries.

From Rev. John J. Considine's *Africa: World of New Men,*[6] we learn how Communism can be defeated in Africa, especially in the Belgian Congo, by missionaries with an adequate program for the natives—a program requiring the pooling of all available spiritual and temporal forces. Similar outstanding achievements have also been made by the missionaries in Asia.

In his book *One Front Across the World,*[7] Douglas Hyde tells of the invisible struggle waged between Communism and Christianity for the soul of Asia. In the front line of Christian resistance, as he sees it, are the missionaries. They realize that the consciousness and sometimes over-consciousness of the Orientals about human dignity or self-respect result, in a large measure, from a dissatisfaction with their own culture and a consciousness of their social backwardness. The role of the missionaries is, therefore, not merely to alleviate material poverty and champion social justice, but, above all, to fill the spiritual vacuum created when peoples discover the inadequacy of their own traditional values and remain unsettled between belief and unbelief, between materialism and spirituality, between Communism and Christianity. Missionaries, properly imbued with the ideals of their calling, are able to draw out the finest there is in the Asians, and to implant in them the finest there is in world culture, in order that they may become not only fully evolved natives, but also fully endowed men created in the image of our common Father in Heaven, and sharing in the common heritage of mankind.

My own three visits to the various countries in the Far East in 1955 and 1956 have also led me to see this present spiritual instability and the immediate need of missionaries. The attitude of Asian peoples in general, and of the Chinese in particular, to the Christian religion, is one of sympathetic understanding and appreciation. A native clergy has been established in many of these countries. However, the native clergy, no matter how strong and competent it may be, is far from enough to cope with the present situation. Many missionaries from the West are needed to fill immediate requirements.

A priest whom I met at Saigon said to me: "The National University of Saigon has been hoping to have some priests on the faculty for years, yet no priest so far is available to satisfy this urgent need." Similar religious need can be detected almost everywhere.

In the case of China, we should review the situation with a sense of urgency. In his article "Red China 'Attack the Heart' of Southeast Asia," John C. Caldwell points out that "in this region Peiping's main weapon is called Kung-sing, which means 'Attacking the Heart,' and its main target is the twelve and one-half million so-called Overseas Chinese. . . . If Red China can compel their allegiance, it will tighten its hold on the whole area."[8] Likewise, he tells in another place how hundreds of Chinese students in Southeast Asia had been disillusioned rather than seduced by Communist propaganda.[9]

The Communists pledged themselves to the protection and promotion of the legitimate rights and interests of Chinese residing abroad. They set a National Commission on Overseas

Chinese Affairs within the government structure and induced some of the wealthiest Chinese abroad to serve as members. They organized local associations in Fukien and Kwangtung for service and assistance to overseas Chinese. Their headquarters doubled as places for good fellowship and centers for propaganda control. The Red regime encouraged student exchanges and good will tours and exploited every means to multiply emigrants' remittances and investments in Chinese industries. It tailored propaganda programs to overseas Chinese and explored ways and means to convert them into fifth columns for possible moments of crisis.[10]

Now, if the Chinese overseas mean so much to the Communists in their quest for control of Asia they must be very important and we should make every effort to reach them.

Overseas Chinese in Free Asia can be reached by many means. Most important, however, they can be reached spiritually. In the history of the Orient there was at times great misunderstanding between the Christian and the non-Christian people. But this is now a thing of the past. Today, the Communist persecution of the Christian religion has made it possible for the peoples in Asia, particularly the Chinese, to realize that all that Communism has propagated is false and that the true purpose of Christianity is the spiritual welfare of all peoples of earth.

The Universal Church, which transcends nationalism and accepts a certain diversity in spiritual unity, can help restore the masses of Asia (with the Chinese overseas as a nucleus) to their destiny of human brotherhood and universal love under God. This is a challenge not only to the missionaries but to all of us. As the late Pope Pius XII said: "Catholics are extraordinarily well equipped to collaborate in the creation of a climate without which a common action on the international plane can have neither substance nor prosperous growth . . . an atmosphere of mutual understanding. . . . No other group of men presents such favorable dispositions, in breadth and in depth, for international harmony."[11] Whether the "New Asia," with China in a major role, turns toward the Church or away from it depends largely upon how Christians the world over can work with, and among, the Chinese in the area!

Thus, missionaries in the usual sense of the word are not enough. This is a challenge to the whole Christian world. Christians, especially those in the United States, have even a greater opportunity, since the United States has enjoyed higher prestige than any other Western Power in the eyes of the Chinese. Communists may prejudice the Chinese against many Western nations because of their colonial records, but this is more difficult with the United States. Chinese have a good memory. They have not forgotten the friendship and assistance which they received from the United States during the past hundred years. They remember only too well that it was Russia who always sought self-advantage from the troubled conditions of the Orient. They look now in a special way to the United States for understanding, sympathy, and aid.

From America, engineers, teachers, doctors, nurses, social workers, and men of all professional and technical fields are needed to answer the call from the East. They will be able not merely to give technical aid or assistance, but to satisfy a deeper desire of Asian peoples—a desire for Christian understanding and sympathy—the basic spiritual need of the common people. By their example of Christian living, lay people can be a tremendous influence in mission areas. They can help to form minds and consciences by mingling with the people and entering places where a priest or religious would often be conspicuous.

Thus, the cultivation of integral Christian-living in Asia can be carried forward with more lay participation from the West. Christian workers of the Western world can be of much aid to the East in social, educational, civic, rural and religious projects. However, they need some kind of special training. A model exists in several institutes for the training of lay missionaries. The

Community House of the Diocese of Paterson is one. Another organization is the new Association for International Development (AID) set up for men under the aegis of the Catholic mission-sending societies of America and with the blessing of Bishop James McNulty of Paterson, New Jersey. It is now training competent workers as lay missionaries, with special attention to developing in the men a necessary humility and respect for native customs. They are trained to plant seed that will flower in an indigenous climate, not to transplant a developed organism from the West that may wither in a new setting, or take no deep root in the strange new soil.

It is urgent because both the Western world, led by the United States, and the Soviet bloc are involved in an economic competition in many nations of Asia. Both are there carrying out technical assistance programs. More and more American-aid missions in various regions of Asia will work side by side with Soviet "colleagues." This already is the case in Cambodia, India, Egypt and other countries.

This is a person-to-person competition at arm's length. Every single act of each individual will produce extensive effects on the entire population. As a Burmese official remarked: "The Russians have been quite amiable in their personal relations. The British, who built our engineering college and polytechnic institute, were very exacting in matters of personal comfort. They demanded select housing for each family, complete with new furniture. With the Soviets we put twenty-odd families into five houses, and give them secondhand furniture. There have been no complaints." (*Time,* Jan. 13, 1958) What is true of the British in Burma is also true of other Westerners in other parts of Asia.

Despite its bad faith, the Soviet bloc is undeniably getting more for its aid-dollar than the United States. The fact that the Soviets make loans rather than gifts is not resented as tightfisted. Instead it flatters the touchy pride of newly independent nations as businesslike dealing between equals. Their apparent aim is to achieve a reputation for being disinterested. They hope that eventually the underdeveloped countries will look to them for leadership and help. Economic bridgeheads, once established, can be expanded into economic dependence. This can bind a country as firmly into the Communist orbit as any political bond.

Therein lies the challenge confronting the Western workers afield. They cannot possibly compete with the Soviet apostolate without a Christian apostolate. This is the reason why Pope Pius XII said at the Second World Congress for the Lay Apostolate: "This fight (against Communism) will be fought to the finish, but with the arms of Christ."

If we have an adequate program which could really instill Christian charity and principle—and I believe it can—into everything concerning the native population, Communist infiltration or propaganda, or both, would be, to say the least, much less effective.

An adequate program would include the following:

1. *The Intellectual Apostolate*

All Asia is now going to school. A rising group of intellectuals is found in every Asian country. The leaders of the people, the professors of the future, the writers, the newspaper editors and columnists, the movie directors, the script writers for television and radio, the social theorists, the political leaders, and, often enough, even the labor leaders will be from this group. If, finally, we have any doubts about the importance of this rising group of intellectuals we need only take note of the importance assigned them in the subversive strategy that emanates from Moscow. Note the importance of student movements in Singapore, in Tokyo, in Seoul, in every major city in India, and in every important center in Asia. Beyond this is the fact that the educated in Asia have always held a special esteem in the eyes of the people. Asia's new culture, Christian or non-Christian, will be predominantly formed from this group. Indeed, if we look back to the missionary history, we note that Ricci, Schall, and Verbiest in the seventeenth century, and Bishop Ford and Father Lebbe in the twentieth century proved that an intellectual apostolate is necessary for the conversion of Asia. They made the beginning. But there was no adequate follow-through. There remains much to be done.

Of course, from the Christian point of view it is souls that count. "God is no respector of persons," and "hath chosen the base things of the world." However, the intellectual apostolate stands in its own right as an integral part of the Christian work in the world. It is also an important instrument of conversion and we should not decline to use it to bring Christianity more effectively to the world. We need only refer to what Newman has said on this point: "It is, indeed, a general characteristic of the course of His Providence to make the few the channels of His Blessings to the many."[12] Surely, the same can be said of China.

Father Francis X. Legrande made a good point:

> To influence Chinese thought to assist in the evolution of China, to permeate Chinese society with Christian principles, to bring China to adopt the Christian concept of life and the living formulae brought by Christ to the world, this is the ideal which must engage the attention of every mission. This intellectual apostolate, to be exercised primarily on the elite and through them on the masses, is by far the most important factor in the Christianization of the country. It is very evident how opportune and how urgent this apostolate is.[13]

The intellectual apostolate involves many things. First of all, we have to undertake an intensive and extensive study of the general cultural and spiritual backgrounds of Chinese life and thought.

In the intellectual approach to the Chinese apostolate, a valuable contribution has been made by Father Thomas Berry, who has taken an active interest in the promotion of a full-developed Chinese Christian culture. "Now is the time to make great advances toward the conversion of China," he said. "If we cannot convert the people, we can convert the culture. For if a people possess a culture, a culture also possess its people. We convert each in and through the other."[14]

How true are these words! In fact, in the Chinese apostolate the conversion of culture should always precede the conversion of the people. This was where Ricci succeeded three centuries ago. This is where we have failed. We have not followed the example of these early missionaries in China, and have not yet established a synthesis of the Christian faith with the native culture.

The directives sent out by the Holy See in 1659 to the priests in China emphasized those principles and methods which were used most effectively in former times and which are as appropriate now as they were three centuries ago. Suffice it here to quote two passages from this document:

By their natural dispositions and manners, they (priest-missioners) should be capable of accommodating themselves to others. They should neither be disagreeable to those who live with them nor offensive or unpleasant to outsiders, but with the Apostle Paul they should be "all things to all men."

Since it is almost a part of human nature to hold in greater love and esteem what is one's own, and particularly to favor what belongs to one's own country over that of others, nothing creates ill feeling and hatred more than attempts of outsiders to change the customs of a people's fatherland. This is especially true of these age-old ways to which they and their fathers have been attached as long as memory records. When the outsider seeks to substitute customs of his own nation in place of those he desires to destroy it is particularly irritating. Therefore, never seek to impose practices on the people among whom you labor. Rather conform yourself with great diligence to their ways.[15]

It is clear then that the missionary must respect, preserve and develop what is genuinely good in the native heritage. This method was faithfully followed by Ricci and the other missionaries in China in the seventeenth century. They began the work. We must continue and perfect it.

That the Church in China is keenly aware of the importance of this subject is evident enough from the words of Dom Pierre-Célestin Lou Tseng-tsiang, O.S.B.:

> In so far as among us—at least in her singing and in the prayers and reading which priests and people recite aloud—in so far as the Catholic liturgy will have been unable to adopt the Chinese literary language (which, as I like to insist, is admirably suited to the Gregorian chant) to that extent the worship which the Church renders to God—the sacrifice of the Mass, the divine office, the liturgy of the sacraments, the admirable Catholic liturgy of the dead—will remain an absolutely closed book for the yellow race. . . .
>
> In default of that measure of adaptation which I believe to be the prerequisite of all important apostolic action, in five hundred or a thousand years evangelizing efforts will not have modified in any considerable fashion the very small proportion represented by the number of Christians and of Catholics in a population which will itself have increased beyond its present numbers in proportions which it is vain to seek to forecast.[16]

This need was revealed to me by a Chinese priest who has been working laboriously among the inhabitants of Taiwan. This is what he wrote me recently: "Kindly pray to our Lord. My difficulties with the apostolate among the natives under the present situation seem humanly unsurmountable. They cling tightly to their native way of worship. Without a genuine appreciation and adaptation of their tradition and ritualistic cult, conversion of these souls appears to be extremely difficult, if not impossible."

Bishop John Niu of Chiayi in Taichung, Taiwan, told me the same thing when I paid him a visit in August 1956. "Christianity has a wonderful opportunity among the natives, but we must reform their cultive life in order to bring them to see the Light."

What the tribal inhabitants cherish most is the popular practice of *Pa-pa.* Literally speaking, no native can live without the observance of *Pa-pa. Pa-pa* is a kind of natural worship with an extravagant display and consumption of food. It provides also an occasion for the family banquet or feast. Therefore, it is a mixture of cultic act and social or clan entertainment. In its present form *Pa-pa* is idolatrous. However, it can be corrected and purified. If we will make a deep study of it, we can certainly find modifications that will transform this ritual into an admirable manifestation of Christian faith and worship. A situation like this is not limited to certain areas of China alone.

In December 1955, I was at Manila to attend the First Asian Congress for the Lady Apostolate.[17] I addressed the assemblage on a theme entitled "Unity and Diversity in Asia." At the following general session, a question which was raised by a delegate from Thailand and directed to me read: "Is it permissible or not for a Catholic to attend his father's funeral which is performed in accordance with the native customs which bears Buddhist touches?" To me, it was, and is, what Americans call a sixty-four dollar question. Fortunately, I was not in the audience when the question was read, thanks to the Maryknoll Sisters who had asked me to give a talk to their college students at the time. Cardinal Gracias, Archbishop of Bombay, India, who presided over the Conference graciously undertook the answer in my behalf by saying: "Without knowing the substance of the native customs, no one, including Doctor Sih and myself, could give the right answer. You had better refer the question to your Bishop, who alone has authority to make the decision."

From this, we can readily understand how many problems concerning religious life remain undecided or doubtful in the hearts of Asian Catholics. These things should be decided, not one by one, but once and for all, through the profound study of competent Catholic scholars and by the final sanction of the Hierarchy.

We might compare our apostolic work to that of a farmer cultivating his fields. He studies two things: the seed and the earth in which he plants the seed. He does not cultivate each seed in the same way. Different soil requires different care, different preparation, different methods of sowing. It would do no good for him to have the best of seeds and to understand perfectly the type of plant it should produce, if he neglected the study and preparation of the soil in which the seed is sown.

So with the Gospel. We have studied our theology and scriptures with very great care. Thousands of theologians and philosophers, scripture scholars and patrologists have studied and are studying the Gospel and its message, the Church and its Mission and the entire body of classical thought handed down to us in the West.

But where are those who should be studying the Asian soil in which the Christian seed is to be sown? For centuries we have worked in these fields and we still have scarcely a score of professional scholars of recognized accomplishment in Oriental Studies, that is, in that part of the orient that is beyond the Bible Lands of the Near East.

Missiology has thus far tended to develop an extensive body of speculation without noticeably influencing practice. The theory and history of the missions are thoroughly studied. But little advance has been made in the spiritual understanding of native thought and religious traditions. Missiology says there should be adaptation. But adaptation to what? There is the question. There is the real need of Orientalists. We understand our theology well enough; we understand the higher spiritual and religious traditions of Asia hardly at all. This is the function of the Catholic Orientalist. Neither the Missionary nor the Missiologist is in a position to do this work. Only when we produce trained Orientalists can the Missiologist and the Missionary do their work with a maximum efficiency. The Orientalist studies the earth into which the seed is to be planted. The missiologist studies the manner of planting the seed. The missionary does the actual planting. This is the basic outline of the team of workers that are needed. Thus far we have produced many missionaries, a few missiologists, almost no orientalists.

In order to remedy this deficiency we need now—right now—a study center which, to borrow the words of Father Thomas Berry, "has three main aspects: (1) purifying the native culture from error; (2) integrating and preserving what is sound in the native culture; (3) elevating the whole of the native life to that higher plane which is attained by contact with Divine Revelation."[18] To this should be added another function, that is, the spiritual interpretation of the scriptures. We all know that Clement of Alexandria succeeded in giving a new vigor to the Faith and adding richness to Christian culture by this method. We also note in the *Confessions* of Saint Augustine that he was positively repelled by the Scriptures until he heard Saint Ambrose expound them in a spiritual sense. The Sixth Book of the *Confessions* is of utmost importance for anyone who would know how to expound the scriptures to the Asian peoples. We read there: "It was a joy to hear Ambrose who often repeated to his congregation, as if it were a rule he was most strongly urging upon them, the text: 'The letter killeth, but the spirit giveth life.' And he would go on to draw aside the veil of mystery and lay open the spiritual meaning of things which taken literally would have seemed to teach falsehood." This method, if handled intelligently, will most satisfy the highly imaginative character of the eastern mentality. Confucius used to teach in allegorical form so that deeper and richer meanings could be communicated to his disciples. This spiritual method, of course, must be used with restraint, and it must be based on the literal meaning of the text. But it is a valid and fruitful way of expounding the true meaning of the Scriptures.

To say all this is to say that in order to promote the intellectual apostolate we are in urgent need of a study center of Asian cultures, a center which would be concerned with the Asian world as a whole and in its distinct parts. This is important, for some spiritual movements, such as Buddhism and Islam, cross over the national boundaries of a large section of Asia. Asia can be and must be understood as a whole as well as in parts. The whole must be understood in the parts and the parts in the whole. Only with depth of appreciation and sympathy of the inner thought and of the fundamental features of the native traditions can we bring about that new cultural synthesis in which the Asian peoples will combine their ancient ways with their new hopes. This is especially true with the Chinese overseas. They can be directly contacted now. Overseas Chinese cling to their native culture even more tightly than the people in China proper. They even retain many of the traditions which have long been lost there. The name of Confucius is more venerated in "Chinatowns" throughout the world than even in Free China. They can be reached through a truly spiritual understanding.

2. *Catholic Leadership-Training*

Overseas Chinese, as well as all peoples in Free Asia, need more churches, schools, hospitals, etc. However, the foremost need is leadership-training for all classes, particularly the intellectual class (students).

We all know, for instance, that in the last fifty years or so prior to the ascendancy of the Communists in China, only one Catholic was a member of the Cabinet. This was not due to any discrimination against Catholics. We just did not have the trained leaders. A similar situation was found in educational and social fields. We cannot blame the Communists wholly for today's situation. We did not do what should have been done.

In this regard, the case of Viet Nam should be an excellent lesson. There we can learn the role a genuine Catholic leadership can play in the fate of a nation. Due to the Christian statesmanship of President Ngo Dinh Diem a seemingly hopeless situation has been saved.[19] In Viet Nam we witness the true force of the Christian faith. Eight hundred thousand Vietnamese refugees streamed from the Communist north to the south after partition. They came to find new homes, new lands, new lives. When I visited Saigon in September 1956, Bishop Ngo Dinh Thuc, Apostolic Vicar of Vinh Long, told me that under the Cai San project forty thousand men and women were already living in a kind of Southeast Asian bamboo Levittown, each family already farming its own land.[20] "This means more than material rehabilitation. It is a manifestation of spiritual rebirth," the Bishop said.

Of course, nothing can be done on a "one-man-show" basis. A nation needs many leaders, many well-trained and competent leaders, just as President Diem told me when I paid him a visit in 1956. "Our constitution is being drafted. We have a complete governmental structure. But that is not enough. We must fill in all the branches of the government with trained people. It is a big job and we are only at the beginning." What is true about the importance of leadership-training in Viet Nam is also true in the rest of the Southeast Asian region.

Among the Catholic institutions here in the United States, Seton Hall University, for instance, with which the author has the honor to be associated, inaugurated more than twenty years ago a scholarship program for foreign students with special attention to Asian youth. The Sino-American Amity founded in 1951 in New York under the Presidency of Archbishop Paul Yu-pin gives special care to the spiritual welfare of Catholic Chinese students in the United States. So does the Crossroads Student Center in Chicago under the directorship of Germaine Ruchand of international Catholic Auxiliaries. In Southeast

Asia, the Pope appointed an Apostolic Visitor, Msgr. Van Melckebeke, who resides in Singapore and who is charged with promoting the apostolate in the communities of Chinese immigrants. The appointment of Msgr. Juan Bautista Velasco, Bishop of Amoy, as Vicar General for the Chinese Catholics of the Archdiocese of Manila has been most useful to the apostolate. The Free Pacific Association, with its headquarters in Saigon, Viet Nam, and under the guidance of a group of internationally minded Christian leaders in the United States, has made outstanding contributions to Christian leadership-training. All these are good and necessary. But they are inadequate and far from enough. Among the five thousand Chinese students in the United States, for example, only seven hundred of them (about one out of seven) are Catholics.[21]

In order to satisfy the present and future need we must have a positive program for scholarship and higher Christian education on a larger and more unified scale. The Protestant United Board for Christian Colleges in China established a few years ago Tunghai University in Taiwan with an entirely new training program.[22] The same organization became, in January 1956, the United Board for Christian Higher Education in Asia in order to foster educational activities in East and Southeast Asia.[23]

There is not a Catholic university for the Chinese in the entire region of Southeast Asia and Taiwan. The Communists have "liquidated" all Catholic schools on the mainland, including Fu Jen, the Catholic University of Peiping which enjoyed so excellent an academic standing in China.[24] But the Communists can never prevent us from restoring it or founding a new one in Free China or elsewhere in Asia.

If we want to bring non-Christians to Christ, we must make them admire and love the Church. To make the Church attractive it is imperative to win the souls of the intellectuals. Thus, a good Catholic university is the minimum requirement for the Christianization of China today. In this connection, I wish to reproduce here a letter addressed by Dr. John C. H. Wu and myself on March 25, 1958, to the late Cardinal Stritch, Archbishop of Chicago, upon his appointment as Pro-Prefect of the Sacred Congregation for the Propagation of the Faith:

With exceedingly joy we learn that Your Eminence has been appointed by Our Holy Father as Pro-Prefect of the Sacred Congregation for the Propagation of the Faith. There is, in this critical time, no greater need than that of unity between the Asian and the Western worlds. Your Eminence's inauguration as the Spiritual Guardian of the mission peoples throughout the world is a great hope and assurance of such spiritual unification.

As Chinese and as Catholics we have a special concern for our own people. We wish at this time to express the hope that increased attention will be given to the young Chinese intellectuals. The Chinese have always had a special esteem for their Scholars. The Scholars in turn have always had a special influence among the people. They have ever been the spiritual guides of the nation. Indeed the Scholars in China have traditionally occupied the position that the priestly class occupies in other lands.

For this reason it is dominantly through them that the new Christian way of life must be brought to its full development in China. We must therefore provide for the Catholic formation of young Chinese scholars. This requires the establishment of a Catholic University in Free China. Such a University we consider the most serious need of the present time. A Catholic University would have far-reaching effects also on that large and extremely influential group of Chinese scattered throughout Southeast Asia and the Pacific Islands.

We know the difficulties of establishing such a University. Yet we believe that no other phase of mission work would be so fruitful or, in the end, so economical. It would become a source for raising up Catholic Teachers for the Schools of China. It would supply vocations for the priesthood. It would provide numerous trained Chinese, clerical and lay, who would join forces with the Priests and Sisters of the West in carrying out an apostolate adequate to the needs of the present and the future. Results, we are sure, would prove the wisdom of this approach. We can, moreover, from direct personal knowledge, assure you that such a University would be most welcome to the Chinese themselves. . . .

In his reply dated March 28, 1958 and sent from Chicago, the late Prince of the Church said that "When I assume my duties as Pro-Prefect of the Sacred Congregation of the Propagation of the Faith, I shall give the contents of your letter my early and serious thought and consideration." Unfortunately, the Cardinal died before he could take up his new Office in Rome. However, the latest report is that competent ecclesiastical authorities are much interested in this project, and that the Divine Word Fathers will in the near future restore the University in Taiwan, at least in some important fields of study.

3. *Liturgical Adjustment and Reform*

Along with the use of intelligence in the Chinese apostolate and Catholic leadership-training for the conversion of China is liturgical adjustment and reform. An understandable liturgy is necessary for those who have embraced the faith, and who are eager to live a fuller liturgical life, as well as for those who have not yet been attracted to the Church.

In accepting the faith Asian peoples must sacrifice much in their former way of life. But not all of their customs are idolatrous. Many of them, if reformed, could be retained and developed.

Indeed, if missionaries are to be really successful, they must become one with the natives in their mission territory; and that means embracing the traditions, language, and customs of the people.

The new liturgical privileges promise much good as was noted in a moving address delivered by Bishop Wilhelm van Bekkum, S.V.D., Apostolic Vicar of Ruteng, Flores, Indonesia, at the International Liturgical Congress in Assisi, September 18-22, 1956. He also cherishes the hope for further development of liturgical living.[25]

First of all, there is the language problem. To intensify divine worship and attract the Oriental heart and soul to the richness of the liturgical life, we must seek a better adaptation of the liturgy to the various peoples of the world. This is primarily a question of language.

While we do not propose that Latin be abolished as the universal language of the Church, we do propose that much more vernacular is needed if liturgy is ever to be effective in Asia. So far as the Chinese language is concerned we have two: the classical language, in which the ancient Chinese thought tradition is contained, and in which serious writings are still done; the modern language, which is mainly employed in newspaper and popular writings. But for liturgical use, a somewhat new language is called for. It should have both the dignity of the classical language and the clarity of the modern language. Such a language is already coming into being in the serious writing that is being done at the present time by Chinese scholars. This is the kind of language that Pope Paul V had in mind when he promulgated in 1615 a papal decree concerning a Chinese liturgy. Catholics of genius could now make a great contribution both to Christianity and to Chinese culture by producing an acceptable native liturgy suitable to the majesty of the Holy Sacrifice and understandable to the people.

As Dr. John Wu puts it, "The all-important thing is the Real Presence of our Lord and our union with Him in offering the Supreme Homage to our Father. But given a genuine spirit of worship and love, I cannot help thinking that the people assisting at the Holy Sacrifice would feel an even more intimate participation in it if they could hear the words in their own mother tongue, as happened in the Cenacle on the first Pentecost in the presence of our Blessed Mother."[26] He actually has expressed the common sentiment and desire of the Chinese faithful, who will say with St. Paul, "I will pray with the spirit, I will pray also with the understanding; I will sing with the spirit, I will sing also with the understanding."[27]

The great majority of the people at the Holy Mass in China and elsewhere in the Orient recite the rosary throughout the sacred ceremonies. There is nothing wrong in manifesting devotion to our Mother in Heaven, but it is a devotion not intended for celebrating the Mass. The faithful must share more fully in offering the Holy Sacrifice; they must not be silent spectators. Personal experience has taught me that the value and the riches of the liturgy can be fully grasped only by an active participation in the sacred ceremonies by the faithful.

In January 1957, with the blessing of Msgr. L. J. Arrell, I was invited to address a Catholic Forum in Fargo, North Dakota. This offered me a good opportunity to attend a Mass at St. Mary's Cathedral there. It was a dialog Mass—the first dialog Mass I had ever attended since I became a Catholic nine years ago. What a wonderful and thrilling experience it was to me! The whole audience was united in one thought and in one spirit. As St. Pius X says, "We do not pray at Mass but pray the Mass." A similar experience was repeated when I participated in another dialog Mass held at St. John's Abbey, Collegeville, Minn., during my recent lecture tour. Since then, I often ask myself: "Could there be any more effective way of leading the faithful in China to live a richer and fuller Christian life than this kind of holy action and worship—worship in a genuine community spirit?"

I am not the first one to make this discovery. Most of the religious and the faithful in China have felt this need long, long ago. The Chinese throughout the ages have always been conscious of corporate worship. Hence the Holy Sacrifice of the Mass offered in the language they could understand would be the greatest boon to conversions. In fact, some preparation has already been made.

As early as 1615, Pope Paul V gave permission for the translation of the Bible and the use of Chinese in the Breviary, at Mass, and in the administration of the sacraments. In this stipulation we find a great deal of wisdom.[28] However, in the past three centuries nothing was done regarding translation. Nevertheless, we understand that in 1939 the Holy See not only renewed the liturgical concessions which had been granted to China by Pope Paul V, but also took certain steps necessary for the production of Chinese liturgical texts.[29] We prayerfully hope that definite results will be achieved in the not too distant future.

To sum up, a constructive program for the Church in China would include: the intellectual apostolate, leadership-training, and the liturgical adjustment. Central to this is the problem of how to incorporate native culture into Christian life wherever this is proper.

In the meantime, serious attempt should be made in liturgical adjustment and reform so as to suit the mentality and culture of different peoples throughout the world. We understand that at the Missionary meeting preceding the International Congress of Pastoral Liturgy in Assisi, resolutions on the liturgical reform were passed. However, in mission lands much more extensive adaptation is urgently needed. The principles, of course, remain everywhere the same, and should lead to a more profound unity in a greater diversity.

This constructive program has already been set in motion in December, 1958, at the Far Eastern Bishops' Conference which convened in Manila under the chairmanship of Cardinal Gregory Peter Agagianian as Pontifical Delegate. I spoke personally with the Cardinal at Rome immediately before his departure for Manila. He mentioned the importance of the Chinese residents in Southeast Asia. Because of this, he took with him, as a member of the delegation, a Chinese priest, Msgr. Peter Tu. The *Fides Report* of November 29, 1958 tells us:

Ordinaries of the Far East will hold the First Eastern Bishops' Conference during the week following the consecration of the Cathedral. This conference will take place in Manila with Ordinaries of the Philippines, Japan, Thailand, Laos, Cambodia, Indonesia, Viet Nam, Formosa, Korea, Malaya, Hong Kong and Macao taking official part in the discussions and deliberations. Ordinaries of India, Ceylon, Burma, Pakistan, Australia, New Zealand and Oceania have been invited to take part as observers.

Among the topics that will be discussed are such matters as seminary training, the various aspects of apostolate for the clergy, education, the lay apostolate, Catholic organizations, social action, liturgy, press, radio and cinema. These and other topics have been assigned and accepted by various Ordinaries for papers in which they will discuss their experience and propose their problems.

An office has been set up at the Apostolic Nunciature in Manila by His Excellency the Most Reverend Egidio Vagnozzi, Apostolic Nuncio, to serve as secretariate of the conference.

All over the Eastern world we find people wonderfully disposed to receive Christianity. They begin to distinguish what is true and what is false in their own religions. The Catholic Church with its inner unity and liturgical richness is wonderfully suited to the flexible, many-sided, synthetic character of the Eastern religious consciousness. This is particularly true of the Chinese who are seeking more earnestly than ever, in silence and agony, the Christian life of faith.

The Crisis in China

In his preface to the author's book *From Confucius to Christ,* Bishop Fulton J. Sheen wrote that Communism is "the death which is spread upon the fields in the winter of discontent as a harbinger for the fruits and herbs of a rich and beautiful springtime."[1] This affirms also the deepest laws proclaimed by Aeschylus: "It is through suffering that learning comes." Pain and purification go hand in hand. It is precisely in this process that China finds, and will find, the turning point in its modern history. There is a Chinese song which reads:

The gourd has still its bitter leaves,
And deep the crossing at the ford.
I wait my lord.

The ford is brimming to its banks;
My lord is late.

The boatmen still keeps backening,
And others reach their journey's end.
I wait my friend.[2]

China has been waiting her Lord and her friends! But it was not He Who was late, it was China who waited in a wrong place. Now, should China have felt as St. Augustine did: "Oh! too late have I loved thee, beauty ever ancient and ever new?"

In the Divine plan nothing will be too late. Through God, with Him and in Him, all things are directed, for God is eternal. We know that it is God Who disposes, but we also know that God wants man to propose. Personally, I can see that because of the suffering inflicted by Communism, man is gradually coming to realize the need of human solidarity and brotherhood under God. For this need, the Communist has nothing to offer. I have found everywhere in the Far East this hunger for a fuller life. Here lies our great opportunity: to speed with moral and spiritual leadership the turn to human unity under Christ.

Christians in China, missionary and native priest and laity, have endured the same torments, been tried before the same judges, been enclosed in the same prisons. This has made them one. Even further, Christians have endured the same torments with non-Christians. This has made them one. A great spiritual communication has passed over the entire country. This new sense of oneness is so precious that it is worth all the suffering that has brought it about. In suffering we find man's great love. As Rev. William G. Most puts it, "Strong love feeds on difficulties, even on suffering."[3] With love, everything is possible. As St. Augustine says, "In love there is either no difficulty, or the difficulty itself is loved."[4]

"The end of life is not happiness, only wisdom," the Chinese used to say. But the only wisdom available in China today is the wisdom of piety and poverty, the wisdom of tears. In this wisdom the Chinese find one asset that is all too rare in life, a sense of fellowship and genuine brotherhood. They are tied together by the usual links of neighbors in the same or isolated communities. But, far more significantly, they are bound to each other by their mutual sufferings. As Pope Pius XII said, "In every country the more noble, far-seeing and mature minds have learned in the school of suffering in the recent past that despite all their differences they have a common element so essential that no one can tamper with it without imperilling the very foundation and the prosperity of his own people."[5] To seek for this "common element so essential" is the task of all Chinese of good will. To survive at all they need the spiritual comfort of the Christian faith and the practical cooperation of each other.

History repeats itself many times, but this repetition is only evident at the time of a civilization's final disintegration. Yet, each time, humanity has elevated itself to nobler, higher levels. Christianity was born of the suffering of a disintegrating Graeco-Roman world. Suffering, in this sense, is the hidden source of wisdom, hope and love. Seeds mature in the dark. It is only in darkness, that the stars are visible.

Will not, then, the tears and blood shed by our brothers and sisters along the Yangtze, the Yellow River, and Si Kiang of China, the Mekong of Viet Nam, and the Yalu of Korea bring spiritual enlightenment and hope to the tormented souls of our brethren in the whole continent of Asia—even to all the peoples of the world?

Suffering can make or break the spirit. It depends upon whether we can see its significance. As Frank Sheed puts it, "God desires men's perfection and whatever the suffering, will give them the strength to bear it—if they will. Only the rebellion of man's will (which is rejection of God) or the collapse of man's will (which is despair) can prevent suffering from enriching life. In the light of this knowledge we can accept all the certainty of purpose."[6] In this view, suffering will increase life; in any other, it will conquer life.

Madame Chiang Kai-shek says: "Purposeless pain, without faith in God, is a tragic waste, a torturous passageway leading to eternal perdition. With faith all human suffering has a purpose, leading to maturity and fulfillment of one's spirit."[7] In the words of St. Paul, "We glory also in tribulations, knowing that tribulation worketh patience; patience trial; and trial hope."[8] In the crisis of suffering, nature suggests pain and despair; but faith offers hope and opportunity.

The word "crisis" has profound meaning. In Greek it means "judgment." In Chinese it is composed of two characters: "danger" and "opportunity." When these two factors exist, there is a crisis. And whenever there is a crisis, there is opportunity. Crisis can be the sharpest goad to our creative energies. The danger is very real. It may challenge our every resource. Yet if we meet it with faith and courage it will bring not disaster but triumph.

Thus the crisis in China presents her at one time with great peril and great opportunity. Christopher Dawson considers that Christianity has a better chance today than it had a hundred years ago.[9] Christians who propose to do anything about China can no longer take a passive stand and react to things after they happen, in a sort of "wait-and-see" policy. We have got to be ahead of events and lead and shape them to the best of our ability.

The United Nations is also in a state of crisis over the question of the admission of Red China. It is a world crisis, but also a world opportunity to reaffirm the most basic principles of international justice. The problem in China is *not* a civil strife. It is *not* some kind of private struggle for power between Chiang Kai-shek and Mao Tse-tung but a decisive phase in the world-wide struggle between freedom and Communist slavery.

Firm adhesion to natural justice and to the sublime truths of Christian revelation is absolutely necessary in our present conflict with forces which display a most degenerate moral sense and extreme defiance of all religion. Material power is useful only when it is employed as an instrument to pursue spiritual ends. Today, we are in agony because of our emphasis on money, material, and manpower, and our neglect of moral principle and religious fidelity. As Rev. Theodore Hesburgh, C.S.C. says, "The heart of the conflict is beyond the physical forces of manpower, strategic bases and nuclear weapons. It is really a battle for the souls of men."[10] If Communism in our times is to be effectively conquered, we must realize how deep-rooted is its philosophy of materialism. Unless the millions of God-fearing people throughout the world carry out in private and public life the logical consequences of their living faith, there can be no easy task of a triumph over materialistic Communism. Dr. Lin Yutang considers that our present struggle against Communism is an ideological war. In his *The Secret Name,* he writes: "An ideological war should be instilled with a high moral passion against evil and against all forms of oppression. It should have a faith which can stir men's souls. It should have a direct, immediate appeal. The voice of propaganda should be the voice of conviction in certain eternal principles, and of certainty (like Communist faith in the materialistic evolution of history)."[11] Evidently, Dr. Lin's words flow from a heart that has known the turbulence of China.

China has had a long and unique experience in this struggle against Communism. For thirty years she has been fighting.

Blood has flowed in every province. Even now in spite of temporary conquest and severe persecution over a period of more than nine years, there is no reason for us to think that the Chinese people will ultimately succumb to an atheistic philosophy of life. In other parts of the world, notably in Hungary, we have similar examples of staunch resistance. We have every reason to believe that with God's grace the crisis of modern times will be, in reality, a glorious opportunity for mankind's return to our Divine Father, to the law of His Love.

In the case of China, she cannot better grasp this opportunity than to follow, like the Magi, the star of grace until it brings her to the heart of the great King. Likewise, China will come to adore the Child bringing the gifts He desires from her—the only gifts He wants: gold, frankincense, and myrrh.

But what do these gifts mean so far as the natural wisdom of the Chinese mind is concerned? With the help of the spiritual insight of Sister Miriam Teresa,[12] I form this analogy: Gold signifies our will and action—the dominant note in the ethics of Confucianism. Frankincense symbolizes our spirit of detachment and contemplation—the central thought of Taoist philosophy. And myrrh connotes, in a measure, our capacity for mortification and purification—the essence of Buddhism. Then, why cannot China lay before the Divine Infant in the arms of the Blessed Virgin, the gold of Confucianism, the frankincense of Taoism, and the myrrh of Buddhism, so that at a single touch by His hands, whatever is false in them is purified, and whatever is genuine is transmuted into supernatural values?

There has been much talk about the meeting of East and West; but we must realize that the East cannot be Westernized, just as the West cannot be Easternized. East cannot meet West in the West; West cannot meet East in the East. We meet only in our common humanity and in Christ. The orginal spiritual traditions of both East and West rise from their one source in our common human nature and seek a common fulfillment in

Christ. Our quest for unity must hold firmly to these facts.

One of the clearest expositions of the organic unity between East and West can be found in the keynote address by Dr. John C. H. Wu at the Second World Congress for the Apostolate of the Laity held in Rome in October 1957. There we see that today's world has needs and aspirations which tend toward a higher synthesis which is beyond the East and West. Let me quote the conclusion of this remarkable speech:

> Christ alone has taught us the truth and mystery of love. Christ alone reconciled the East and the West on the Cross and gave birth to the *new man* beyond all distinctions of race, sex, nation, and class. Christ alone has made it possible for us to be in the world and yet not of it. It is providential that at the present time both the East and the West are hurling a joint challenge at us to lead and cultivate a real and true interior life: the East, in that we must show to it that the kingdom of God within us is the living reality of which all its ancient philosophies have been but foreshadowings; the West, in that only by developing our interior life to a point surpassing in vigor and splendor its material civilization can we transmute the deadening weight of matter into an enlivening vessel of the Holy Spirit.
>
> The true East and true West are only to be found in Christ. If the East does not find the West in Christ, it will never meet the West and love it. If the West does not find the East in Christ, it will never meet the East and love it. If the East is westernized apart from Christ, it will become worse than the West. If the West is easternized apart from Christ, it will become worse than the East. If East and West are wedded outside of Christ and His Church, in a moment of infatuation, the union will not last and will only produce monsters. Only when the East and the West are united in the bosom of Christ will they love each other with the love of Christ. Only then will their union be like "the tree that gives life, bearing its fruit twelvefold, one yield for each month," and whose "leaves bring health to all nations."
>
> Christ is all in all. Without Christ, there is war even in peace. With Christ, there is peace even in war. Without Christ, material civilization is mere husks for the swine. With Christ, adversity and poverty are blessings in disguise. Without Christ, the "intellectuals" are fools. With Christ, the simple are wise. Without Christ, life is death. With Christ, death is life. Without

Christ, the more hopeful the more nopeless. With Christ, the more helpless the more hopeful. Christ is the only hope of mankind, the sole need of the world.

We are absolutely certain that there can be no real antipathy between the higher spiritual traditions of the East and the West, but only a profound unity which we instinctively feel to be present but which we cannot yet bring to full expression. However, we are now being forced to a more perfect mutual understanding because of the Communist attack against all that is sacred in both traditions.

The East hungers for knowledge, for new things, for a new order to strengthen its own heritage and traditions. It is the East that is coming to the West. The West cannot approach the East declaring, "We think your religions are as good as ours," or try to put the old on a par with the new, by saying Confucius is equal to Christ. The East is experiencing an acute spiritual hunger which the Christian West can satisfy, or should be able to satisfy.

Whatever else Russia may have, it does not have and does not pretend to have what we call spiritual values—the essence of civilization. Communism has made the headway in Asia or elsewhere, not by its strength, but our weakness, by our failure to make full use of these spiritual assets. The Soviet sputniks have awakened us to the necessity of accelerated research in science. Scientific education must be made more effective, but it must be developed within the context of total education for spiritual growth and religious fidelity. We must always remember that besides scientific reality there is a higher, divine reality. To counteract the materialistic, atheistic philosophy of Communism we need the spiritual resources of all the world.

So far as the East is concerned the spiritual resources of China are pre-eminent. They are also well suited for union with the spiritual resources of other traditions. What appears today a divided China is, after all, a passing phenomenon. Sooner or later, Red China will disappear, so will this division. There is everywhere a burning desire for unity rooted in our common humanity, and in Christ. China needs the world, the world needs China. This mutual need assures the dawning of the new Christian age. We are given the interval between now and the end to form a new united world. Christians the world over must exert their full effort and work for the realization of a new spiritual order and a new Christian Humanism. Then, and only then, will China's aspirations and hopes, hidden in this crisis, find their fulfillment, when she, too, will possess Christ, the Way, the Truth, and the Life.

Epilogue: American Policy Towards China: A Reappraisal

Admission of Red China to the U.N. would be a severe blow to an organization that even now lacks the support it needs from the major powers.

The Communist Chinese regime in Peking and the Government of the United States have been in a state of intense opposition ever since the Communist regime was established in 1949. The opposition between these two reached a state of severe military conflict in Korea during the years 1951-1953. In recent years the scene of conflict has shifted to Southeast Asia where Communist forces, supported by Red China, have taken over North Vietnam, have set up a Communist-orientated neutralist government in Cambodia, have taken over direct control of a large part of Laos, and are now carrying on an intensive guerrilla warfare in the remainder of Laos and in South Vietnam.

It is a critical period. Seeing the difficulties that we face in this continuing conflict some writers and speakers are now suggesting that we ease the situation by giving in on a number of points, especially by:

(1) Accepting Red China into the U.N.
(2) Granting diplomatic recognition to Red China.
(3) Establishing trade and aid programs.
(4) Withdrawing our military commitments in Southeast Asia.

These proposals affect all nations of the Free World. But since the United States is the leader of the Free World both in its practical material assistance to besieged nations and in its commitment to the ideals of political and personal liberty throughout the world, this country is under special critique for its consistent refusal to accept these points and to give in to the Chinese Communist regime, a government that is rapidly becoming the leading world force in aiding subversive movements throughout Asia, Africa, and South America.

In reality the official policy pursued by the United States has been thought out by capable men with extensive information and long experience in dealing with the Communist movement in East Asia. There have been flaws in the planning and execution of the program, but the basic pattern has been extremely sound. If implemented faithfully it could carry us, and the entire Free World, through our present difficulties into a better period of man's historical development.

This is particularly true because our efforts to limit the military advance of communism by counter military measures is associated with a sound program to help the peoples of Asia and the other parts of the world accomplish their social revolutions in a creative manner which would lead them into a new period of freedom and security rather than into a period of oppression and fear. President Kennedy, the main architect of the program in recent years, was very sensitive to the political and social needs of the new age. The work he developed and advanced so forcefully must be continued. He realized, and we must realize, that we are involved in a long process. Our enthusiasm must be sustained over a long period of years. Our main problem will be to sustain this program without growing discouraged over the amount of time needed for fulfillment.

However, these ideals of a creative social revolution brought about by the use and expansion of political independence and personal freedom are being challenged and threatened with subversion by a social revolution that is carried on by violence and which leads to the extinction of political and personal freedom. Until recently this force was led by Soviet Russia. Now Red China is challenging Soviet Russia for leadership of the world Communist Revolution and is succeeding to a striking degree. We have, in the West, found ways of bringing about a balance of force with Soviet Russia. The more aggressive challenge is now coming from Red China. The challenge exists on several continents but its focal point at present is in East and Southeast Asia.

It would be difficult to exaggerate the inner violence of the clash between the ideals and the practices of Red China and the United States. Great political wisdom, military strength of a new type and sustained effort will be needed to cope with this situation, which may be expected to go through a number of critical phases.

Thus far the advance of East Asian communism has been halted in Korea, Taiwan, and India. The crucial line of defense at the moment is Southeast Asia. In Laos and Vietnam, the struggle has grown intense since the forces of

Ho Chih-min, backed by Red China, are infiltrating in increasing numbers to the south.

If Laos and Vietnam should fall into Communist hands, it would be difficult to see how the spread of communism could be halted anywhere in Asia. If it can be contained approximately at the present lines of conflict then the Communist regimes of East and Southeast Asia may well prove disappointing to their peoples to be modified and eventually replaced by governments of a more humane and more acceptable type.

At this critical moment, when our main effort should be to show the effectiveness of our military power to prevent Communist conquest and subversion by raw force, some are making the catastrophic proposal that we abandon our efforts and conciliate the Peking regime.

(1) First there is the proposal that we admit Red China into the United Nations.

The answer to this is simply that admission of Red China into the U.N. would bring about unendurable confusion and frustration in an organization which is not even now receiving the support, moral or economic, that it needs from major powers (especially Soviet Russia); it would bring into the U.N. the bitter antagonism that exists between the Peking regime and the Nationalist Government; it would turn the U.N. into an arena of struggle between Peking and Moscow; it would enable Red China to work at its world subversive program on a high level, it would eventually give Red China a seat on the Security Council with a veto on the activities of that most important international body, an international body specifically designed to keep the peace that Peking is constantly breaking.

Beyond these effects admission of Red China would be a betrayal of the Chinese people, for it would strengthen the present tenuous hold an oppressive government still has on a people who show their dissatisfaction more intensely each year.

As a result of this Red China presence, confidence in the U.N. might wane, to a disastrous degree, in the popular feeling of those countries which are now its firmest supporters.

(2) Next, there is the proposal that we grant diplomatic recognition to Red China.

This, at the present time, is one of the most difficult of all proposals to understand. Red China is at war with the United States and with the Free World in Korea and throughout Southeast Asia. A diplomatic rapprochement between Red China and the United States would destroy all confidence in our determination to help these other peoples of Asia over the long period of time needed for them to establish their independence on a secure basis and to carry through the social renewal that is now in process.

Nor would recognition give us any advantage. Great Britain recognized Red China long ago and has not yet attained any significant benefit from this fact. France may have gained some slight trade benefits and some international prestige – but only by generally weakening the cause of the Free World. Finally, diplomatic recognition would afford Red China continual opportunity to embarrass and to harass us before the entire international community.

(3) Then there is the proposal that we establish trade and aid relations with Red China.

The answer to this is that aid given in this manner would, under this present Chinese regime, only strengthen the forces at the top of this oppressive system. The food and other benefits would go first and mainly to Red officials and their supporters, and to the military personnel. Only a minimum would ever get to the people. Even that little would never get to anyone not in total sympathy with the present regime.

Such aid to Red China would also increase the capacity of that country to aid subversive movements abroad. Even when the people of China were in one of their worst periods of starvation, the present regime shipped 1,200,000 tons of food to Albania, Cuba, and other nations, for the sake of prestige and propaganda. Trade or aid to Red China would decidedly help to bolster Communist subversion of freedom in Asia, Africa, and South America.

It is true that the people of China need food and aid from the Free World. We should see that they get it. But it cannot be gotten to them under the present regime. For the welfare of the Chinese people themselves, we must insist on a change of regime. This is much more possible than is generally recognized. The hold of this regime is neither absolute nor eternal. In fact, it has shown great weaknesses recently.

(4) Finally, there is the proposal that the United States withdraw its military commitments to Southeast Asia.

This would evidence a weak, vacillating attitude that easily gives in to sustained pressures. Such weakness would only encourage the aggressive tactics of Red China. The Nationalist Chinese defenders of Quemoy have shown that any position can be held against Red China if men will firmly resolve to hold it. Confronted by such determination, the Communist forces have consistently stopped short. In Korea their forces were checked, again in Malaya, and in the Philippines.

In Southeast Asia there are new and difficult complications which demand even greater wisdom and more sustained effort. Yet these positions can be held, if only we will to do so. Any wavering or uncertainty is fatal.

We are committed to this region both in fact and in principle. It is foolish to recoil from this task because some people are afraid that a major war might result. A major war is made much more possible by a lack of strength rather than by a show of strength. It was weakness, not strength, indecision rather than decision, that produced World War II. It was a vague uncertain idealism, not a firm realism based on principle that resulted in that terrible conflict.

There are several final points to be noted in concluding this discussion. These are all most important.

First, we must never forget that Red China acts according to the dialectical process outlined by Mao Tse-tung in his essay *On Contradiction.* This central treatise of the Chinese Communists insists that all development comes out of creative tensions. When one tension or one antipathy is resolved, another must be created. Thus whenever the opposition wearies of one tension or conflict and gives in to the Chinese Communists, the Chinese Communists immediately create another conflict and again increase the discomfort until we give in again, again, and again. By giving in to these tensions we will never attain release. It is an illusion with absolutely no basis in fact to think that we can ease the situation between ourselves and

Red China by any concessions whatsoever. So long as the present regime exists in Peking, the only possible way to peace is to strengthen counter-tensions until our endurance and our command over the situation at least equals theirs. This has been done in Korea and in Taiwan. It can be done in Southeast Asia.

The only alternative is to begin the disastrous process of retreat, on diplomatic and military fronts, throughout the entire world, to leave complete freedom of action to this fanatical group of men in Peking whose powers of damaging the Free World of Asia, Africa , and South America would increase in geometric proportion as we retreated from one position to another

Concerning the possibility of supporting Red China as a counter-force against Soviet Russia, could we not foster the opposition between them and thus bring benefits to the rest of the world by this confrontation between the two major forces of the Communist world? This proposal is frequently used as a reason for diplomatic recognition of Red China, for bringing Red China into the U.N., for granting trade and aid to Red China, and for easing the situation in Southeast Asia.

The answer is simply that there are no advantages to be gained in proportion to our losses in such a program. There is already sufficient bitterness between the two on the ideological plane. There is also a sufficient balance of force between the two to serve as a watch on each other. Actual war between the two is unlikely. Neither would a war serve any purpose for Red China, the Soviet, or the rest of the world.

It is especially to be noted that except for propaganda purposes and political expediency there are no great territorial conflicts between Red China and the Soviet. Those who know nothing of inner Asia speak of the vast lands of inner Asia which China once controlled and which she now seeks to regain from the Soviet. *There are no such lands.* Except for Outer Mongolia, there is no significant amount of territory in Central Asia now claimed by the Soviet which was ever under Chinese control.

The extravagance of language in which China and the Soviet accuse each other at the present time arises out of an ideological conflict for leadership of the world Communist movement. This war of words is in no manner a preparation for military action.

Nothing that we can do will change this Sino-Soviet relationship to our advantage. In fact, it may well change the situation to our disadvantage if we meddle in this conflict. Certainly it offers no basis for offering concessions to Red China. It might rather upset what constructive relations we now have with the Soviet Union. These are themselves very tenuous. But they are at least endurable at the present time. A balance of force and political action has been achieved between the U.S. and the Soviet Union in Europe, and, to some extent in Africa and South America. Thus it is difficult to see just what people mean when they talk about aiding China over against the Soviet Union. It really has no meaning at all.

This brings us back to our basic proposition. The pattern of diplomatic, military, and economic activity that the United States is presently committed to in East and Southeast Asia is basically sound. The work of many years, the expenditure of billions of dollars, and the very future of many nations in Asia and throughout the Free World are imperiled by granting Red China any of the four basic concessions outlined.

In conclusion, we must say that there is hardly anything so preposterous as to blame the United States for the lack of recognition of mainland China, for mainland China's absence from the U.N., or for a lack of trade with the mainland. Mainland China could long ago have had all of these things if Peking really wanted them; if rulers of Peking had dealt in a properly civilized manner toward its own people; if Peking had only refrained from aggression in Korea; if Peking showed a proper respect for the international community; if Peking had ceased its support of subversive movements throughout Asia, Africa, and South America.

But this is the strange thing about communism in China as in Cuba. Commitment to this doctrine brings about the subversion of the very ends it proclaims to seek, especially the economic relief of the people. The United States and other countries throughout the world are anxious and more than anxious to help the Chinese people. But this is precisely what the Peking regime will not permit. It might be considered one of the triumphs of Communist propaganda throughout the world to have the United States bear such a large part of the blame for a situation brought about deliberately by the Peking regime, a situation to which Peking is so absolutely committed that we have no reason to believe the policy will change until the existing regime is changed.

The evidence at present is that the pressures of Red China on the Free World will increase rather than diminish. The only answer is counter-pressure, which stopped the

Soviet in Europe, which stopped Cuba in the Western hemisphere and which has already stopped Red China in Korea and Taiwan.

We have in Soviet Russia itself an excellent illustration of how "reasonably" these Communist countries can be made to talk. The most "reasonable" bit of Soviet talking we have had yet was the talking done by Khrushchev on the occasion of President Kennedy's demands during the Cuban crisis.

The men in Peking likewise must learn this lesson in the same way. The result eventually in both cases we can well believe, will be new and different – non-Communist regimes.

Selected Bibliography

THE LIST of books and articles that follows does not include all the written material consulted in the course of the current project. It includes materials of which the writer has made use and also material he recommends to persons desiring further reading.

Abegg, Lily. *The Mind of East Asia,* trans. by A. J. Crick & E. E. Thomas. London, New York: Thamas & Hudson, 1952.

Ballantine, Joseph W. *Formosa: A Problem for the United States Foreign Policy.* Washington, D. C.: The Brookings Institution, 1952.

Bate, H. Maclear. *Report from Formosa.* New York: E. P. Dutton, 1952.

Bau, Mingchien Joshua. *The Open Door Doctrine in Relation to China.* New York: Macmillan, 1923.

Bauer, Thomas J. *The Systematic Destruction of the Catholic Church in China.* New York: World Horizon Reports, 1954.

Beloff, Max. *Soviet Policy in the Far East, 1944-1951.* New York: Oxford University Press, 1953.

Berry, Rev. Thomas. "Our Need of Orientalists." *Worldmission,* Fall 1956.

Binyon, Laurence. *The Spirit of Man in Asian Art.* Cambridge, Mass.: Harvard University Press, 1935.

Bodde, Derk. *China's Gifts to the West.* Washington, D. C.: American Council on Education, 1942.

Brandt, C., Schwartz, B. and Fairbank, J. K. *A Documentary*

History of Chinese Communism. Cambridge, Mass.: Harvard University Press, 1952.

Buck, John Lossing. *Chinese Farm Economy*. Chicago: University of Chicago Press, 1930.

———. *Farm Tenancy in China*. Chengtu, 1944. Pp. 455-66 of *Economic Facts*, No. 33 (June 1944).

———. *Land Utilization in China*. Shanghai, Commercial Press, 1937.

Buss, Claude A. *The Far East*. New York: Macmillan, 1955.

———. *War and Diplomacy in Eastern Asia*. New York: Macmillan, 1941.

Buxton, L. H. D. *China, The Land and The People*. London: Oxford University Press, 1929.

Caldwell, John C. *South of Tokyo*. Chicago: Henry Regnery Co., 1957.

Carnegie Endowment for International Peace. *Treaties and Agreements With and Concerning China, 1919-1929*. Washington, 1950.

Cary-Elwes, Columba. *China and the Cross: A Survey of Missionary History*. New York: P. J. Kenedy & Sons, 1956.

Chan, Wing-tsit. *Religious Trends in Modern China*. New York: Columbia University Press, 1953.

Chang, C. M. "Mao's Strategem of Land Reform." *Foreign Affairs*, July 1951.

Chang Chi-yun. *China of the Fifty Centuries*. Taipei: China Culture Publishing Foundation, 1953.

———. *The Centenary Celebration of Sino-American Intellectual Friendship*. Taipei: China Culture Publishing Foundation, 1953.

———. *The Essence of Chinese Culture*. Taipei: China News Press, 1957.

Chang Kia-ngau. *China's Struggle for Railroad Development*. New York: John Day, 1943.

Chang Kuo-tao. "Mao—A New Portrait by an Old Colleague." *New York Times*, Magazine section, August 2, 1953.

Chao Kuo-chün, comp. *Selected Works in English for a Topical Study of Modern China, 1840-1952* (mimeo.). Cambridge, Mass.: Regional Studies Program on East Asia, Harvard University, November 1952.

———. *The Communist Movement in China: A Chronology of Major Development, 1918-1950*. Russian Research Center, Harvard University, 1950.

Chapman, H. O. *The Chinese Revolution*, 1926-1927. London, 1928.

Chen, Theodore Hsi-en. "China: Communist Reform." *Current History,* November 1953.

———. "Education and Propaganda in Communist China." *Anals of the American Academy of Political and Social Science,* September 1951.

———. "The 'Three-Anti' and 'Five-Anti' Movements in Communist China." *Pacific Affairs,* March 1953.

Cheng, Tien-fong. *A History of Sino-Russian Relations.* Washington, D. C.: Public Affairs Press, 1957.

Chennault, Major General Claire L. *Way of a Fighter.* New York: G. P. Putnam's Sons, 1948.

Chiang Kai-shek. *China's Destiny.* New York: Macmillan, 1947.

———. *Soviet Russia in China.* New York: Farrar, Straus & Cudahy, 1957.

———. *The Collected Wartime Messages of Generalissimo Chiang Kai-shek, 1937-1945.* New York: John Day, 1946.

Chiang Soong Mei-ling. Sian: A Coup d'État. Shanghai, 1937.

China Handbook. Chungking, 1937-1945; New York, 1950; Taipei, 1951-1957.

China Year Book. New York, 1912-1919; Tientsin, 1921-1930; Shanghai, 1931-1939.

Chinese Delegation to the League of Nations. *Japanese Aggression and the Nine Power Conference.* Geneva: League of Nations, 1937.

Chinese Delegation to the United Nations. *China Presents Her Case to the United Nations.* New York, 1949.

Clyde, Paul H. *International Rivalries in Manchuria.* Columbus, Ohio, 1928.

———. *The Far East.* New York: Prentice-Hall, 1948.

Communist China Problem Research Series. A mimeographed topical series put out by the Union Research Institute, P. O. Private Bag K-1, Kowloon, Hong Kong, since November 1953.

Compton, Boyd, trans. *Mao's China: Party Reform Documents, 1942-1944.* Seattle: University of Washington, 1952.

Constantine, Leonard. Series of articles on Red China. *Manchester Guardian Weekly* from 23 November 1950 to 8 February 1951.

Cressey, George B. *Asia's Lands and Peoples.* New York: McGraw-Hill, 1951.

———. *China's Geographic Foundations.* New York: McGraw-Hill, 1934.

———. *Land of the 500 Million, A Geography of China.* New York: McGraw-Hill, 1955.

Creel, H. G. *Chinese Thought: From Confucius to Mao Tse-tung.* Chicago: University of Chicago Press, 1953.

———. *Confucius: The Man and the Myth.* New York: John Day, 1949.

———. *The Birth of China.* New York: John Day, 1937.

Dallin, David J. *Soviet Russia and the Far East.* New Haven, Conn.: Yale University Press, 1948.

———. *Soviet Russia's Foreign Policy, 1939-1942.* New Haven, Conn.: Yale University Press, 1942.

Danton, George H. *The Cultural Contacts of the United States and China.* New York: Columbia University Press, 1931.

De Jaegher, Rev. Raymond J. and Kuhn, Irene Corbally. *The Enemy Within.* New York: Doubleday, 1952.

Dewey, Thomas E. *Journey to the Far Pacific.* New York: Doubleday, 1952.

Dunlap, A. M. *Behind the Bamboo Curtain.* Washington, 1956.

Eberhard, Wolfram. *A History of China.* London: Routledge and Kegan Paul, 1950.

Eckel, Paul E. *The Far East Since 1500.* New York: Harcourt, Brace and Co., 1948.

Epatein, Israel. *The Unfinished Revolution in China.* Boston, 1947.

Feis, Herbert. *The China Tangle.* Princeton, N. J.: Princeton University Press, 1953.

Fitch, Geraldine. *Formosa Beachhead.* Chicago: Henry Regnery Co., 1953.

Fitzgerald, C. P. *China, A Short Cultural History.* London: Cresset Press, 1935.

Flynn, John T. *The Lattimore Story.* New York: Devin-Adair, 1953.

Forman, Harrison. *Changing China.* New York, 1948.

———. *Report from Red China.* London, 1946.

Friedman, Irving S. *British Relations with China: 1931-1939.* New York: Institute of Pacific Relations, 1940.

Fung, Yu-lan. *A History of Chinese Philosophy.* Vol. 1. Period of the philosophers (from the beginning to *c.* 100 B.C.) Trans. Derk Bodde. Peking and London, 1937. Vol. II. The Period of Classical Learning (from the 2nd century B.C. to the 20th century A.D.) Trans. same. London, 1953.

———. *A Short History of Chinese Philosophy.* New York: Macmillan, 1948.

Gallagher, Louis J., trans. *China in the Sixteenth Century: The Journals of Matthew Ricci: 1583-1610.* New York: Random House, 1953.

Giles, Herbert Allen. *A History of Chinese Literature.* London: Wm. Heinemann, 1901; New York: Appleton, 1903.

Goffart, P. *Life of Father Lebbe.* Louvain: University of Louvain, 1950.

Goodrich, L. Carrington. *A Short History of the Chinese People.* New York: Harper & Brothers, 1951.

———. *Scientific Developments in China.* The Sino-Indian Cultural Society, 1954.

Greenberg, Michael. *British Trade and the Opening of China, 1800-1842.* Cambridge, 1951.

Greene, Rev. Robert W. *Calvary in China.* New York: G. P. Putnam's Sons, 1953.

Griswold, Alfred Whitney. *The Far Eastern Policy of the United States.* New York: Harcourt, 1938.

Guillam, Robert. *600 Million Chinese.* New York: Criterion Books, 1957.

Herrmann, Albert. *Historical and Commercial Atlas of China.* Cambridge, Mass.: Harvard University Press, 1935.

Ho, Franklin L. "The Land Problem of China." *Annals of the American Academy of Political and Social Science,* July 1951.

Holcombe, Arthur N. *The Chinese Revolution: A Phase in the Regeneration of a World Power.* Cambridge, Mass.: Harvard University Press, 1930.

Holland, William L., ed. *Asian Nationalism and the West.* New York: Macmillan, 1953.

Hornbeck, Stanley K. *The United States and the Far East.* Boston, 1942.

Hsiung, S. I. *The Life of Chiang Kai-shek.* London, 1948.

Hu Shih. "China in Stalin's Grand Strategy." *Foreign Affairs,* October 1950.

———. "My Former Student, Mao Tse-tung." *Freeman,* July 2, 1951.

———. "The Natural Law in the Chinese Tradition." Barrett, Edward F. ed. *University of Notre Dame Natural Law Institute Proceedings.* Vol. V. Notre Dame, Ind.: University of Notre Dame Press, 1953.

Hughes, E. R., trans. *Chinese Philosophy in Classical Times.* New York: E. P. Dutton, 1942, 1944.

———. *The Invasion of China by the Western World.* New York: Macmillan, 1938.

Hummel, Arthur W. *Eminent Chinese of the Ch'ing Dynasty.* 2 vols. Washington, D. C.: Government Printing Office, 1943.

———. "Some Basic Principles in Chinese Culture." *Proceedings of the American Philosophical Society,* 1951.

Hunter, Edward. *Brain-Washing in Red China.* New York: Vanguard Press, 1951.

Hutheesing, Raja. *The Great Peace.* New York: Harper & Brothers, 1953.

Hyde, Douglas. *One Front Across the World.* Westminster, Md.: Newman Press, 1956.

Isaacs, Harold R. *The Tragedy of the Chinese Revolution* (revised ed.). Stanford, Calif.: Stanford University Press, 1951 (original ed., 1938).

Kiang, Wen-han. *Chinese Student Movement.* 1948.

King, John Kerry. *Southeast Asia in Perspective.* New York: Macmillan, 1956.

King, Wunsz, ed. *V. K. Wellington Koo's Foreign Policy.* Shanghai: Kelly and Walsh, 1931.

Kirby, E. Stuart. "The British and the Chinese." *Far Eastern Survey,* April 18, 1951.

———. "Hong Kong and the British Position in China." *Annals of the American Academy of Political and Social Science,* September 1951.

Ladany, S. J. *China News Analysis.* A weekly printed newssheet published in Hong Kong since August 25, 1953.

Latourette, Kenneth Scott. *A History of Christian Missions in China.* New York: Macmillan, 1929.

———. *A History of Modern China.* Melbourne, London, Baltimore: Penguin Books, 1954.

———. *The Chinese: Their History and Culture.* New York: Macmillan, 1949.

Leclerq, Chan J. *Vie du Père Lebbe, Le tonnerre qui chante au loin.* Paris: 1955.

Lee, Shao-ch'ang, comp. *China's Cultural Development.* East Lansing, Mich.: Michigan State University Press, 1952.

Legge, James. *Chinese Classics* (with a translation, critical and exegetical notes, prolegomena and copious indexes). 5 vols. First ed. Hong Kong, 1861-72, revised ed. of Vols. 1 and 2, Oxford: University Press, 1893-1895.

———. *The Religions of China.* New York: Charles Scribner's Sons, 1881.

Levi, Werner. *Modern China's Foreign Policy.* Minneapolis: University of Minnesota Press, 1954.

Li Chien-nung. *The Political History of China, 1840-1928* (ed. and trans. by Ssu-yu Teng and Jeremy Ingalls). New Jersey: D. Van Nostrand Co., 1956.

Li, Tien-yi. *Woodrow Wilson's China Policy, 1913-1917.* University of Kansas Press, 1952.

Lin Mousheng. *Men and Ideas*. New York: John Day, 1942.
Linebarger, Paul M. A. *The China of Chiang Kai-shek*. Boston: World Peace Foundation, 1941.
Ling, Nai-jui. "Three Years of Communist Rule in China." *The Review of Politics*, January 1953.
Liu, Shaw-tong. *Out of Red China*, trans. by Jack Chia and Henry Walter. New York: Duell, Sloan and Pearce, 1953.
Liu, Wu-chi. *A Short History of Confucian Philosophy*. Pelican Books A-333, 1955.
Lou Tseng-tsiang. *Ways of Confucius and of Christ*. London: Burn Oates, 1948.
Lyons, D. "The Chinese in Occidental Countries." *China Missionary Bulletin*, April 1953.
MacMurray, John van A. *Treaties and Agreements With and Concerning China*. 2 vols. Washington, 1921.
MacNair, Harley F. *China in Revolution*. Chicago: University of Chicago Press, 1931.
Mallory, Walter H. "Chinese Minorities in Southeast Asia." *Foreign Affairs*, January 1956.
Mao Tse-tung. *New Democracy*. New York: New Century Publishers, 1945.
———. "The Chinese Revolution and the Communist Party in China." *China Digest*.
Maurer, Herrymon. *Collision of East and West*. Chicago: Henry Regnery Co., 1951.
Mei Yi-pao. *The Ethical and Political Works of Motse*. London: A. Probsthain, 1929.
Min, U Kiaw. *Through the Iron Curtain via the Back Door*. Rangoon: Burmese Advertising Press, 1952.
Monsterleet, Rev. Jean. *Martyrs in China*. Chicago: Henry Regnery Co., 1956.
Moorad, George. *Behind the Iron Curtain*. Philadelphia, 1946.
Moore, Charles A., ed. *Philosophy East & West*. Princeton, N. J.: Princeton University Press, 1946.
Moraes, Frank. *Report on Mao's China*. New York, 1953.
Morse, H. B. *International Relations of the Chinese Empire*. 3 vols. Shanghai, 1910-1918.
Moule, A. C. *Christians in China Before the Year 1550*. New York: Macmillan, 1930.
Needham, Joseph. *Science and Civilization in China*. 7 vols. Two published. Cambridge: Cambridge University Press, 1954.
North, Robert C. *Kuomintang and Chinese Communist Elites*. Stanford, Calif.: Stanford University Press, 1952.

———. *Moscow and Chinese Communists.* Stanford, Calif.: Stanford University Press, 1953.
Northrop, F. S. C. *The Meeting of East and West.* New York: Macmillan, 1947.
Palmer, Norman D., and Shao Chuan Leng. "Organization of the Chinese Communist Party." *Current History,* July 1952.
Perleberg, Max. *Who's Who in Modern China* (from the beginning of the Chinese Republic to the end of 1953). Hong Kong: Ye Olde Printerie, 1954.
Plattner, Felix Alfred. *Jesuits Go East, a record of missionary activity in the East, 1541-1786.* Dublin, 1950.
Reichelt, Karl L. *Truth and Tradition in Chinese Buddhism* (tr. from the Norwegian). Shanghai: Commercial Press, 1927. 1934.
Reichwein, Adolf. *China and Europe* (tr. from the German by J. C. Powell). New York: Knopf, 1925.
Riggs, Fred W. *Formosa Under Chinese Nationalist Rule.* New York: Macmillan, 1952.
Rigney, Rev. Harold W. *Four Years in a Red Hell.* Chicago: Henry Regnery Co., 1956.
Ring, George C. *Religions of the Far East.* Milwaukee: Bruce, 1950.
Ripa, Matteo. *Memoirs, during 13 years residence at the court of Peking, in service of the emperor of China.* Trans. F. Prandi. London, 1846.
Rosso, Antonio Sisto. *Apostolic Legations to China of the Eighteenth Century.* South Pasadena, Calif.: P. D. and Ione Perkins, 1948.
Rostow, W. W. *The Prospects for Communist China.* New York: John Wiley & Sons, 1954.
Rowley, H. H. *Prophecy and Religion in the Ancient China and Israel.* New York: Harper & Brothers, 1956.
Rowbotham, A. H. *Missionary and Mandarin, the Jesuits at the Court of China.* Berkeley, Calif.: University of California Press, 1942.
Saeki, P. Y. *The Nestorian Monument in China.* London, 1916.
Schwarz, B. L. *Chinese Communism and the Rise of Mao.* Cambridge, Mass.: Harvard University Press, 1950.
Sheed, Frank J. *Communism and Man.* New York: Sheed & Ward, 1938.
Sheen, Bishop Fulton J. *Communism and the Conscience of the West.* New York: Bobbs-Merrill, 1948.
Shen, T. H. *Agricultural Resources of China.* Ithaca, N. Y.: Cornell University Press, 1951.

Shirley-Price, L. *Confucius and Christ, a Christian estimate of Confucius.* Westminster Press, 1951.
Sih, Paul K. T. *Chinese Culture and Christianity.* Taipei: China Culture Publishing Foundation, 1957.
———, ed. *Democracy in East Asia.* Taipei: China Culture Publishing Foundation, 1957.
———. *From Confucius to Christ.* New York: Sheed & Ward, 1952.
———. "The Natural Law of Mencius Philosophy." *New Scholasticism,* July 1957.
Soothill, W. E. *The Three Religions of China.* Oxford: Oxford University Press, 1923.
Steiner, Arthur H. *Chinese Communism in Action.* Los Angeles: University of California Press, 1953.
———. "Mainsprings of Chinese Communist Foreign Policy." *The American Journal of International Law,* January 1950.
———. *Report on China.* Annals of the American Academy of Political and Social Science, September 1951.
Stettinius, Edward. *Roosevelt and the Russians: The Yalta Conference.* New York, 1949.
Stimson, Henry L. *The Far Eastern Crisis.* New York, 1936.
Straelen, Henry Van. *Through Eastern Eyes.* Loveland, Ohio: Grailville, 1951.
———. *The Far East Must be Understood.* London, Luzac, 1945.
Stuart, John Leighton. *Fifty Years in China.* New York: Random House, 1945.
Suigo, Father Carlo. *In the Land of Mao Tse-tung.* London, 1953.
Sun Yat-sen. *Memoirs of a Chinese Revolutionary.* London: Hutchinson, 1927.
———. *San Min Chu I, The Three Principles of the People.* Trans. by Frank W. Price. Shanghai: China Committee, Institute of Pacific Relations, 1927.
Tamagna, Frank M. *Banking and Finance in China.* New York: Institute of Pacific Relations, 1942.
Tang, Peter S. H. *Communist China Today: Domestic and Foreign Policies.* New York: Frederick A. Praeger, 1957.
Tennien, Rev. Mark. *No Secret Is Safe.* New York: Farrar, Straus and Young, 1952.
Tong, Hollington K. *Chiang Kai-shek.* Taipei: China Publishing Co., 1953.
———. *Dateline: China.* New York: Rockport Press, 1950.
Trigault, Nicholas, S.J. *The China that Was: China as discov-*

ered by the Jesuits at the close of the 16th century. Trans. by L. J. Gallagher, S.J. Milwaukee: Bruce, 1942.
Tsui Chi. *A Short History of Chinese Civilization.* London: Victor Gollancz, 1942.
Utley, Freda. *The China Story.* Chicago: Henry Regnery Co., 1951.
U. S. Department of State. *United States Relations with China, 1944-1949.* Washington: Government Printing Office, 1949.
U. S. 81st Congress 1st Session, Comm. on Foreign Affairs, House of Representatives. *Communism in China,* Supplement III-C to the Strategy and Tactics of world Communism. Washington, Government Printing Office, 1949.
Victoria, Sister Mary. *Nun in Red China.* New York: McGraw-Hill, 1953.
Vinacke, Harold M. *A History of the Far East in Modern Times.* New York: Crofts, 1941.
———. *The United States and the Far East, 1945-1951.* Stanford, Calif.: Stanford University Press, 1952.
Waley, Arthur. *The Analects of Confucius Translated and Annotated.* London, 1938.
———. *Three Ways of Thought in Ancient China.* London: Allen & Unwin, 1939.
Walker, Richard L. *China Under Communism.* New Haven, Conn.: Yale University Press, 1955.
———. "Communist China Looks at the United States." *Yale Review,* Autumn 1951.
Wallace, Henry A. *Soviet Asia Mission.* New York, 1946.
Weber, Max. *The Religion of China.* Ed. and trans. by Hans H. Gerth. Glencoe, Ill.: The Free Press, 1951.
Wei, Francis, C. M. *The Spirit of Chinese Culture.* New York: Scribner, 1947.
Wei, Henry. *China and Soviet Russia.* New Jersey, D. Van Nostrad, 1956.
Weigh, Ken-sheng. *Russo-Chinese Diplomacy.* Shanghai, 1928.
Wilhelm, R. *A Short History of Chinese Civilization.* Trans. by J. Joshua. New York, 1929.
William, Maurice. *Sun Yat-sen Versus Communism.* Baltimore, 1932.
Willoughby, W. W. *Foreign Rights and Interests in China.* 2 vols. Baltimore, 1920.
Wolferstan, Bertram. *The Catholic Church in China from 1860-1907.* London, 1909.
Wright, Stanley F. *China's Struggle for Tariff Autonomy: 1843-1938.* Shanghai, 1938.

Wu, Aitchen K. *China and the Soviet Union.* New York: John Day, 1950.
Wu, John C. H. *Beyond East and West.* New York, Sheed & Ward, 1951.
———. *Confucius: The Man and His Ideas.* South Orange, N. J.: Seton Hall University Press, 1952.
———. *The Interior Carmel.* New York: Sheed & Ward, 1953.
———, ed. and trans. "Lao Tzu's The Tao and Its Virtue." *T'ien Hsia,* 1939.
Wu, Yuan-li. *An Economy Survey of Communist China.* New York: Bookman Associates, 1956.
Yang, Lien-sheng. *Topics in Chinese History.* Cambridge, Mass.: Harvard University Press, 1950.
Yeh, George and Fitzgerald, C.P. *China, A Short History.* London, 1950.
Yen, Maria. *The Umbrella Garden.* New York: Macmillan, 1954.
Yu-pin, Archbishop Paul. *Eyes East.* Paterson, N. J.: St. Anthony Guild Press, 1945.

Notes

Prologue

1. Cf. Northrop, *Jurisprudence in the Law School Curriculum,* I. J. of Leg. Ed. 484, 487, (1949).

2. Two hundred ten million people inside the Soviet Union, 550 million Chinese, 25 million Poles, 6 million Latvians, Lithuanians, and Estonians, 12 million Czechs and Slovaks, 18 million Germans, 16 million Rumanians, 10 million Hungarians, and 7 million Bulgarians.

3. For a detailed study of Red China's military affairs, cf. *Communist China, 1955.* (Hong Kong: Union Research Institute, 1956), pp. 129-36.

4. Suez development prompted a significant demonstration of parallel action by the Soviet Union and Red China. On November 10, 1956, the Soviet government officially announced that it would permit "volunteers" to go to Egypt to fight the "aggressors," if Britain, France, and Israel refused to withdraw their forces from Egyptian territory. Red China followed suit with an offer of 25,000 "volunteers." Cf. Ivar Spector, "Russia in the Middle East" (*Current History,* February 1957) p. 86.

5. The *New York Times,* March 14, 1957.

6. *Reader's Digest,* January 1957.

7. Chinese immigrants dominate the economic life of Southeast Asia. In Hong Kong, with a population of about 2,500,000, more than 99 per cent of the population is Chinese. The following table is arranged in the order of size of the ethnic Chinese compared with the total population of each area:

Chinese in Southeast Asia

Country	*Chinese*	*Total Population*	*Percent Chinese*
Malaya (and Singapore)	3,000,000	5,900,000	50.8
British Borneo	220,000	880,000	25.0
Thailand	3,000,000	19,000,000	15.8
Indo-China	1,000,000	27,000,000	3.7
Indonesia	2,000,000	78,000,000	2.6
Burma	300,000	18,000,000	1.7
Philippines	150,000	21,500,000	0.7
Total:	9,670,000	170,280,000	5.7

Cf. Walter H. Mallory, "Chinese Minorities in Southeast Asia" (*Foreign Affairs,* January 1956). For more detailed figures of an earlier date see *The Chinese in Southeast Asia* by Victor Purcell (New York: Oxford University Press, 1951).

8. *See* p. 54 of this text.

9. For a brief account of the Catholic Church's work among the Chinese overseas, cf. D. Lyons, "The Chinese in Occidental Countries" (*China Missionary Bulletin,* April 1953).

Breadth and Depth

1. In the Yuan dynasty (1277-1367) China was ruled by the Mongols, and in the Ch'ing dynasty (1644-1911) she was ruled by the Manchus.

2. Chang Chi-yun, *China of the Fifty Centuries* (Taipei: China Culture Publishing Foundation, 1953) p. 25.

3. Alfred N. Whitehead, *Science and the Modern World* (New York, 1941) p. 8.

4. Laurence Binyon, *The Spirit of Man in Asian Art* (Cambridge: Harvard University Press, 1935) p. 13.

5. Dom Pierre-Célestin Lou Tseng-tsiang, *Ways of Confucius and Christ* (London: Burns Oates, 1948) p. 107.

6. Paul K. T. Sih, *From Confucius to Christ* (New York: Sheed & Ward, 1952) pp. 44-45.

Origins and Developments

1. There exists an ancient, extremely popular Taoist book, the *Kung Kuo Ko,* which means literally "manual of creditable

actions and misdeeds." According to this work, one's morality can be computed on a mathematical basis.

2. Kenneth S. Latourette, *The Chinese: Their History and Culture* (New York: Macmillan, 1949) p. 613.

3. Thomas F. Ryan, S.J., *Chinese Through Catholic Eyes* (Hong Kong: Catholic Truth Society, 1941) p. 13.

4. Lily Abegg, *The Mind of East Asia,* translated by A. J. Crick & E. E. Thomas (London, New York: Thamas & Hudson, 1952) p. 197.

5. According to Confucius, the cultivation of human perfection and family solidarity serves the basis for the common good of society, community, country and world. The first passage of *Ta Hsueh (The Great Learning)* reads: "What the Great Learning teaches is . . . to illustrate illustrious virtue; to renovate the people; and to rest in highest excellence." (Legge translation)

6. According to Mencius, Heaven has will, intelligence, creative power and protective love—an idea much more clear than that of Confucius. Commenting on Mencius' philosophy, the late Msgr. R. V. Kavanagh of Carroll College, Helena, Montana, once wrote me: "Although Mencius is less abstract than Aristotle, he has a concept of human nature very much like the dynamic developmental concept of the Greek philosopher." There is a great deal of truth in these words. But it is not exactly "dynamic concept," rather an organic interpretation of a human nature in accordance with the law of nature.

7. *The Mencius,* Bk. 7, p. 1, ch. 1.

8. For a general treatment of the natural-law philosophy of Mencius, cf. Paul K. T. Sih, "Mencius' Natural Law Philosophy" (The *New Scholasticism,* July 1957).

9. H. G. Creel, *Confucius: The Man and the Myth* (New York: John Day, 1949) pp. 110-11.

10. For a study of Chang Tsai's pantheist ideas, cf. Fung Yulan, *A History of Chinese Philosophy,* translated by Derk Bodde (Princeton, University Press, 1953) Vol. II, pp. 477-84.

11. Creel, *op. cit.,* p. 258.

12. *Ibid.*

13. *St. John* 2, 10.

14. "The Philosophy of Mariology" (Boston: The *Catholic Alumni Sodality Bulletin,* October 1952) p. 6.

The Early Contacts

1. Professor Soo teaches Chinese Literature at the Cheng Kung University in Taiwan. Her work, *The Chinese Tradition*

and the Old Testament, was published in Chinese by the Catholic Truth Society in Hong Kong, 1950.

2. For a brief summary of St. Thomas' alleged visit to China, see A. C. Moule, *Christians in China Before the Year 1500* (New York: Macmillan, 1930), pp. 10-26.

3. Moule, *op. cit.,* p. 23.

4. The Nestorians, or Christians of the Eastern or Syriac Church, claimed that there were distinct divine and human personalities in Christ and that Mary was the Mother of the Man Christ, but not the Mother of One Who was really God. For a study of the Nestorians in China, see Columba Cary-Elwes, *China and the Cross* (New York: Kenedy & Sons, 1956), pp. 14-35.

5. *The China Year Book,* 1944-1945, p. 887.

6. *The Catholic Encyclopedia* (New York: Robert Appleton, 1908), Vol. III, p. 670.

7. Latourette, *op. cit.,* pp. 275-76.

8. *The Catholic Encyclopedia* (New York: Gilmary Society), Sup. II, 4th Sec., Vol. XVIII, part on "China."

9. Arnold Toynbee, *The World and the West* (Oxford Press, 1953), p. 64.

10. Thomas J. Campbell, *The Jesuits: 1534-1921* (New York: Encyclopedia Press, 1921), Vol. I, p. 255.

11. Louis J. Gallagher, S.J., *China in the Sixteenth Century: The Journals of Matthew Ricci, 1583-1610* (New York: Random House, 1953), p. xx.

12. Paschal M. d'Elia, *Missionary History of the Catholic Church in China,* in Chinese (Shanghai: Commercial Press, 1934), p. 60. English translation is made by the author.

13. Paul Siu was baptized on February 11, 1603, by Father Joannes di Roccia. Speaking of Catholicism, he once said: "The doctrine of the Church is notably able to supplement what the teachings of the Confucian school have left unexpressed and to correct what the cult of Buddhism has misrepresented. . . . All the commandments and the teachings of the Church are intimately related to the natural law. Whoever obeys them with devotion can certainly attain the highest goodness and uproot all kinds of evils." See Msgr. Stanislau Lokuang, *The Life of Paul Siu,* in Chinese (Hong Kong: Catholic Truth Society, 1953).

14. Gallagher, *op. cit.,* p. 155.

15. Maurus Fang Hao, "Notes on Matteo Ricci's De Amicitia" (*Monumenta Serica,* Tokyo: S.V.D. Research Institute, 1949-1955), p. 576.

16. *Ibid.,* p. 577.

17. Antonio Rosso, O.F.M., *Apostolic Legations* (South Pasadena, Calif.: P. D. & Iona Perkins, 1948), p. 65.

18. For this version Ricci coined many new ecclesiastical terms. See Piero Tacchi Venturi, S.J., *Opere Storiche del P. Matteo Ricci* (Maceratta, 1911), Vol. II, p. 266. For a full study of Ricci's works, see Pasquale d'Elia, S.J., *Fonti Ricciane* (Vol. I, Rome, 1942; Vols. II and III, Rome, 1949). A review of this work in English by Heinrich Busch, S.V.D. appeared in *Monumenta Serica,* 1949-1955, pp. 600-03.

19. Rosso, *op. cit.,* p. 66.

20. Venturi, *op. cit.,* Vol. I, pp. 85-92; Vol. II, pp. 386-87. See Msgr. Stanislau Lokuang, *La Sapienza dei Cinesi, il Confucianismo* (Roma: Officium Libri Catolici, 1945), p. 19ff, 72ff.

21. D'Elia, *op. cit.,* p. 60.

22. Schall's life was given in detail by Remusat in his *Melanges Asiatiques,* Vol. II, p. 217.

23. Campbell, *op. cit.,* p. 256.

24. During the years 1650-1664 the Dominicans baptized 3,400 Chinese, administered 21 churches, 11 residences. During 1633-1660 the Franciscans baptized 3,500 Chinese, administered 3 churches, 1 residence. In 1671, according to a report submitted by Father Intorcetta to Rome, it was estimated that under the Jesuit jurisdiction there were 256,880 Catholics, 156 churches, 41 residences, while the other missionaries also made substantial progress. See *Compendiosa Narratione* (Rome, 1672), pp. 7-9; D'Elia, *op. cit.,* pp. 67-68.

25. In the petition which Nicolas Trigault presented to Pope Paul V, he begged the Pope to allow the Bible and the Roman Missal, Ritual and Briviary to be translated into Chinese, and to permit the Chinese to use their own language in the liturgy and in the administration of the sacraments. . . . Paul V, who took a lively interest in the Jesuit missions in China, did not meet the unusual request with a flat refusal but handed it to the Congregation of the Inquisition for examination; and since, in the discussion, no less a personage than Bellamine spoke in favour of the concession, the Congregation passed a favourable verdict, on March 26th, 1615. Basing himself on this resolution, by a decree of June 27th, 1615, Paul V gave permission for the translation of the Bible and the use of Chinese in the Brivary, at Mass, and in the administration of the Sacraments. . . . At the same time, in consideration of the fact that, according to Chinese conceptions, solemn functions may not be carried out with head uncovered, the Pope allowed the missionaries to wear at Mass a head-dress resembling the biretta worn by the Chinese literati. Armed with these weighty concessions and accomplished by new missionaries, Trigault was back in China in 1619. However, the only privilege of which the missionaries availed themselves was

that of saying Mass with head covered" (Pastor, *The History of the Popes,* Vol. XXV, pp. 356-58).

26. For an interesting study of this problem, see Joseph Jennes, C.M.C.M. (Scheut), "A Propos de la Liturgie Chinoise: Le Bref Romanae Sedia Antistes de Paul V (1615)," published in the *Neue Zeitschrift für Missionswizaenschaft* (Suisse: Beckenried, 1946), pp. 241-54; see also Stanislaus Chen, *Historia Tentaminum Missionariorum Societatis Jesu Pro Liturgia Sinica in Saeculo XVII* (Rome: Propaganda College, 1951). The Decree of the Holy Office (March 26, 1615) as well as the Brief of Paul V (June 27, 1615) is reproduced in the Appendix of Chen's *Historia.* The originals of both documents are preserved in the Archivo Segreto Vaticano, Sec. Brevia, Vol. 536, ff 111-13. The Decree reads as follows:

In the general Congregation of the Holy Roman and Universal Inquisition held in the Apostolic Palace at St. Peter's in presence of Our Most Holy Lord Paul V by divine providence Pope, and of the Most Illustrious and Reverend Lords . . . [There follow the names and the titular churches of the six Cardinals who composed the commission.]

Having read the memorial of the Jesuit Fathers residing in the Kingdom of the Chinese, called "China" in the vernacular, Our Most Holy Lord the Pope has granted to them, and to other Catholic priests, that in the celebration of Mass they may keep the head covered, since in that region to go about or to act bareheaded is not reverence but irreverence, and engenders scandal, not devotion. The said Fathers and other Priests will take care, however, that in the celebration of Mass they use not an ordinary headdress of common wear, but a special one and of the same color as the other vestments; and if this cannot conveniently be done, at least they will use the bonnet they are wont to wear in preaching the word of God and in other sacred functions, not that everyday one they ordinarily use. This concession the same Holy Father intends and declares to be lasting as long as it shall not be declared otherwise by the Holy See.

Likewise His Holiness has permitted to the same Fathers that they may translate the Holy Bible into Chinese, not however into the popular tongue, but the cultivated and that proper to the scholars; and then to use the books thus translated. At the same time He orders that in the translation of the Bible they use the utmost and exacting diligence, so that the translation be a most faithful one; and in the same Chinese language the divine offices of Mass and the Canonical Hours may be celebrated by Chinese.

Lastly, He has permitted that in the same literary language of China the sacraments may be administered and other ecclesiastical functions performed by Chinese, when they are legitimately promoted to Holy Orders and found worthy by the one having authority and are admitted to the performing of the said ecclesiastical functions, in which they are bound to conform themselves to the rite of the Holy Roman Church. However, if it ever happens that a Bishop or Bishops be constituted in these parts, this permission is not to be prejudicial to the episcopal office and jurisdiction.

27. Campbell, *op. cit.*, pp. 261-62.

The Chinese Rites Controversy

1. Speaking of these three sects in China, Ricci held that "the oldest one being of the scholars (Confucianists), who now, as in the past, control China. The other sects (Taoists and Buddhists) were worshipers of idols but had differentiating characteristics of their own. These two were always at odds with the scholars. Although the sect of the scholars never gave itself up to things supernatural, the ethics it professed was almost in complete accord with Catholic principles." See Rosso, *op. cit.*, p. 68.

2. Venturi, *op. cit.*, Vol. I, p. 90.

3. Rosso, *op. cit.*, p. 82.

4. George C. Ring, S.J., *Religions of the Far East* (Milwaukee: Bruce, 1950), p. 41.

5. For details, see Rosso, *op. cit.*, pp. 111-20.

6. Venturi, *op. cit.*, Vol. I, p. 92.

7. It was not, however, a clear-cut controversy between the Jesuits on one hand and the Franciscans and Dominicans on the other. It is true that upon the arrival of the Dominican, Morales, in China (1633) the disputes over the rites began. It is equally true that it was the Dominican, Navarrete, who first launched the attack on the Jesuit method of dealing with Chinese traditions in his work, "Tratadoa Históricos." But it was also a Dominican, Father Sarpetri, who sent a solemn denunciation of the "Tratadoa Históricos" to Rome. He declared that the practice of the Jesuits in allowing such rites was not only irreproachable from every point of view, but also necessary in propagating the Gospel. Another Dominican (a Chinese), Gregorio Lopez, Bishop of Basiles and Vicar-Apostolic of Nanking, sent the Sacred Congregation a "memoir" in favor of the Jesuits.

It was a Franciscan, Father Carlo Horatij, who was largely responsible when the Holy See issued the definite condemnation of the rites (1742). Yet, in 1718, he himself had introduced an amended form of the ancestral tablet which represented an earnest and sensible attempt to accommodate himself to the Jesuit view on the subject.

To all this controversy and confusion was added the open rivalry between the Portuguese and French Jesuits at the Court of Peking. In reference to the above material see Rosso, *op. cit.*, pp. 111-20; Campbell, *op. cit.*, p. 257; Rosso, *op. cit.*, p. 134n, 135, 234-35.

8. Ring, *op. cit.*, p. 42.
9. Rosso, *op. cit.*, pp. 138-40, 143.
10. Campbell, *op. cit.*, p. 261.
11. For the full text of the decree, see Rosso, *op. cit.*, p. 243.
12. Campbell, *op. cit.*, p. 261.
13. Rosso, *op. cit.*, p. 189.
14. *Ibid.*, p. 192.
15. Ring, *op. cit.*, p. 42.
16. Ryan, *op. cit.*, p. 60.
17. As a result, China suffered a great decrease of the faithful (from 300,000 in 1700 to 200,000 in 1800). See D'Elia, *Misssionary History, op. cit.*, p. 82.
18. Ring, *op. cit.*, p. 42. These important concessions have been properly safeguarded against abuse. By way of an interpretative norm, a letter was sent by the Sacred Congregation to the Apostolic Delegate in China, which is printed in *Cill, S.C.*, June 1941. Father Gustav Voss, S.J. discussed the whole question thoroughly in *Theological Studies*, Vol. IV, No. 4, pp. 525-60.

Entry by Force

1. As early as 1842, Richard Cobden (1804-1865) commented, "although the Chinese are undoubtedly guilty of much absurd phraseology, and of no little ostentatious pride and of some excess, justice in my opinion is with them. . . . We, the enlightened and civilized Christians, are pursuing objects at variance both with justice and with religion." See E. R. Hughes, *The Invasion of China by the Western World* (New York: Macmillan, 1938), p. 25. Gladstone himself stated that if the British government favored a war with China and demanded indemnity for confiscated opium, history would record this as England's war in defence of the "poppy interests."
2. In October, 1856, a craft, the *Lorcha Arrow,* owned by Chinese and with a Chinese crew, but registered at Hong Kong,

having a British captain, and flying the British flag, was boarded by Chinese officers while at Canton. Most of the crew were arrested on the ground that they had been engaged in a recent act of piracy, and the British flag was hauled down. The British declared that British sovereignty had been violated and their flag insulted. Thus hostilities began. As they started with the incident on the *Lorcha Arrow,* the conflict is historically named the Arrow War.

3. See note 12, this section.

4. Russia disclosed her political and territorial purpose in the Far East, by securing successive concessions from China in the Treaties of Nerchinek (1689), Kiachta (1727), Kiachta (two trade Conventions, 1768, 1792), Kuldja (trade, 1851), and finally in the Treaty of Aigum, 1858, (following her friendly intervention in the Arrow War) which brought her to the Pacific at Nikovlaievsk, and three years later to Vladivostok.

5. For a documentary study of the Yalta Agreement with special reference to Port Arthur, Dairen, and the special interests of Russia in Manchuria, see Herbert Feis, *The China Tangle* (Princeton University Press, Princeton, N. J., 1953), pp. 233, 245, 246, 247, 249, 252n.

6. Ten years after the Opium War, the Tai Ping Rebellion took place. The uprising, starting from the Kwangsi Province, soon spread to the Yangtze Valley. Nanking was taken in 1853, made the capital, and held till 1864. The rebellion which lasted 14 years and extended to 12 provinces, was devastating in results: 600 cities, mostly in the southeast, were laid waste, and the list of casualties—the loss of life inflicted by war and famine—amounted to some 20 millions of people. See Chang Chi-yun, *op. cit.*, p. 24.

7. The American Open Door Policy involves, in essence, two principles: the equal opportunity of trade, and the integrity of China. That is, the United States maintained that she or her nationals should have equal opportunity of trade in the markets of China, and that the integrity of China be respected. These two principles were set forth in John Hay's two famous documents which gave birth to the policy: the first issued on September 6, 1899, and the second on July 2, 1900. Professor Paul E. Eckel remarks: "To this Policy goes a large part of the credit for mobilizing public opinion against further dismemberment of China." See *The Far East since 1500* (New York: Harcourt, Brace, 1948), p. 277.

8. As Dr. Chang Chi-yun remarks: "The friendliness on the part of China toward America was due in no small degree to the

decision taken by the United States not to allow her citizens to have anything to do with the opium trade." See *The Centenary Celebration of Sino-American Intellectual Friendship* (Taipei: China Culture Publishing Foundation, 1953), p. 12.

9. Secretary John Foster Dulles's maternal grandfather, General John W. Foster, who had been Secretary of State under President Benjamin Harrison, was invited in 1895 by the Imperial Chinese government to serve as mediator at the peace conference which ended the war. In recognition of General Foster's contribution, Li Hung-chang, who represented China at the conference, wrote to Secretary Dulles a letter upon the General's death. On this matter Secretary Dulles remarked: "One of my most prized possessions is a letter I received when eight years old from Li Hung-chang, then the great Chinese elder statesman. The opening sentence of the letter reads: 'To the little grandchild of General Foster, my friend and counsellor in my hours of perplexity and trouble.' " See *Department of State Bulletin*, Vol. XXIV, No. 621, May 28, 1951, p. 842.

10. China's complete confidence in the United States is clearly expressed in the fact that during the American Civil War, President Lincoln appointed Anson Burlingame as Minister to China, and upon the expiration of his term in 1867, Burlingame was appointed by the Chinese government as China's special envoy to the United States and the other countries in Europe—a precedent which probably has never been repeated in modern diplomatic history. For a brief account of Burlingame's mission in China, see Hollington K. Tong, *What Is Ahead for China?* (Washington, D. C.: Chinese Embassy, 1957), pp. 156-58.

11. A military court-martial acquittal of a United States Army Sergeant Robert R. Reynolds accused of slaying a Chinese citizen touched off a riot on May 24, 1957 in Taipei, Taiwan.

12. The French Convention of 1860 gave further sanction to the promise made in the imperial edict of 1846 that the Chinese government would restore to Roman Catholics the religious and benevolent establishments confiscated during the persecutions of the preceding century and a half.

13. To the author's memory, among those few foreigners who protested against the sign was Dr. John W. Cline, who was President of Soochow University, a Methodist institution.

14. The Spanish Dominicans were in Fukein. The working field of the Paris Foreign Mission Society covered Szechuan, Kweichow, Yunan, Kwangtung, Kwaingsi, Manchuria, and Tibet. The Franciscans labored in central and eastern parts of China. The Lazarists, who took over the missionary work left

by the Jesuits since 1785, made substantial achievements in Hupei, Kwangsi, Honan, and Chekiang. Since 1842 the Jesuits have worked in Kiangsu, Anwei, and southeastern part of Hupei. See D'Elia, *Missionary History, op. cit.*, pp. 87-88.

15. The Pontifical Institute of Mission Expansion of Milan (PIME) arrived in Hong Kong in 1858 and carried out its missionary program in Honan in 1869. The Scheut Fathers, not long after the founding of their congregation, preached in Mongolia in 1865. The Augustinians, who had interrupted their activities in China for more than one hundred years, returned to Honan in 1879. The Roman Seminary of SS. Peter and Paul was founded in 1885 and sent its members in the same year to work in Shensi. The Steyl Society of the Divine Word did not come until 1879; it started to work in 1882 in a district of Shantung. Among others, there were the Trappists in Yangchiaping (1883), the Brothers of the Christian School in Hong Kong (1870), and the Little Brothers of Mary in Shanghai (1893). *Ibid.*, pp. 88-89.

16. The Sisters of Charity arrived in China in 1842. Then came the Sisters of St. Paul de Chartres (1848), the Canossian Sisters (1860), the Helpers of the Holy Souls (1867), the Portieux Sisters of Providence (1875), the Franciscan Missionaries of Mary (1885), and the Dominican Sisters (1889). The Carmelite Sisters did not come to China until 1869. *Ibid.*, p. 89.

17. Bishop Raymond A. Lane, *Stone in the King's Highway* (New York: McMullen, 1953), pp. 262-63.

18. Chiang Kai-shek, *China's Destiny,* translated by Wang Chung-hui (New York: Macmillan, 1947), pp. 78-79.

The Struggle for Reform

1. H. G. Creel, *Chinese Thought From Confucius to Mao Tse-tung* (University of Chicago, 1953) pp. 236-37.

2. His Holiness Pius XII says: "The nineteenth century is the one largely responsible for juridical positivism." Cf. Pius XII *Discorsi agli Intellectuali: 1939-1954,* p, 211.

3. Yen Fu, a conservative translator of many philosophical Western works, set up as desiderata of translation, "Accuracy, Intellgibility, Elegance."

4. Cf. *Catholic Encyclopedia* (Gilmary), *op. cit.,* Supplement II, 4th Sec. Vol. XVIII, 1953, on "Intellectual Evolution of Modern China, 1898-1950."

5. For an interesting study of Weng T'ung-ho's reform pro-

gram, cf. Kung-chuan Hsiao, "Wang T'ung-ho and the Reform Movement of 1898," *Tsing Hua Journal of Chinese Studies,* Taipei, Taiwan, No. 2, April 1957.

6. For a full account of the reforms of 1898, cf. Meribeth E. Cameron, *The Reform Movement in China* (Stanford University, 1931) ch. 2.

7. Among them there were four European missionary priests and fifty-two Chinese laymen. For details, cf. *Mission Bulletin,* Hong Kong, May 1955, pp. 367-69.

8. For a brief description of the rise of the Boxers, suppression of the Uprising and the peace settlement, cf. Eckel, *op. cit.,* pp. 281-90.

9. For a summary of the reform program, cf. Paul Hibbert Clyde, *The Far East* (New York: Prentice-Hall, 1948) pp. 319-28.

Trial and Error

1. For the text of San Min Chu I, cf. F. W. Price, trans. *Sun Yat-sen, San Min Chu I: The Three Principles of the People* (Chungking, 1943). Cf. also L. S. Hsu, *Sun Yat-sen, His Political and Social Ideas* (Los Angeles, 1933).

2. Cf. Li Chien-nung, *The Political History of China, 1840-1928,* edited and translated by Sssu-yu Teng and Jeremy Ingalls (New Jersey: D. Van Nostrand, 1956) p. 257.

3. For a summary account of these seven attempts, cf. Li, *op. cit.,* pp. 221-25.

4. *See* p. 55.

5. Li, *op. cit.,* pp. 257-58.

6. *Ibid.,* p. 288.

7. For a detailed account of the monarchy movement, cf. H. M. Vinacke, *Modern Constitutional Development in China* (Princeton, 1920) pp. 179-211.

8. For a summary of the internal struggle among the war lords in China during this period, cf. Li, *op. cit.,* pp. 351-400 *passin.*

The Intellectual Revival

1. D'Elia, *Missionary History, op. cit.,* p. 94.

2. The Salesians in Macao (1902), the Parma Foreign Mission Society in Honan (1904), the Little Sisters of the Poor in Shanghai (1904), the Servants of the Holy Ghost in Shantung (1905), the Missionary Sisters of the Immaculate Conception of Canada

in Kwangchow (1909), and the Franciscan Missionary Sisters of Egypt in Hopei (1910). Cf. *Ibid.*, p. 95, p. 97.

3. Morrison left the United States in the "Trident." He was in the United States only twenty days, but Madison, then Secretary of State, gave him a letter to Carrington, the United States Consul. Morrison arrived at Macao, September 4, 1807. Cf. George H. Danton, *The Cultural Contacts of the United States and China* (New York: Columbia Press, 1931) p. 30.

4. *Ibid.*, p. 44.

5. For a brief description of these enterprises, cf. *Ibid.*, p. 44-71.

6. Dr. Sun Yat-sen, for instance, became a Protestant in 1884 when he was a student in Hong Kong.

7. *U. S. Foreign Relations*, 1907, p. 1, pp. 174-75; cf. also *Ibid.*, 1908, pp. 64-65, pp. 71-72.

8. The Maryknoll Fathers in Kiangmen, Kwangchow (1918), the Columban Fathers in Hanyang (1920), the Passionist Fathers in Honan (1921), The Picpus Brothers in Hainan (1922), the Betharramite Fathers in Yunan (1922), the Benedictines from Pennsylvania in Peiping (1925), the Maryknoll Sisters of St. Dominic in Hong Kong (1920), the St. Mary-of-the-Woods Sisters and the Sisters of Providence in Honan (1920). Cf. D'Elia, *Missionary History, op. cit.*, p. 95, p. 97.

9. Cf. Harold W. Rigney, S.V.D., *Four Years in a Red Hell* (Chicago: Henry Regnery, 1956) p. 3. Father Rigney was Rector of the Fu Jen University of Peiping before he was expelled from China by the Communists in 1955.

10. Latourette, *op. cit.*, p. 656. Before the Communists ruled the Chinese mainland in 1949, there were 13 Protestant colleges and universities, largely supported by American, British and Canadian funds, with an aggregate enrollment of 11,688 for 1947-48. There were 2,301 Protestant middle schools in 103 cities in China, with a total registration of 74,320 boys and girls in 1948. The three Catholic institutions of university standing had about an enrollment of 3,500 students during the same period. There were 155 Catholic middle schools; 85 per cent of the students were non-Catholics. It may be also added that in 1946 there were 31 national universities, with an enrollment of 1,495,874 students. Cf. *China Handbook, 1950* (New York: Rockport Press) pp. 28-29, p. 640, p. 643.

11. Dr. Sun Yat-sen says: "The aim of the revolution in China is directly opposite to that in Europe. Europeans resorted to revolutions because they had too little liberty; whereas in China we have had too much liberty without organization and resisting

power. . . . We must free ourselves into a strong cohesive body." Cf. Chiang, *China's Destiny*, *op. cit.*, p. 208.

12. Cf. Tien-yi Li, *Woodrow Wilson's China Policy, 1913-1917* (University of Kansas Press, 1952).

13. Frank J. Sheed, *Communism and Man* (New York: Sheed & Ward, 1939) p. 136.

14. Latourette, *op. cit.*, p. 480, p. 484.

15. The Peking National University, nicknamed Pei-ta, was one of the few institutions created during the abortive *Hundred Days Reform* of 1898 that had not been destroyed by the Empress Dowager's counter-reformation. Having its origins in a reaction against traditional Chinese culture, it endured as a center of experimental thought.

16. Cf. Rev. Mark Tsai, "Bertrand Russell and Chinese Tragedy" (The *Catholic World*, September 1952) p. 440.

17. Cf. Wing-tsit Chan, *Religious Trends in Modern China* (New York: Columbia Press, 1953) pp. 224-25.

18. Chan, *op cit.*, p. 225.

19. We read in the editorial of *Life*, March 31, 1958: "The worthwhile innovations in methods brought by Dewey's educationists should be kept. But their exclusive devotion to techniques and group adjustment should never again be allowed to hide the fact that American education exists first of all to educate the individual in a body of learning, with a tradition and purpose behind it. A man so educated is far better equipped as a democratic citizen than the merely 'well adjusted.' For he will have not only the social ease to make his civilization comfortable, but the intellectual discipline to help save it."

20. For a discussion of the Communist study of the monkey as human origins, cf. Liu Shaw-tong, *Out of Red China*, translated by Jack Chia and Henry Walter (New York: Duell, Sloan & Pearce, 1953) pp. 154-57.

21. Lao Sze-kwang, "Know Thyself" (*China Weekly*, in Chinese, Hong Kong, May 7, 1956) p. 168. English translation by Paul K. T. Sih.

22. Quoted by Vincent Cronin in his *The Wise Man From the West* (New York: Dutton, 1955) p. 285.

23. Apocalypse 3, 17-18.

24. *The China Monthly*, New York, October 1947, p. 342.

A Spiritual Vacuum

1. John C. H. Wu, "Adolescence in China: Its Problems and Aspirations" (The *China Monthly*, New York, October 1947) p. 341.

2. In 1919 the Soviets issued a manifesto offering to negotiate with China on the basis of the renunciation of all special privileges of Russia and Russians in China, the cancellation of further payments on the Boxer indemnity, the restoration to China, without compensation, of the Chinese Eastern Railway and the mines and forests acquired by the Czar's government from China, and the return of territory seized by the former regime. This action of Moscow was not from such disinterested generosity as might at first appear. It was good policy. Russia hoped for the spread of the Communist revolution into the Far East. (Cf. Latourette, *op. cit.*, p. 423.)

3. For a brief account of this agreement of collaboration, cf. *Catholic Encyclopedia* (Gilmary) *op. cit.*, Supplement II, 4th Sec., 1953.

4. Hollington K. Tong, *Chiang Kai-Shek* (Taipei: China Publishing Co., 1953) p. 44.

5. For the text of Dr. Sun's inauguration speech to the First National Party Congress on January 20, 1924, cf. Li, *op. cit.*, pp. 444-45.

6. *Ibid.*, pp. 453-55.

7. Chiang Kai-shek, *Soviet Russia in China* (New York: Farrar, Straus & Cudahy, 1957) p. 219.

8. W. W. Rostow, *The Prospects for Communist China* (New York: John Wiley, 1954) pp. 11-12.

9. Tong, *Chiang Kai-shek, op. cit.*, p. 46.

Unfinished Business

1. *Ibid.*, pp. x-xi.

2. Chiang, *China's Destiny, op. cit.*, pp. 81-84.

3. *Ibid.*, pp. 77-78.

4. John C. H. Wu, "President Chiang and the Translation of the New Testament," *Selected Essays of the History of Chinese Culture,* Vol. IV, in Chinese (Taipei: China Culture Publishing Foundation, 1956). English translation is made by the author.

5. Hollington K. Tong, *Dateline: China* (New York: Rockport Press, 1950) p. 200.

6. Only two of the six original Bishops consecrated by Pope Pius XI are still alive. Neither is able to act as Ordinary. One is Bishop Simon Chu, S.J., of Haimen, in Kiangsu province. Now 90 years old he is kept from his people by the Red regime. The other is Bishop Joseph Hu, C.M., of Taichow, in Chekiang province. He is in jail. (The *Advocate,* Newark, New Jersey, May 12, 1956.)

7. When Bishop Tien came to Rome in February 1946 to receive the Red Hat, the author, in the capacity of Chargé d'Affaires with ministerial rank of the Chinese Embassy in Italy, was privileged to give an official dinner party in his honor.

8. The number of Chinese priests having received episcopal consecration, or nominated Apostolic Prefects or Administrators, up to 1952, is as follows:

Bishops:	45
Apostolic Prefects:	23
Apostolic Administrators:	7
Total	75

It has to be noted that 9 Apostolic Prefects have been consecrated bishops, so that the total number must be reduced to 66. Cf. *Christ to the World,* Rome, Vol. I, No. 2, 1955, p. 72.

9. For a study of Father Lebbe's life, see *Thunder in the Distance* by Jacques Leclercq, Sheed & Ward, New York, 1958.

10. The Catholic Chinese mission was at that time still under the French Protectorate. All transactions with the Chinese Government were conducted by the French; and—irrespective of whether he was a Catholic or not—the French Consul was the official representative of the Catholic missions. This situation persisted until 1922 when the first Apostolic Delegate was sent to China by the Holy See.

11. For the text of the pastoral letter, cf. *The Voice of the Church in China* (New York: Longmans, 1938) pp. 37-39.

12. A Chinese priest, Father Gregory Lo Wen-tsao, O. P., called Lopez by the Spaniards, had been consecrated Bishop of all China in 1685; but centuries had passed, and Rome had never nominated another Chinese Bishop. For the significance of Father Lebbe's audience with Cardinal Van Rossum, cf. Raymond J. de Jaegher, *The Apostle of China: Father Lebbe* (London: Catholic Truth Society, 1954) p. 17.

13. Besides China, priests of S.A.M. are to be found working under native Bishops in other places: in Viet Nam, in India, in Ceylon, in Japan and in Central Africa. Father Antony Cotta, a great friend of China, died of old age at Maryknoll, New York, on April 28, 1957. For a study of his work and life in China, cf. Raymond J. de Jaegher, "The First Chinese Bishops and Father Cotta" (*Worldmission,* New York, Fall 1955) pp. 267-77.

14. 138 foreign missionaries and 52 nuns belonging to numerous countries and congregations are happy to work in Taiwan as auxiliaries of a Chinese bishop. Two of them, Msgr. Petrone

M. Lacchio, O.F.M., the archbishop of Changsha and Msgr. Philippe Cote, S.J., the bishop of Hsinchow, are working as simple auxiliaries under the jurisdiction of Msgr. Joseph Kuo, Archbishop of Taipei. Cf. *Christ to the World,* Rome, Vol. I, No. 2, 1955, p. 73.

15. For a brief account of the relations between China and the Holy See, cf. Paul K. T. Sih, "The Papacy and China," *Integrity,* June 1953.

16. The *New Life Movement,* at its inauguration, announced eight principles: (1) Regard yesterday as a period of death, today as a period of life. Let us rid ourselves of old abuses and build up a new nation. (2) Let us accept the heavy responsibilities of reviving the nation. (3) We must observe rules and have faith, honesty and shame. (4) Our clothing, eating, living and travelling must be simple, orderly, plain and clean. (5) We must willingly face hardships. We must strive for frugality. (6) We must have adequate knowledge and moral integrity as citizens. (7) Our actions must be courageous and rapid. (8) We must act on our promises, or even act without promising. (Cf. Tong, *Chiang Kai-shek, op. cit.,* p. 155.)

17. Chen Li-fu who has spent almost his whole life in a most uncompromising way against Communism is now leading a retired life on a farm in New Jersey. Chang Chia-ngau is a professor at Loyola University in Los Angeles.

The Folly of Co-Existence

1. Claude A. Buss, *The Far East* (New York: Macmillan, 1955) p. 509.

2. *Ibid.,* p. 510.

3. Hu Shih, "China in Stalin's Grand Strategy" (*Foreign Affairs,* October 1950) p. 30.

4. *Ibid.,* pp. 33-34.

5. Remarks made by Mao Tse-tung in his two speeches to Chinese Communist party leaders in Peiping on February 27 and March 12, 1957 as reported by the *New York Times,* June 13, 1957.

6. *Collision of East and West* (Chicago: Henry Regnery Co., 1951) p. 236.

7. Harold M. Vinacke, *The United States and the Far East, 1945-51* (Stanford Press, 1952) p. 31.

8. For a study of the crisis about Stilwell in China, cf. Feis, *op. cit.,* pp. 185-99.

9. For a summary of Wallace's mission to China, cf. *ibid.*, pp. 145-56.

10. China took up the fight against Japan in 1931 for the defense of the rights in Manchuria. By virtue of the Yalta Agreement, China lost not only Manchuria, but also Outer Mongolia, Port Arthur and Dairen. The injury inflicted upon the prestige and dignity of Chiang Kai-shek and the National government was almost inconceivable. The price China was to pay Russia for her entry into the Pacific War in this Agreement included these grave items: (1) the loss of Outer Mongolia which has an area twelve times larger than the State of New York; (2) the lease of Port Arthur as a naval base of the Soviet Union; (3) Russian control of the Port Dairen; (4) Russian control of the railway system in Manchuria. The combination of the last three items, of course, meant the real and effectual control of the whole of Manchuria. (For a summary review of the Yalta Agreement, cf. Feis, *op. cit.*, pp. 240-54.)

11. Statement made before the Political and Security Committee of the United Nations General Assembly in Paris as reported in the *New York Times*, January 27, 1952. For the really important faults found with the Yalta Agreement, cf. Feis, *op. cit.*, pp. 252-54.

12. For a summary account of General Marshall's mission to China, cf. Feis, *op. cit.*, pp. 413-30.

13. Vinacke, *op. cit.*, pp. 47-48.

14. The *Senate Judiciary Committee's Report*, 82d Congress, 2d Session (No. 2050, 1952) pp. 204-06. The Senate Committee in charge of investigating the issue of how China was lost is composed of many eminent lawyers such as Senator Willis Smith of North Carolina, a former president of the American Bar Association; Senator O'Connor of Maryland, a State's Attorney and former president of the National Association of Attorneys General; Senator Ferguson, a former circuit judge in Michigan; and Senator McCarran, one-time Chief Justice of the Supreme Court of Nevada.

15. Tien-fong Cheng, *A History of Sino-Russian Relations* (Washington, D. C.: Public Affairs Press, 1957) p. 223.

16. Vinacke, *op. cit.*, p. 54.

17. *Senate Judiciary Report*, No. 2050, *op. cit.*, p. 186.

18. John Leighton Stuart, *Fifty Years in China* (New York: Random House, 1954) pp. 271-72.

19. Quoted by Arthur Krock in his article "Chiang Kai-shek and our Post-War Policy" published in the *New York Times*, February 10, 1956.

20. Cf. General Wedmeyer's article "Let's Draw the Line Now," *Collier's* November 17, 1951; General Chennault's *Way of a Fighter* (New York: G. P. Putnam's Sons, 1948); *The Forrestal Diaries,* edited by Walter Lillis with the collaboration of E. S. Duffield, 1951, entry February 10, 1956.

21. Chiang, *Soviet Russia, op. cit.,* p. 242.

22. Chicago: Loyola University Press, 1954, p. 449.

23. Jeremias 2, 13.

24. Chiang Kai-shek writes: "Upon the abolition of unequal treaties at the end of the war, China's national equality and freedom were assured. We had a wonderful opportunity for reconstruction. At this juncture the Chinese Communists and their front organizations spread defeatism while international Communists launched a spearing campaign against our country and our Government. All our efforts at psychological reconstruction were thus nullified." Chiang, *Soviet Russia, op. cit.,* p. 221.

25. *Ibid.,* p. 212.

26. *Worldmission,* Fall 1955, p. 324.

27. Reported in the *New York Times,* October 12, 1958.

Silent Thunder

1. The *New York Times* (magazine section) March 27, 1955.

2. Rev. Albert O'Hara, "Phony Progress in Red China" (*America,* June 13, 1953.)

3. *The Great Peace* (New York: Harper, 1953) p. 174. Raja Hutheesing is a noted Indian journalist, and a brother-in-law of Prime Minister Nehru.

4. Quoted by the *Sign,* May 1956, p. 8. For an eye-witness account of Red China under totalitarian despotism, cf. Robert Guillain, "I Saw Communist China" (The *Saturday Evening Post,* May 19, May 26, June 2, 1956.)

5. *The Catholic World,* August 1958.

6. F. Engels, *Anti-Duhring.*

7. The so-called language reform committee in Peiping, headed by Wu Yu-chang, ordered the replacement of more than 2,000 Chinese characters by a Latin alphabet in Nov. 1956. In a manifesto issued on Dec. 15, 1956, twelve cultural organizations in Taiwan declared that the introduction of Latin alphabet was a prelude to introduction of the Slavic language throughout mainland China. The manifesto stated that the Red elimination of the written Chinese characters was an insidious

weapon to facilitate the domination and enslavement of the Chinese people's mind by the Soviet Union. At a meeting of the "National Committee of the Chinese People's Political Consultative Conference," Chou En-lai, Communist Prime Minister, called for nation-wide support and widespread publicity for the new alphabet "so that the Chinese language can be steadily and positively changed to suit the needs of Socialist construction." The *New York Times,* Jan. 12, 1958.)

8. In the first two years of the Communist rule, the two oldest and largest publishing houses of China, the Commercial Press and the Chunghwa Book Company were compelled . . . to burn the existing stocks of books in some 22,000 categories, a total of 500,000 volumes. (The *Freeman,* in Chinese, Hong Kong, Nov. 10, 1951.)

9. Address made by Dr. Hollington K. Tong at Seton Hall Commencement Exercises, June 8, 1957.

10. As reported by the British-owned daily *South China Morning Post* upon the educator's return to Hong Kong in January, 1956 from a Peiping-sponsored three-week tour of the mainland.

11. Robert Guillain related this unpleasant experience to a *Central News Agency* correspondent in Tokyo on Feb. 25, 1956.

12. *The Marriage Law* (Peiping: Foreign Language Press, 1950) gives the text as well as the two articles discussing the law. For the ill effects of this law, cf. Richard L. Walker, *China Under Communism* (Yale Press, 1955) p. 348, note 30.

13. The Communist attack on the family is documented in numerous publications of the United States Hong Kong Consulate General. Cf. also C. K. Yang, *The Chinese Family in the Communist Revolution* (Cambridge: Center for International Studies, M. I. T., 1953) 373 pp.

14. The *New York Times* (magazine section), June 15, 1958.

15. *Ibid.*

16. The Chinese people are very particular about their descendents. The more children they have, the more glory there will be to the family. If one member of the family dies without children, they adopt a boy to continue his generation in the direct line. They would never permit that line to be left open. So the last and the most hideous curse that can be used on anyone in China is "May you be childless and generationless forever!"

17. *The Mencius,* Bk. 4, p. 1, ch. 26.

18. With its belief in the dualistic principle of *Yin* and *Yang*

and in mystic union with the ultimate Reality, Taoism was distorted, in its later days, into a speculative doctrine believing in magic and divination, and aiming solely at prolonging this life on earth. For this, Taoist belief has often been associated with secret societies.

19. Walker, *op. cit.*, p. 189.

20. The *Department of State Bulletin,* Vol. XXX, No. 768, March 15, 1954, p. 400.

21. Walker, *op. cit.*, p. 186.

22. Raymond J. de Jaegher and Irene C. Kuhn, *The Enemy Within* (New York: Doubleday, 1952) pp. 46-47.

23. *Time,* March 5, 1956.

24. Mr. Lucian Taire is a businessman whose personal fortune, built up in more than 30 years of labor in China, was wiped out by the Communists. His story appeared in *U. S. News & World Report,* May 18, 1956.

25. During the 15 years in which the Bolsheviks were consolidating the power in Russia, an estimated 15 million Russians were killed or died of planned or accidental starvation. (*Reader's Digest,* June 1956.)

26. The *New York Times,* May 5, and May 8, 1958.

27. *Ibid.,* Jan. 13, 1958.

28. *Ibid.,* April 13, 1958.

29. In mid-May, 1958, the *People's Daily* counseled all Peiping's 3,000,000 inhabitants to watch one another so there would be "6,000,000 eyes ferreting out those evil persons commonly called counter-revolutionaries." (Reported in the *New York Times,* May 18, 1958.)

Crossed Fingers

1. The *New York Times,* June 25, 1957.

2. *Ibid.,* (magazine section), June 15, 1958.

3. *Ibid.,* June 2, 1958.

4. At the 19-day closed session of the eighth National Congress of the Chinese Communist party during the period May 5-May 23, 1958, the official report on agricultural production over the period from the winter of 1955 to the spring of 1958 presented a rather darker picture than had been painted earlier and suggested that the adverse effects of mass collectivization on Chinese agriculture might have been greater than originally admitted. (*N. Y. Herald Tribune,* June 4, 1958.)

5. In China it is easy to see the close relationship between the

farm and the family system. "The Western world knows little of the intensity of effort required for subsistence in Asiatic agriculture in overpopulated areas—notably India, China, and Japan. The required intensity of effort was forthcoming in China when the system was based on private holdings rooted in the family. Chinese agriculture has thus been based in a particularly direct way on private family incentive." Cf. W. W. Rostow, *The Prospects for Communist China* (New York: John Wiley & Technology Press of M.I.T., 1954) p. 149.

6. *Foreign Affairs,* October 1957.

7. The *New York Times* (magazine section), June 15, 1958.

8. Chou's report to the central committee of the Chinese Communist party in Jan. 1956, as reported in the *New York Times,* April 15, 1956.

9. The intelligentsia in China, as elsewhere, is a complex group. Strictly speaking it embraces all literate persons. As of the end of 1952 those undergoing education in some form under Communist rule were officially stated to be just under 60 million, as follows:

College and university students	203,000
Middle-school students	3,280,000
Primary-school students	55,000,000

Cf. Rostow, *op. cit.,* p. 134.

10. The editorial of *Wen Wei Pao,* in Chinese, Shanghai, March 28, 1956.

11. *Mission Bulletin,* Hong Kong, May 1957, p. 284.

12. The *New York Times,* July 15, 1957. According to an official dispatch by the Communist *Hsinhua News Agency,* the vice chancellor of the National University of Peiping, Kiang Ling-chi, told a subcommittee of the so-called the National People's Congress that the University "has been used as a center for disseminating anti-Communist views and a base of 'rumor mongering.' " (*Ibid.,* June 28, 1957.)

13. The annual income per capita of a peasant is less than $66 in Communist currency which amounts to less than 30 U. S. dollars.

14. According to the *People's Daily* in Peiping dated March 21, 1957 the number of livestocks in June 1956 in the North-Eastern area and the four provinces of Shantung, Honan, Hopei, and Shensi was 1,900,000 less than two years ago.

15. A list of anti-Communist guerrilla forces, compiled from the texts of the Communist delegates' report shows that these forces are found in no less than 16 provinces. They are said to be

responsible for frequent skirmishes with local Red garrisons. (Cf. *Chinese News Service,* New York, May 18, 1956.) For a detailed account of the troubles brewing in Red China, cf. *U. S. News & World Report,* July 13, 1956.

16. *Time,* July 15, 1957.

17. For an interesting study of the anti-Communist movements in mainland China, see James W. Berner's article "Peiping Harassed by Burgeoning Anti-Communist Movements," published in *Free Front,* April 1958, Saigon, Viet Nam.

18. The *New York Times,* June 17, 1957.

19. *Ibid.*

20. *Ibid.,* March 9, 1957. General Chiang, eldest son of President Chiang Kai-shek, is considered to be the best-informed man in Free China about the internal situation on mainland China.

21. A summary account of Mao's two speeches was published in the *New York Times,* June 13, 1957. Mao laid down the new line in a speech made before the so-called Supreme State Council on February 27, 1957. It was further discussed by Mao in his speech of March 12 of the same year before the National Propaganda Work Conference. The official edited Peiping version of Mao's February speech appeared in the *New York Times,* June 19, 1957.

22. Mao himself conceded in his February speech that "Certain people in our country were delighted when the Hungarian events took place. They hoped that something similar would happen in China, that thousands upon thousands of people would demonstrate in the streets against the People's Government." (Cf. official edited Peiping text published in the *New York Times,* June 19, 1957.)

23. Tingfu F. Tsiang, Permanent Representative of China to the United Nations, said the continuing carnage stands "somewhere over 20,000,000." Two American diplomats also challenged Mao. Assistant Secretary of State for Far Eastern Affairs Walter S. Robertson said: "Mao's henchmen have slaughtered some 18,000,000 of mainland Chinese in seven years." Former Undersecretary of State Joseph C. Grew said: "Since 1949 the Chinese Reds, like animals who devour their young, have killed 20,000,000 Chinesee—their own people." (*New York Journal-American,* June 14, 1957.)

24. The *New York Times,* June 29, 1957.

25. Both had faithfully toed the Communist party line. The two were accused of "aiding with counter-revolutionaries" by the Peiping *People's Daily* on June 8, 1957 because of their outspoken criticism against the Communist regime.

26. The *New York Times,* June 14, 1957.

27. *Time,* April 7, 1958.

28. Chang Po-chun, the Red Communication Minister; Chang Nai-chi, the Red Food Minister, and Lo Lung-chi, the Red Timber Industry Minister, lost their Cabinet posts in Jan. 1958 for "rightist activities." They were also suspended from the standing committee of the so-called Chinese People's Political Consultative Conference, which is the government's vehicle for maintaining a united front between Communist and other political parties. (The *New York Times,* March 18, 1958.)

29. *U. S. News & World Report,* April 4, 1958.

30. Edward Hunter, *The Black Book on Red China* (New York: Bookmailer, 1958) p. 163.

31. The *New York Times,* May 28, 1958.

32. Dennis Bloodworth of The *London Observer* wrote in his article "Reds Dream of Plenty in Farm Co-operatives": "The peasant received nothing for his land any more. He was once more a paid laborer. . . . His wage is about $42 a year." (*N. Y. Herald Tribune,* Oct. 2, 1958.)

33. The *New York Times,* Sep. 28, 1958.

34. The first Empire of China which brought about the unification by military conquest of the powerful Emperor Ch'in Shih-huang lasted only fifteen years (2212-06 B.C.). Emperor Wang Meng of "New Dynasty" between the Western Han and the Eastern Han Dynasties who based his authoritative regime on land-reform lasted only fourteen years (9-23 A.D.). Emperor Y'ang Ti of Siu Dynasty which carried out military adventure in Korea as impressive as the present Communist regime lasted 37 years (581-618 A.D.).

35. Wen Tien-hsiang died as a martyr, when the Sung Dynasty (960-1279) was overthrown by the Mongols. Upon execution, he wrote: "Confucius advocates righteousness; Mencius upholds justice. It is only when justice is done that righteousness will prevail. This is what we should learn from the writings of the sages. Henceforth I shall not feel ashamed of myself." For an English translation of Wen's *Cheng Chi K'e,* cf. H. A. Giles, *A History of Chinese Literature* (London: Wm. Heinemann, 1901; New York: Appleton, 1903) pp. 248-49; also Carsun Chang, *The Development of Neo-Confucian Thought* (New York: Bookman Associates, 1957) pp. 348-53.

36. *The Mencius,* Bk. 2, p. 1, ch. 3, 2.

37. *The Mind of East Asia, op. cit.,* p. 202.

38. N. Y. *Herald Tribune,* Oct. 6, 1958.

Wings to God

1. Sheed, *op. cit.,* p. 85.
2. *Time,* Sep. 19, 1955.
3. For a detailed account of the Chinese faithful who died as martyrs early in the nineteenth century and the cause of beatification of these martyrs, cf. Ryan, *op. cit.,* pp. 61-62.
4. *Red Book* (Rome: Catholic Action)—a 378-page volume which gives the Red record of persecution, country by country, in documented detail.
5. As of September 1956 there remained in Red China twenty-four foreign missionaries, a Bishop, the Most Rev. James E. Walsh of Maryknoll, three priests with limited freedom, nine priests in prison and eleven Franciscan Missionary of Mary Sisters who, in Peiping, were conducting a school for foreign children. (*Catholic Sunday Examiner,* Hong Kong, Nov. 30, 1956, p. 8.)
6. Jean Monsterleet, *Martyrs in China* (Chicago: Henry Regnery, 1956) pp. 251-52.
7. 166 missionaries have been killed by the Communists or died in prison: 127 Chinese and 39 foreigners. 346 foreign missionaries have been imprisoned for terms from two months to four years. The Chinese priests put in jail are very much more numerous still. For a detailed account, cf. Thomas J. Bauer, M.M., *The Systematic Destruction of the Catholic Church in China* (New York: World Horizons Reports, 1954). Even though foreign missionaries were entirely removed, the Catholic Church would remain fervent, solidly established, and directed by some thirty Chinese Bishops under the leadership of Bishop Ignatius Kung. With regard to the imprisonment of Bishop Kung by the Reds, see p. 152.
8. *Mission Bulletin,* Hong Kong, Sep. 1954, pp. 606-08.
9. The author was privileged to address the student body of this college, a Jesuit institution, at the personal request of Father Beda Chang in Oct. 1957, before he became a Catholic.
10. *China Missionary Bulletin,* Nov. 1952, p. 727. "Upon Father Beda Chang's death, all churches in the whole diocese of Shanghai were packed at the special Masses, and many wept publicly. . . . It was decided by Bishop Ignatius Kung of Shanghai that all Catholics in the city should mourn for Father Chang by wearing a white flower for a week. But the people with white flowers could be seen in churches and schools even after two or

three weeks had elapsed." (*Worldmisson,* Summer 1952, pp. 207-08.)

11. In the preceding year (1950), 22 Chinese priests died under the Red regime by execution in North China, including Father Francis Hsiao who died after torture in Wanhsiao on Good Friday, Father Wang who died in jail in Ipin and Father Thadee Lin of Pakpoi who was beaten to death.

12. *The Advocate,* Newark, Dec. 28, 1957; Jan. 11, 1958, and Mar. 22, 1958.

13. *Ibid.,* Mar. 22, 1958.

14. *Chinese News Service,* New York, April 10, 1958.

15. *Ibid.*

16. *Time,* August 18, 1958; *N. Y. Herald Tribune,* Oct. 3, 1958.

17. The *New York Times,* May 19, 1958.

18. St. John 12, 24-25.

The Church In Torment

1. Joseph M. C. Kung, "God Help China!" (*America,* August 11, 1956). Mr. Kung, a nephew of Bishop Ignatius Kung of Shanghai whose imprisonment by the Communists is referred to in page 152, came to the United States from Hong Kong in July, 1955. He is the only member of the Kung family outside Red China.

2. Thomas J. M. Burke, S.J., ed. *Mary and Modern Man* (New York: America Press, 1954) p. 75.

3. Columba Cary-Elwes, *op. cit.,* p. 279.

4. Val Erian, "Shanghai Reds and the Lady in Blue," *Worldmission,* Fall 1953, pp. 320-21. For a detailed account of the Communist persecution of the Legion of Mary in China, cf. Rev. Albert V. Fedders, "Communism and the Legion of Mary," *China Missionary Bulletin,* October 1952, pp. 649-54; November 1952, pp. 736-40.

5. *Worldmission,* Fall 1953, pp. 321-22.

6. Of the three Catholic universities, 189 secondary and 2,343 prayer schools providing education for some 30,000 students before the Communist rule, hardly one school remains Catholic today. (*China Missionary Bulletin,* January 1953, p. 2.)

7. *Ibid.,* October 1952, p. 646.

8. *America,* August 11, 1956, p. 442.

9. *Imitation of Christ,* II, ch. vi.
10. For a detailed account of the arrest, cf. Jean Lefeuvre, S.J., *Shanghai: Les Enfants dans la Ville* (Paris: Témoignage Chrétien).
11. "One example of how the persecutors are defeating themselves in Red China is the recent mock trial of Bishop Ignatius Kung (Kiung Pin-mei) of Shanghai. To each humiliating accusation a group of 4,000 persons cried out 'Long live our Bishop!' The trial had to be stopped and the Bishop dragged off to prison again." (The *New York Times,* May 14, 1956.)
12. A Communist official publicly declared: "The Legion is a spiritual force. We can't see it and shoot it!" (*China Missionary Bulletin,* October 1952, p. 649.)
13. The *Advocate,* Newark, N. J., April 13, 1957.
14. During his six years under the Reds Bishop Donaghy spent six months of them in prison. He came back to the States in 1956 and is now in Taiwan.
15. *No Secret Is Safe* (New York: Farrar, Straus & Young, 1952) p. 216.
16. *China Missionary Bulletin,* October 1952, p. 648.
17. Monsterleet, *op. cit.,* p. 144.
18. *China Missionary Bulletin,* May 1953, p. 240-41.
19. Psalm 92, 19 (Vulgate).
20. *The Interior Carmel* (New York: Sheed & Ward, 1952) pp. 215-16.
21. Monsterleet, *op. cit.,* p. 284.
22. In his article "Religion Will Survive in Russia," Dr. Walter W. van Kirk, an American churchman who came back from Soviet Russia, reports that though Soviet officials still inveigh against God, five times as many churches are open as in 1935, and millions go to them. (*Collier's,* June 8, 1956.)
23. Peter I, 2, 9.

The Chinese Are Chinese

1. *The Mind of East Asia, op. cit.,* p. 69.
2. Psalm 17 (Vulgate).
3. Preface to Paul K. T. Sih, *Chinese Culture and Christianity* (Taipei: China Culture Publishing Foundation, 1957) pp. 6-7.
4. The Hierarchy was established in Taiwan on October 25,

1952. Msgr. Joseph Kuo was consecrated as first Archbishop of Taipei.

5. In the National Taiwan University, there are Chinese priests and missionaries of different nationalities on the teaching staff. The Ministry of Education granted permission to a lay Catholic woman-educator, Mrs. Helen Chang, to found the Tsai Hsing Primary School in Taipei conducted with a Catholic spirit. It is the only private elementary school in Free China. That the Chinese Minister of Education, Dr. Chang Chi-yun, has exemplified himself as a valiant promoter of democracy in the Far East was clearly expressed in the citation for an honorary degree of Doctor of Laws presented to the Chinese educator on June 8, 1957 by Seton Hall University: "We salute him as a leading scholar and distinguished educator in China and as a great friend of the United States, whose work and life have exemplified devotion and unremitting effort in making democratic principles effective in the land of Confucius."

6. The increase has beeen progressive and in a breakdown of the figures we find the following:

Year	*Catholics*
1952	20,112
1953	25,075
1954	32,530
1955	48,517
1956	80,661

There was an increase of 32,144 Catholics for the twelve-month period ending June, 1956, and at that time there were 59,993 catechumens registered for the coming year. (*Catholic Sunday Examiner,* November 30, 1956, p. 6.)

7. A Chinese priest in Taiwan who is serving on the faculty of the National Taiwan University wrote me in February, 1956 that "this is my seventh year in Taiwan. In these seven years, I baptized about 1,000 souls. Among them, 438 came from various walks of life, including high school boys. The other 570 were university students."

8. For details, cf. *Catholic Life,* March-April 1956, p. 17.

9. *Poverty,* translated by Rosemary Sheed (New York: Sheed & Ward, 1950) p. 182.

10. As Father F. Legrand says, "The present persecution in China is perhaps *a providential opportunity to work at the conversion of the Chinese* in Formosa and in the dispora: they are 20 million, 8 in Formosa and 12 scattered all over the world." (*Christ to the World,* Vol. I, No. 2, 1955, p. 79.)

The Turning Point

1. For a general study of Chinese Communist influence in Southeast Asia, see C. M. Chang, "Communist China in Asian Affairs," published by the Institute of Ethnic Studies, Georgetown University, Washington, D. C., April 26, 1958.

2. *Communism and Christianity,* Penguin Books, 1956, p. 188.

3. *Eyes East* (Paterson, New Jersey: St. Anthony Guild Press, 1945) p. 180.

What Can We Do?

1. For the importance of the Chinese overseas in relation to the fate of Southeast Asia, cf. James Reston, "Chiang's Stock Rises," The *New York Times,* April 2, 1954.

2. *Ibid.,* March 14, 1957.

3. *Ibid.*

4. *Ibid.,* June 4, 1957.

5. *Ibid.,* June 29, 1957.

6. New York: Dodd, Mead & Co., 1954.

7. Westminster: The Newman Press, 1956. Mr. Hyde is a former news editor of the *London Daily Worker* who renounced his Communism for the Catholic faith.

8. *Reader's Digest,* January 1957.

9. *Ibid.,* April 1957.

10. Buss, *op. cit.,* p. 534.

11. To delegates to a Study-Week of Italian C. A. on "Catholics and International Life," July 16, 1952.

12. *Parochial and Plain Sermons,* Vol. I, No. XXII.

13. *The Intellectual Apostolate* (Hong Kong: Catholic Truth Society, 1947) p. 6.

14. "Our Need of Orientalists," *Worldmission,* Fall 1956, p. 301.

15. *Collectanes,* Vol. I, p. 42.

16. "The Case for a Chinese Liturgy," *Tablet,* London, February 2, 1946.

17. The Congress was ably organized by Dr. Vittorio Veronese, Secretary General of the Permanent Committee of International Congresses for the Lay Apostolate, in collaboration with Catholic Action of the Philippines and under the guidance of Archbishop Vagnozzi, Nuncio to the Philippines.

18. *Op. cit.,* Worldmission, Fall 1956, p. 314.

19. In the citation for an honorary Doctor of Laws degree presented to President Ngo Dinh Diem by Seton Hall University on May 12, 1957, we read: "In June, 1954, following the French disaster at Dien Bien-Phu, President Ngo Dinh Diem was presented with the difficult task of forming a government under the most trying circumstances. Under his leadership, the whole nation is experiencing the true force of Christian faith. By his political wisdom, by his high statesmanship and by his Christian spirit . . . he has accomplished what appeared to be the impossible."

20. On the last day of November, 1955, President Diem agreed with American officials on a resettlement plan, the Cai San project, involving 150,000 acres of *abandoned* rice lands capable of providing food for 100,000 men, women and children.

21. With the generous cooperation of Catholic American institutions, Father John T. S. Mao, under the guidance of Archbishop Paul Yu-pin, succeeded in the last ten years in sponsoring about 700 Chinese youth to be educated in this country.

22. Tunghai University initiated a student-labor training program based on the experience of Berea College, Berea, Kentucky. Cf. *New Horizon* (New York: United Board for Christian Higher Education in Asia, April 1956).

23. At its annual meeting in 1955 the Protestant United Board for Christian Higher Education in Asia declared that "the basic purpose of the United Board is to foster Christian higher education, especially in East and Southeast Asia, developing needed institutions, supporting programs where support is justified, and using whatever other educational means may be indicated . . . in an effort to make Christian higher education in that area a truly effective force in the life of Church and of nation." Cf. *ibid.*, p. 1.

24. For a complete story of Communists' seizure of Fu Jen University, cf. Rigney, *op. cit.*

25. For a brief study of Bishop Wilhelm van Bekkum's address, cf. Paul K. T. Sih, "The Conversion of China," *Worship,* September 1957.

26. "In Our Own Language," *The Catholic World,* May 1957.

27. I Cor. 14, 15.

28. *See* p. 27.

29. In an address given in Rome in 1956 on "Pope Piux XII and the Missionary Renewal" (published in *Eglise Vivante,* Sept.-Oct., 1956, pp. 317-334), Cardinal Celso Costantini stated: "Our Holy Father Pius XII in 1942 authorized (for China) a

translation of numerous parts of the Ritual and, later, taking up again a concession made in 1615 by Paul V, he permitted Chinese priests to celebrate the Mass, except for the Canon, in the liturgy language of China. Of course, the obligation to learn Latin remains" (p. 329). This history-making permission was granted in 1949, and knowledge of it has become quite general; its official promulgation, however, awaits the Roman approval of an acceptable Chinese translation of the biblical and liturgical texts, which is in the making. (Cf. *Worship,* September 1957, p. 488.)

The Crisis in China

1. Sih, *op. cit.,* pp. x-xi.
2. Translated by Miss Helen Waddell, *Lyrics from the Chinese.*
3. *Mary in Our Life* (New York: Kenedy, 1954) p. 69.
4. *De Bono Viduitatis,* XXI, xxvi.
5. Quoted by Dr. John C. H. Wu in his *Beyond East and West* (New York: Sheed & Ward, 1951) p. 329.
6. Sheed, *op. cit.,* p. 191.
7. *The Sure Victory* (New Jersey: Revell, 1956) p. 21.
8. Rom. 5, 3-4.
9. Cf. *The Revolt of Asia* (London: Sheed & Ward, 1957).
10. Address on "The Necessity of Faith for a Living Democracy" given at the annual conference of Staff Chaplains of the U. S. Air Force, as reported in the *Advocate,* Newark, New Jersey, Feb. 23, 1957. Rev. Theodore Hesburgh is President of Notre Dame University and was named in May, 1957 by Pope Pius XII as permanent representative of Vatican City to the international Atomic Agency, as United Nations atom-for-peace organization.
11. *The Secret Name* (New York: Farrar, Straus & Cudahy, 1958) p. 245.
12. Sister Miriam Teresa, whose cause of beatification has entered the stage of apostolic process, compared gold to our will, frankincense to our intellect and myrrh to the bitterness of life. Cf. *Greater Perfection* (New Jersey: St. Anthony Guild, 1953) pp. 244-46.

Index

Asia in the Modern World, No. 10

PAUL K.T. SIH, Editor

Also in this series:

No. 1
THE CHINESE REVOLUTION of 1911
by Chin-tung Liang

No. 2
CHINA AT THE PARIS PEACE CONFERENCE in 1919
by Wunsz King

No. 3
CHINA AND THE WASHINGTON CONFERENCE, 1921-1922
by Wunsz King

No. 4
CHINA AND THE BRUXELLES CONFERENCE, 1937
by Tsien Tai

No. 5
CHINA AND THE LEAGUE OF NATIONS
by Wunsz King

No. 6
THE SINISTER FACE OF THE MUKDEN INCIDENT
by Chin-tung Liang

No. 7
THE KUOMINTANG: SELECTED HISTORICAL DOCUMENTS, 1894-1969
by Milton J. T. Shieh

No. 8
FOUNDATIONS OF THE CHINESE REVOLUTION, 1905-1912
by Ta-ling Lee

No. 9
THE STRENUOUS DECADE: CHINA'S NATION-BUILDING EFFORTS, 1927-1937
Ed. with an introduction by Paul K.T. Sih

A Symposium in Celebration of the St. John's University Centennial, 1870-1970